Baby & Toddler Sleep Solutions For Dummies®

Cheat Sheet

What to Check if Your Child Wakes

- **Diaper:** Is she wet?
- **Appetite:** Is he hungry or crying for a lost pacifier? (Is he using the *I'm hungry* ploy to get attention? Don't offer a snack unless you're sure he's hungry.)
- **Tummy problems:** If this is a rare event, cuddle her until she feels better. (A little rocking and jiggling can help her pass gas if she needs to.)
- **Clothing:** Check for scratchy tags or parts that hurt or itch.
- **Symptoms of illness:** Is he feverish, congested, or looking sickly? See Chapter 13 for dealing with colds, flu, and other bugs. If you feel that there is any chance it could be serious call your pediatrician right away. Is he scratching? Check for mosquito bites and other annoyances. Diaper rash? Slather on the petroleum jelly.
- **Her routine:** Is she excited about an upcoming event or stressed by a hectic day? Try soothing music and a reassuring pat. Keep lights low and voices quiet. See Chapter 14.
- **Schedule:** Did he take an extra-long nap, stay up late, or go to bed early? His sleepy schedule is a little off track so you can cut him a little slack.
- **Milestones:** Is she learning to sit up, walk, or talk, or is she teething? Expect a few days of disrupted sleep. Remember that normal development calls for your child to find her way to normal adaption, so when progress interrupts sleep, let her find her own (and therefore best) solution.
- **Separation anxiety:** Is he having trouble letting go of Mommy or Daddy? For strategies, see Chapter 6.
- **Bad dreams and night terrors:** A nightmare calls for cuddles and reassurance. But a night terror doesn't respond to either (your best strategy is to wait it out). See Chapter 7.
- **Distractions:** Is the room too noisy? Too light? Turn off the TV, keep your conversations low, and turn off lights near her room. If you can't get rid of annoying noise, try music or white noise (see Chapter 15).
- **Temperature:** Is he too hot or cold? Unless he's premature, he's comfy at the same temperature as you. Be careful not to overdress him.

Average Hours of Daytime and Nighttime Sleep

The stats in this chart are just averages, based on thousands of tots, so don't be surprised if your child sleeps more or less each day than what's on this chart.

Age	Nap Time (Hours)	Nighttime Sleep (Hours)	Age	Nap Time (Hours)	Nighttime Sleep (Hours)
1 week	8	8	1 year	2	11
1 month	7	8.5	2 years	1	12
3 months	5	9	3 years	0.5	11
6 months	4	10			

For Dummies: Bestselling Book Series for Beginners

Baby & Toddler Sleep Solutions For Dummies®

A Sleepytime Shopping List

Make sure your beddy-bye tool kit includes these essentials.

For babies:

- Sleepers of varying weights (so blankets are unnecessary)
- Pacifiers (if your child takes one)
- Petroleum jelly or ointment for the diaper area of baby's skin
- Safety equipment: Socket plugs, cord protectors, closet door locks, and so on

For toddlers:

- Puzzles and other quiet pre-bed toys
- Comfy jammies — if it's toilet-training time, make sure they're easy to adjust for potty breaks
- A cuddly stuffed animal or doll
- A nightlight or easy-to-turn-on bedside light if your toddler is learning to use the bathroom on his own

For all ages:

- Soothing CDs — either music or nature sounds
- Bedtime stories
- Blackout curtains if too much light is an issue
- A white-noise generator if noise is an issue

Tips for Traveling

A little planning before a flight or road trip can help ensure your baby's or toddler's sleep stays on schedule:

If you're driving:

- Try to time your trip to coincide with your tot's naptime.
- Stop every few hours to let your tot walk or get a cuddle.
- Use a window shade to keep the sun out of his eyes.
- Keep meals on schedule to keep sleep on schedule. Pack more food than usual, just in case delays pop up.
- If you're a threesome, have one person keep your baby or toddler company in the back seat.
- Play lullaby CDs to lull your tot to sleep.

If you're flying:

- For very young babies, ask ahead whether the airline supplies *skycots*, miniature beds that attach to the wall in front of front row seats on the plane.
- If you're flying across time zones, gradually adjust your tot's feeding schedule. Try moving each meal forward or back by 15 minutes.
- Bring the following in your carry-on:
  - A few pacifiers to help your baby relax and help pop her ears if cabin presure bothers her
  - A couple of light-weight blankets to keep her cozy and block light
  - Simple snacks, in case of delays
  - Quiet-time toys, some bedtime stories, and a small, stuffed animal

For Dummies: Bestselling Book Series for Beginners

Baby & Toddler Sleep Solutions

FOR

DUMMIES®

Baby & Toddler Sleep Solutions

FOR

DUMMIES®

by Arthur Lavin, MD and Susan Glaser, MA

BICENTENNIAL
1807
WILEY
2007
BICENTENNIAL

Wiley Publishing, Inc.

Baby & Toddler Sleep Solutions For Dummies®

Published by
Wiley Publishing, Inc.
111 River St.
Hoboken, NJ 07030-5774
www.wiley.com

WILEY

About the Authors

Arthur Lavin, M.D., F.A.A.P., is a pediatrician who's been in private practice for over 20 years and is also an associate clinical professor of pediatrics at Case Medical School in Cleveland, Ohio. He was trained and then taught at Harvard and MIT in pediatrics and the specialty of newborn medicine and has published original research in such journals as *Science*. He is also the coauthor of *Who's the Boss: Moving Families from Conflict to Collaboration* (Collaboration Press, 2006), a book presenting a new paradigm of parenting with specific guidance on managing the most common challenges of parenting young children such as toilet training, sibling rivalry, and discipline.

Lavin's professional experience includes training by T. Berry Brazelton, M.D. and Mel Levine, M.D. He has served on a number of national committees of the American Academy of Pediatrics, helping to create standards for community pediatrics and to draft manuals for teaching American pediatricians to care for children with special health care needs. In 1998, Lavin accepted an invitation by the United States government to participate in an overseas health partner mission. In addition, Microsoft showcased Lavin's office, Advanced Pediatrics, in its launch of Office 2003. He is married and has three children.

Susan B. Glaser, M.A., is an educational psychologist and early childhood educator with more than 30 years of experience in supporting families of young children. She graduated from Case Western Reserve University, where she worked with noted educator Jane Kessler, Ph.D. in a school for children with special needs; she received her master's degree from John Carroll University.

Glaser served for 15 years as the Director of Early Childhood Services for the Jewish Community Center of Cleveland. She currently works as a national consultant, traveling the United States and Canada to assess early childhood centers and present workshops for parents and teachers. She contributes to the parent Web site of the national association of Jewish Community Centers.

Glaser is the chairperson of the Infant/Toddler Network of the Coalition for Alternatives in Jewish Education (CAJE), a national group devoted to furthering and improving education. She is also a member of the Universal Pre-K Committee of Cuyahoga County, Ohio. Her articles on parenting appear in newspapers and national publications in the field of early child development. She coauthored *Who's the Boss: Moving Families from Conflict to Collaboration* (Collaboration Press, 2006) with Dr. Lavin. Glaser is married and has three grown children.

Dedication

To Laurel, Rebecca, Joshua, Jeremy, Abigail, and Hannah.

Authors' Acknowledgments

We acknowledge with love and gratitude the support, love, and inspiration from our spouses, Richard Glaser and Diane E. Lavin, without whom this work could not have been completed. It was they who helped us reach, explore, learn, and share. With our gratitude and love, we also want to acknowledge our children. It was they who taught us with their love how to guide and still love.

We thank Alison Blake, who has done an extraordinary job of helping us fashion this book into a format that is enjoyable, and familiar to all the world that loves the *For Dummies* series. To our acquisitions editor, Tracy Boggier, we remain grateful for the initial idea of this book, the opportunity to make it so widely available. To our project editor, Kristin DeMint, and our copy editor, Pam Ruble, many thanks for a wonderful working relationship and invaluable editing as our manuscript came to life. Finally, to our agent, Margot Maley Hutchison, thank you for bringing us together with Wiley Publishing, bringing our insights and passion for parenting to light.

Dr. Lavin: No one learns alone, and I would like to thank those who most helped me think about caring for children and their families: Dr. T. Berry Brazelton, Dr. Mel Levine, Dr. F. Sessions Cole, Dr. Phil Hill, Dr. Jerry Hass, Dr. Alan Nauss, Dr. Francis Rushton, Dr. Cal Sia, and the Division of Community Pediatrics of the American Academy of Pediatrics. All the important threads in my professional development came together in our office, Advanced Pediatrics. I thank our wonderful team of staff and professionals who every day reach out to families and offer what is needed most: a listening ear, an eagerness to help, and a commitment to offer the best expertise possible. Ultimately the greatest honor is to be asked to help someone, so I deeply thank the families who have placed the greatest gift, their trust, into my hands.

Ms. Glaser: I wish to thank Dr. Jane Kessler, who was my mentor at the Mental Development Center of Case Western Reserve University; Eleanor Wiesberger, who inspired me to write a book about parents based on practical, developmentally appropriate ideas that work; my colleagues at the Jewish Community Center, especially Cindy Bruder and Barb McDonald, who were my touchstones for sharing ideas and strategies; and Judith Pitlick and Devra Adlestein, with whom I shared long walks and longer discussions about children's development. And most of all, I thank the young parents who have entered my life and allowed me to become part of theirs while their families grew and developed.

Publisher's Acknowledgments

We're proud of this book; please send us your comments through our Dummies online registration form located at www.dummies.com/register/.

Some of the people who helped bring this book to market include the following:

Acquisitions, Editorial, and Media Development

Project Editor: Kristin DeMint

Acquisitions Editor: Tracy Boggier

Copy Editor: Pam Ruble

Technical Editor: Robert Needlman, M.D.

Senior Editorial Manager: Jennifer Ehrlich

Editorial Assistants: Erin Calligan Mooney, Joe Niesen, Leeann Harney

Cover Photos: © Flying Colors/Getty Images

Cartoons: Rich Tennant (www.the5thwave.com)

Composition Services

Project Coordinator: Heather Kolter

Layout and Graphics: Brooke Graczyk, Joyce Haughey, Shane Johnson, Laura Pence

Anniversary Logo Design: Richard Pacifico

Proofreaders: Laura Albert, Aptara, Brian H. Walls

Indexer: Aptara

Special Help: Alison Blake

Publishing and Editorial for Consumer Dummies

> **Diane Graves Steele,** Vice President and Publisher, Consumer Dummies
>
> **Joyce Pepple,** Acquisitions Director, Consumer Dummies
>
> **Kristin A. Cocks,** Product Development Director, Consumer Dummies
>
> **Michael Spring,** Vice President and Publisher, Travel
>
> **Kelly Regan,** Editorial Director, Travel

Publishing for Technology Dummies

> **Andy Cummings,** Vice President and Publisher, Dummies Technology/General User

Composition Services

> **Gerry Fahey,** Vice President of Production Services
>
> **Debbie Stailey,** Director of Composition Services

Contents at a Glance

Table of Contents

Introduction

$\bullet$ $\bullet$

Are you starting to wonder whether you'll *ever* sleep through the night again? If so, you're not alone! Being a new parent is joyful and thrilling, but it's also a prescription for sleepless nights. And those nights can get mighty long and frustrating when nothing seems to soothe your oh-so-demanding little cherub to sleep.

Luckily, however, that's about to change. In *Baby & Toddler Sleep Solutions For Dummies,* we offer time-tested strategies that encourage even the most wide-awake tot to snooze peacefully through the night. With the help of our easy, step-by-step plans, your bedtime battles give way to sweet dreams so you and your child can both be well-rested and full of energy for your daytime adventures.

If you're completely at the mercy of that little person in the crib, this book shows you how to lovingly and firmly take charge of the sleepy-time schedule in your home. Whether your sweetie fusses at tuck-in-time, squawks all night long, or hops out of his bed and into yours, we have the answers that help you take control of the night (and naptimes, too). So cheer up — help is here, and a peaceful night's sleep is on the way.

About This Book

If you feel like you're flat out of answers trying to get your sweetie to snooze, you're not alone. Millions of parents try those one-size-fits-all sleep strategies, and find out that — guess what — they don't fit every tot or every parent.

That's not surprising, because one-size *doesn't* fit all babies and toddlers. And that's why we don't recommend a cookie-cutter approach to sleep issues. Instead, we help you tailor a strategy that's a custom fit for you and your sweetie. We base our techniques on a simple, tried-and-true principle: The best way to solve any baby or toddler issue is to let your child participate in the solution. Between the two of us, we've helped more than 10,000 families use this strategy successfully — and that's a lot of peace and quiet!

Making your child an active player in the sleep game avoids the twin pitfalls of tough love (crying it out) or passively hoping the problem will go away. Here's the foundation for our successful approach: Your child creates the problem of interrupting your sleep (and often your privacy), so only your child can solve this problem — with your loving guidance. Two elements are key to your role in this process:

✔ Your expectation that you're entitled to the sleep and privacy you need.

✔ Your knowledge that your angel can't be traumatized by your loving but firm guidance as she finds the solutions to her sleep issues.

When you put these pieces into place and combine them with the clear-cut, easy-to-use interventions we offer, you're on the road to peaceful nights and happy, well-rested days.

Conventions Used in This Book

To help you find what you want quickly, we use a few conventions in our typeface.

✔ *Italic* is used to highlight new terms that we define in the text.

✔ **Boldface** is used to indicate the action part of numbered steps.

✔ `Monofont` is used for Web and e-mail addresses.

What You're Not to Read

Of course, you can read every word if you want to! In fact, we'll be very happy if you do. But if you want to cut to the chase, feel free to ignore the sidebars (the gray boxes sprinkled throughout these pages). These sidebars are filled with valuable and entertaining tidbits, but you can ignore them and still master the sleep strategies we describe. You can also browse past the paragraphs marked with a *Technical Stuff* icon. That icon points out useful information, but it isn't essential if you want the need-to-know info so you can get in and get out of the book.

Foolish Assumptions

In writing this book, we tried to picture what our readers are like and what information they need the most. Here's what we assume about you:

✔ You're fairly new at the parenting game — not necessarily a first-time parent but probably not the parent of a dozen kids either.

✔ You have a child — whether an infant or a growing toddler — who just won't sleep the way you think he should.

✔ You're a kind and caring parent who's looking for sleep strategies that are both effective and loving.

✔ You want simple, no-frills advice without lots of jargon or technical details.

✔ You can't wait to jump in and get started so you can finally get a good night's sleep!

How This Book Is Organized

Baby & Toddler Sleep Solutions For Dummies is divided into five parts so you can quickly find the information that's just right for your child's age, your needs, and any special circumstances that affect your tot's sleep. Here's a quick look at what you'll find in each part.

Part 1: From A to ZZZZZ: The Basics of Sleep

In this part, we offer the background info that helps set the stage for a successful sleep strategy. In Chapter 1, we introduce the most important themes about sleep and explain how to tell the difference between your child's *wants* and *needs* — a big key to taking charge of the nights around your house. Chapter 2 describes the basics of baby and toddler sleep including what it is and how it develops so you know what to realistically expect from your angel, whether she's 3 days or 3 years old. In Chapter 3 we talk about the important role that personality — both yours and your tot's — plays in designing a sleep plan that works for everyone in your household.

Part II: I Have a Dream: Winning Sleep Strategies for Every Age

Part II is where you find sleep-promoting approaches for each age and stage of your baby's or toddler's development. If your sweetie is under 6 months old, turn to Chapter 4 for info about when and how to establish a sleep schedule. Chapter 5 offers advice for the

6-months-to-1-year-old crowd including how to establish a bedtime routine and how to manipulate mealtimes to promote longer stretches of sleep. In Chapter 6, you find out how to cope with a 12- to 18-month-old and get important advice on handling that big sleep disruptor called *separation anxiety.* Chapter 7 talks about toddlers in the 18-month to 2-year range. We cover how to use language to enhance your sleep strategies; how to handle nightmares, night terrors, and sleepwalking or sleep-talking; and how (and when) to make that big switch from crib to bed. Chapter 8 covers the 2-to-3-year-old gang including that all-important question: How do you juggle a sleep schedule with potty training?

Part III: Sleep Decisions that Involve the Whole Family

This part takes a look at sleep issues that affect every person in your household. In Chapter 9, we examine the advantages and drawbacks of co-sleeping — that is, sharing your bedroom or even your bed with your tot — and explain how to co-sleep safely. Chapter 10 focuses on siblings and includes tips on twins and sleep issues that arise if you adopt. In Chapter 11, we talk about babysitters, childcare, and preschool, and we explain how to ensure that your child-care decisions foster sound sleep at night.

Part IV: Dealing with Special Circumstances

This part offers additional advice for parents dealing with some of life's big and small challenges. In Chapter 12, we talk about the sleep issues of premature infants; we describe swaddling and other techniques to enhance an early bird's slumber. Chapter 13 discusses what to do if your sweetie comes down with a short-term bug or has a long-term medical issue. And in Chapter 14, we explain how life's changes, major or minor, can send your tot's sleep schedule into a tailspin — and what you can do to restore peace and quiet.

Part V: The Part of Tens

In this special *For Dummies* feature, we offer fun and helpful tips to round out your sleep know-how. Chapter 15 provides 10 of our best ideas for getting babies and toddlers to sleep. Chapter 16 does just the opposite; it describes 10 sleep pitfalls to avoid. And in Chapter 17, we offer 10 of the all-time best songs, games, and stories for bedtime.

Icons Used in This Book

As you're reading, you'll spot icons in the margins next to the text. These can steer you to information that's useful, informative, funny, or important to your child's safety. These icons can be real time-savers if you're looking for specific information, so keep an eye out for them.

We know that talking about parenting — especially when it comes to sleep — is a lot easier than putting it into action because everyone's situation is different. This icon highlights individual situations where parents implemented our advice. We think you'll find them helpful.

When you see this sign, look for critical information to keep in mind. It's worth repeating — and remembering.

Wherever you see this icon, you'll find in-depth details on a sleep-related topic. (Not into the technical nitty-gritty? Then feel free to skip these sections.)

This icon draws your attention to a piece of advice that deserves special attention — for instance, a key part of your sleep strategy.

This icon can help you avoid dangerous situations and mistakes that can derail your tot's sleep routine.

Where to Go from Here

We know you have your hands full. What parent of a little tyke doesn't? That's why we don't waste your time by making you wade through lots of information you don't need. Instead, we organized this book so you can pick and choose the topics that interest you. Let your fingers do the walking through the Table of Contents — or just open the book at any point and dive in. We also offer handy cross-references so you can easily find the additional information you need.

When you picked up this book, you took the first step on the road to a good night's sleep for you and your child. What's your next step? If you're still gathering your nerve to tackle the bedtime battles, we recommend Chapter 1. Interested in the hows and whys of sleep? Then Chapter 2 is a good place to start. We recommend Chapter 3 if you want to get a handle on the personality issues that affect your sweetie's sleep.

If you'd rather just dive in and start on your new sleep plan tonight, then pick the age-appropriate chapter in Part II and go for it! Add Chapter 9 if you're co-sleeping (or considering this choice) and Chapters 10 or 11 if you're dealing with sibling or school issues. And be sure to check out Part IV if your sweetie arrived prematurely, has health issues, or is going through big or little life changes.

Wherever you start, you'll be doing yourself and your tot a big favor by using the tips we offer. And the better you and your sweetie rest at night, the happier you'll both be in the daytime — which means that the bedtime battles can end in a win-win situation. So congratulations on taking charge of your tot's nightlife . . . and sweet dreams!

Part I

From A to ZZZZZ: The Basics of Sleep

"Getting her to sleep is like going to the opera. It takes place in stages, there's a lot of yelling, and by the end everyone's starting to nod off."

In this part . . .

Your new life as a proud parent is filled with joys and thrills . . . *and* plenty of sleepless nights! But with a little luck — and the help of our practical tips — you'll be snoozing soundly before long. In Chapter 1, you discover why your *game face* is so important to success in the sleep wars. Chapter 2 first tells you how and why babies and toddlers sleep and then what you can expect as your baby's sleep patterns mature. And in Chapter 3, we describe why ß isn't just a song title — it's also a key to tailoring sleep strategies for your tot's (and your!) needs.

Chapter 1

Taking Charge of Your Dream Team

In This Chapter

▶ Accepting the rules of the first few months

▶ Getting it straight: Trauma versus disappointment, wants versus needs

▶ Plotting a new, improved course of action

▶ Trading up: From guilt to self-confidence

*Y*ou're a grownup, smart and experienced. And you have lots of skills — you can scramble an egg, ride a bicycle, and balance a checkbook. Your child, in contrast, is a little person. He's smart too, but he really doesn't know much yet.

So you're probably wondering, "Why does *he* keep winning the bedtime battles?"

The answer is simple: Right now, your child is deciding when it's sleepytime and when it isn't. But the solution is also simple: You need to change the rules.

Luckily, you can accomplish this mission in a loving way that strengthens the bond between you and your sweetie. In fact, when you help him sleep on his own, you lay the groundwork for a strong, happy relationship. In this chapter, we tell you when and how to prepare for this big step — and, most importantly, why it's the right one for both you and your child.

In the Beginning . . . Baby's in Charge

The whole world is new to your baby, but she enters it fully equipped for those all-important basics: eating, sleeping, peeing, and pooping. The catch, of course, is that she does these on her

schedule, not yours! That's okay when it's peeing and pooping —
but those non-stop wake-up calls in the middle of the night can
leave you bleary-eyed and fuzzy-brained.

However, when your newborn hollers every few hours, she's doing
just what she's supposed to do. In the early weeks, your baby
simply isn't ready to sleep through the night. (Yes, we know, a few
tots do — but they're the exception, not the rule.)

Your newborn needs you to wait on her each time she wakes up
because she's growing like a weed and has to eat every few hours
to meet her calorie demands (see Chapter 4). Besides, her sleep
cycles are too immature for her to make it through the night. In
Chapter 2, we explain why sleep is more than just closing your
eyes and why your baby needs to grow into mature sleep patterns
before she can conk out for more than a few hours.

When your little angel gets past those calorie and sleep-pattern
hurdles, she's ready for an all-night snooze. Almost all children hit
this mark between 4 and 6 months of age. Of course, each tot's
unique, and some reach this point a few weeks after birth — but
the closer she gets to 4 months of age, the more certain you can be
that your infant can sleep all night without interruption. (For ways
to make her even *more* ready, see Chapter 5.) But at that point,
another question arises: Are *you* ready?

Conquering Your Fears about Taking the Big Step

Even though you can now pick your moment for getting your
sweetie to doze through the night, one qualm may hold you back —
the fear that somehow you'll emotionally damage your little love-
bug by being firm with him.

But the fact that you're reading this book means you want to handle
your tyke's sleep problems in a kind and nurturing way. So here's
good news: Helping your babe figure out how to fall asleep on his
own doesn't hurt him a bit. In fact, you'll do him — and you — a
world of good.

The big misunderstanding: Trauma versus disappointment

The first secret to raising kids is knowing the huge difference
between *trauma* and *disappointment.* Yes, you'll disappoint your

sweetie when you stop letting him call the shots at bedtime — but no, he won't be the least bit traumatized. In fact, he'll take a giant step toward becoming a well-adjusted little person.

So what's the big difference between trauma and disappointment? Check out the following explanations:

- ✔ A *trauma* is a terrible event that shakes a child to the core, challenges his belief that the world is a safe place, and causes long-term emotional distress — for instance, the death of someone he loves or abandonment by the people he trusts. Traumas occur when serious needs are denied, and they cause grave harm.

- ✔ *Disappointments,* on the other hand, are tiny clouds that pass, causing no harm at all. They're simply unanswered desires that occur when people create expectations that can't be fulfilled — and they're the stuff of daily life.

Fortunately, traumas happen far less often than disappointments. Of course, everyone wants to skate through life free of both traumas *and* disappointments — and caring parents certainly strive to keep both to a minimum. But it's important not to mistake minor disappointments for serious traumas because this mistake can hinder both you and your child. What's more, it's a common trap for parents.

Why is it so easy to make this mistake? To get an idea, picture an 8-month-old crying up a storm at 2 a.m. Because his parents weaned him from the nighttime bottle two months ago, they know he isn't hungry. They're also sure he isn't sick, in pain, or simply stuck. In reality, he's just trying to wake up Mommy and Daddy, get them out of bed, and enjoy a little snuggle. But even after they make sure nothing's really wrong (see the yellow tear-out card at the front of this book), his parents *believe* they're hearing the primal scream of a child terrified by the impending trauma of parental abandonment. It's a classic case of mistaken identity — the disappointed infant masquerading as a broken-hearted child in a life crisis.

Why does this confusion matter? Because if you think your infant is about to suffer irreparable harm, your only option is to give in. In fact, when you let this mistaken idea direct your actions, you're unable to offer your child any guidance — now or later — for fear that lifelong damage may ensue. And this fear can leave you paralyzed by doubt and worry, making any effective course of action impossible and inevitably getting in the way of your tot's growth and development.

What's more, the impossible task of preventing all disappointments can leave you exhausted and resentful. You're much smarter to show your little huggy-bear that frustrations come with all new life skills — from tying his shoes, to playing with friends, to managing a Fortune-500 company — and sleeping on a schedule is one of the very first.

So as you get ready to turn over a new leaf in your household, brace yourself for a very interesting turn of events as you put your tot in charge of his own sleep. If you hear complaints — and we're pretty sure you will! — see them for what they are: reactions to a minor disappointment, not a major trauma. Remember, too, that this is an exciting moment. When you tell your sweetie in words and actions that he's ready to sleep through the night, you're demonstrating your confidence in his ability to master this first big-kid skill.

Your biggest challenge: Distinguishing between wants and needs

Watching your sweetie's face scrunch up and hearing her wail when she doesn't get what she wants can be tough, we know. But you can expect this reaction more than once when you implement your sleep strategy.

However, the key to your child's sleep — and every other aspect of her life — is remembering that *wants* aren't *needs.* As a parent, you make sure your child has everything she *needs,* but that doesn't mean you give her everything she *wants.*

For the first few months of your baby's life, you can easily distinguish her wants from her needs — because she needs you for everything! Somewhere around that 4- to 6-month mark, however, she doesn't need you as much as you think.

With each passing month, your little one is able to do more, understand more, and be more independent. However, she's also accustomed to being with you — her 24-hour on-call buddy — and she's not going to give up that arrangement easily.

Like a kid in a candy store, your tot has trouble knowing the difference between what she wants from you and what she needs from you. And as a loving, nurturing, and very tired parent, you don't always know the difference either. But if you can make this distinction between wants and needs *and* make it early in the game, your life and your child's can be happier.

Of course, older kids' wants and needs are easier to sort out than babies' and toddlers'. (In fact, we outline different sleep strategies for kids at different ages and stages in Part II of this book because what works for an 8-month-old can be very different from what works for a 3-year-old.) But making the distinction is key to your sleep strategy. To help you tell the difference, here's a quick run-down of your little one's needs versus her wants.

Your baby *needs* the following from you:

- ✔ Plenty of food — on demand at first, and at regular intervals later on
- ✔ Love, cuddles, rocking, gentle touching, and the sound of your voice
- ✔ Safety and security
- ✔ Interaction that develops her language and stimulates her development
- ✔ Consistent caregivers to help her develop trust and attachment
- ✔ Proper medical care to keep her happy and healthy
- ✔ Lots of diaper changes!

In contrast, here's what your baby or toddler *wants* from you:

- ✔ **You, you, you,** every minute of every day and — as the old Beatles' song goes — "eight days a week."
- ✔ **Lots of inappropriate stuff** — like your permission to stick her finger in a light socket or put the cat in the toilet — especially in those first months of toddlerhood, when she discovers the amazing wonders of the world around her (more on this stage in Chapter 6).
- ✔ **Power**

  Power is simply the ability to change what someone else does, and politicians and movie villains aren't the only power-mad people. The average tot is quite able — and very willing — to use her power when she desires control over Mommy or Daddy.
- ✔ **Everything else her little heart desires — right now!**

Do you see a lot of overlap between the preceding wants and needs lists? Nope. Yet loving parents often worry so much about upsetting their children that they give into every demand, no matter how unreasonable. As a result, they keep their little ones from finding the boundaries all children seek: the line where their parents say "No" *and* the rules their parents really care about.

Understanding the need for limits

Of course, your child can get what he wants — he just can't get what he wants *every time,* and some of his demands will simply be unreasonable. When he's 6 years old, for instance, he'll want the fad toy that costs a fortune and breaks on the first day. At 10, he'll beg for junk food every day. And when he's 16, he'll want you to buy him a brand-new sports car you can't afford.

You know parents who give in to all of their kids' demands, whether they're sensible wishes or not. These kids scream for candy in the grocery store and have ear-splitting tantrums on the playground when they don't win every game. They stay up till 2 a.m. watching television and then struggle through school half-asleep the next day. Somewhere along the line, their parents find out the hard way that children actually crave and need limits. A kid whose every wish is granted keeps pushing and expanding his demands, always seeking the line his parents never draw.

When you draw that line, you give your child a gift that's second only to love: guidance. And coupled with your love, this guidance tells him you'll keep him safe and sound. A child whose Mom and Dad set loving limits learns early to have reasonable expectations and be very happy when they're met.

Changing Your Tot's Expectations — and Yours

If you're the Queen of England, you have pretty high expectations. Your tiara needs to sparkle, your palaces need to be spotless, and high tea had better include those little cucumber sandwiches.

If you're a regular person, however, you're probably happy if your partner cooks breakfast or your dog fetches the paper. And if the next-door neighbor drops off a batch of home-made cookies, you're in heaven.

What's our point? That people base much of their happiness on what they expect from life. You don't expect dozens of servants to wait on you hand-and-foot, so you're perfectly happy without them. The queen, however, would be mighty unhappy if she had to scrub your toilet and water your ficus.

Babies and toddlers, just like grownups, are happy when life meets their expectations. But right now, that's a problem for you because your child expects you to appear on demand at any hour of the night. As a result, he'll be as mad as a queen with a tarnished tiara if you don't show your face on schedule.

To tweak his royal stance, you need to change his expectation — but it isn't likely to change until you take the first step, by changing *yours.*

Refocusing your thoughts

Before your munchkin can change her expectations, you need to change two of your own. First, expect her to take charge of the issue at hand: her. Second, expect her to put up a fuss when you ask her to do this. Be prepared to react (or *not,* as the case may be) to this resistance.

You can help change your expectations by keeping these facts in mind:

- ✔ **You and your tot have different jobs.** Your sweetie's job is to demand lots of stuff because that's how she figures out what's reasonable and what isn't. Your job, in turn, is to set limits so she can figure out the rules of life.

  For instance, if she says, "I want an elephant," your job *isn't* to rush out and get her one. Your job *is* to explain why she's not getting one.

- ✔ **To maintain a healthy lifestyle, both you and your child need regular, uninterrupted sleep.** A good night's sleep is important for your whole household, and your tot will still love you every bit as much when you stop popping out of bed at all hours to entertain her. When you recognize these truths, you're halfway down the road to a solid sleep solution. At this point you're ready to gently and lovingly teach your child a brand-new expectation: I'm not going to get lots of attention if I squawk when I wake up, so I'll just happily go back to sleep on my own. Period.

- ✔ **Giving in has a big downside.** When you cave in and satisfy an unreasonable demand, your child's first thought is something like, "Wow! I got Mommy and Daddy to give me a bottle when I didn't need it!" But her next thought is something like, "Hmm . . . now, how do I get a bottle *twice* a night? How far can I push my demands before they draw the line?" And if you never set reasonable limits, she's likely to start worrying, "Uh-oh — how can I feel safe if Mommy and Daddy don't really respond to my pushing the limits?"

Strengthening your hand at the negotiating table

Many families have at least one tot who simply refuses to sleep through the night. This is the tyke who figures out how to keep the rest of the family members popping up like prairie dogs all night long for months, even years.

Often, the mommies and daddies in these families are skilled negotiators — lawyers, sales people, or even CEOs who negotiate for a living. Yet every night, these parents get outmaneuvered by a tiny being. How is this possible?

The answer is that even very young babies negotiate — and often they drive hard bargains! Most people think of negotiation as a tough adults-only event, like union bosses sitting at a table with corporate lawyers or company administrators discussing big mergers. But negotiation is simply a situation in which two people want different outcomes; they interact to see how it'll turn out.

In your case, negotiation occurs whenever your baby wants something different than you do at bedtime. At the outset, you're in opposing corners: Your baby wants to be awake with you, and you want to sleep all night. Only a negotiation can settle the difference.

Right now, your baby is winning that negotiation hands down because he's using his one big tool: screaming. If you think about it, that's all he has to throw at the situation. He can't e-mail you, write a letter, call you on the phone, talk it over, or even pay you to come see him at 2 a.m. But then, he doesn't need to, does he?

As long as you go to your tot each time he opens his mouth and yells, you lose at the parent-child negotiation game. The instant you realize that you hold the moral high ground (because a good night's sleep is beneficial for both of you), you can stop investing so much power in your tyke's strategy and start setting your own terms. In Part II of this book, we tell you how to change the rules of the nighty-night game and walk away from the bedtime negotiations with a deal that works for both of you.

Factoring in your tot's personality and other issues

If a single blueprint could solve every tot's sleep problems, this book would be about six pages long. However, because each child is unique, you need to take your tot's personality — in addition to her age and development — into account. These factors, as well as your own unique style, play a big role in planning your approach to the bedtime negotiations, as we explain in Chapter 3.

In addition, your bedtime strategy needs to make allowances for a host of special circumstances that can influence your expectations of your little sweetie. Among them:

✔ A 4-month-old premature baby can't snooze through the night, and a tot with asthma can't doze peacefully if she's wheezing. In Chapters 12 and 13, we look at adaptations that promote sleep if your tot is an early bird or has medical issues.

✔ A little darling who's coping with a big life-change like a new sibling or her parents' divorce has more trouble sleeping than a tot whose life is on an even keel. As a result, she needs a little special handling — a topic we cover in Chapter 14.

✔ If you're co-sleeping with your tot, something we discuss in Chapter 9, you need to handle the big switch when your sweetie heads off to her own bed.

✔ Potty-training adds a new twist to the bedtime story, and you need a strategy for making a good night's sleep *and* dry pants a reality (an issue we cover in Chapter 8).

✔ Is your sweetie a sleepwalker or sleep-talker? Does she experience those bizarre episodes called *sleep terrors?* If so, you need to know why these events occur and what you should and shouldn't do about them — a topic we discuss in Chapter 7.

✔ If your little cub is starting day care or preschool soon, you can expect some sleep setbacks. Chapter 11 offers advice on getting her back on track.

Sleep routines get even more complicated when you have more than one child because each tyke comes with her own set of needs, wants, and personality quirks — and if the sibs are twins or triplets, you really have your hands full! (We offer tips on all of these topics in Chapter 10.)

Setting Yourself Up for Success

Ready to say "Goodbye" to sleepless nights and "Hello" to sweet dreams? If so, it's time to get in the right frame of mind for the challenge ahead. Here are two more key pieces to put in place before you start.

Losing the guilt

Still feeling a twinge of guilt about expecting your tot to sleep through the night? If so, you're only human. (In fact, if you're not feeling guilty about *something* on a regular basis, you're not yet a parent!)

Maybe you're thinking, "I'm doing this for my own sake because I'm so tired of getting up." And of course, that's true — you have needs, and one of them is sleep! In truth, however, you're really taking this step for your child because

- This is the first big solution he gets to come up with in his little life.

- When he figures out how to comfort himself to sleep and stay in his own bed all night long, he gets a big shot of confidence.

    This self-assurance makes future steps toward independence (staying with a babysitter, using the potty, and so on) much easier for him to master.

- When your sweetie sleeps long and soundly, he's rested and ready to face the day.

Even more important, your child needs *you* to be well-rested! Just think of all the jobs you do and why you can do them better when you're not droopy and baggy-eyed:

- **You're his personal driver.** Not surprisingly, a rested driver is a safer driver. About 100,000 car crashes occur in the United States each year because drivers are sleepy.

- **You're his best teacher.** Exploring the wonderful world together is lots more fun when you're bright-eyed and bushy-tailed.

- **You're the light of his life.** Your baby adores you, and he needs you to stay happy and healthy. Staying well-rested helps protect you from lots of medical problems (including postpartum depression if you're a new mom). In fact, according to an important study in *Pediatrics* (May 2007), moderate or severe sleep problems in infants nearly double the chance that mothers will experience severe psychological distress and poor overall health — even if they have no mental health issues before delivery. For dads, the odds of developing poor overall health go up 50 percent when infants have significant sleep problems.

    As professionals, we've met thousands of new parents. The happiest ones are the parents who lovingly set limits on sleep and other aspects of their tots' lives, not the ones who wearily (and then resentfully) cater to their tot's whims.

> ✔ **You're his rudder.** Whether he realizes it or not, your little cherub counts on you to guide him through the sometimes choppy waters of childhood. If you don't offer guidance at the simpler stages early on — and sleep is one — he won't be confident that you can help him through more difficult times that are sure to come.

To keep all of your family strong, happy, and full of bounce (and to strengthen your relationship with your little one), nothing beats a good night's sleep.

Gaining the confidence that leads to success

Your baby's birth begins a lifelong dance. Sometimes she leads and you follow; other times, you need to take her firmly by the hand and show her some new steps. The trick is knowing when to lead and when to follow because your goal is to give her everything she needs while encouraging her to stand on her own two feet (or lie on her own pillow, in this case!).

Earlier generations of parents had an easier time making these decisions. For centuries, people raised their kids very much like their own parents, grandparents, and even great-grandparents did. But today's families often live hundreds of miles from their closest kin. As a result, Moms and Dads have a harder time knowing whether they're doing the best they can for their tots.

Making sure you're in good shape

Depression is very common, affecting up to 25 percent of all people at any one time. And it's also one of the most common threats to feeling good as a new parent; in fact, at least 10 percent of all mothers experience postpartum depression.

Our advice? Always seek treatment for depression. In fact, as a new parent, you have an especially good reason: your baby's well-being. A parent's depression strongly affects a newborn, infant, or child, and in particular can result in sleep problems.

So as you prepare to tackle your tot's sleep issues, be sure to start with this question: Do I have any signs of depression? These signs include sadness, change in appetite, loss of energy (beyond what you'd expect as a new parent), and loss of interest in life or in your baby. If you have any concerns, call your obstetrician or a qualified counselor right away. Also, see *Postpartum Depression For Dummies* by Shoshana S. Bennett and Mary Jo Codey (Wiley).

Stories from the crib: A declaration of independence

Latrice, a nurse with three kids under the age of 4, felt guilty about her middle child, Lamont. Lamont was only 1 year old when Latrice became pregnant with his little brother, and she felt bad that Lamont didn't get to be the baby for long. To add to her guilt, Lamont — unlike his brothers — didn't adjust well to childcare.

At 2 years of age, Lamont still woke up twice each night. Latrice offered him a bottle each time to get him back to sleep. She dragged through her work days and dreaded the nights, but she couldn't break the cycle.

Finally, Latrice attended a parenting workshop where she learned to tell the difference between Lamont's needs and his wants. She also realized that her guilt kept her trapped in an intolerable routine.

Using the strategies from the workshop, Latrice devised a sleep plan and stuck to it. First, she weaned Lamont from his middle-of-the-night bottles. Next, she stopped running to him when he cried and let him comfort himself to sleep.

A few weeks later, Latrice showed up at the parenting group and announced, "My life has changed!" Lamont was now sleeping through the night, and the newly-energized Latrice could offer him quality time in the mornings and evenings — instead of at 2 a.m.!

If your child's lack of sleep is causing stress in your life, you're not alone; at least one-third of all families have the same problem! We've counseled more than 10,000 of these families, and with very rare exceptions (usually when the tots or their parents have other, very serious life issues), the techniques we describe in this book work like a charm.

In the following chapters we offer you lots of information and plenty of advice because we want you to tackle your tot's sleep routine with confidence. We believe the more you know about sleep and good strategies, the more easily you can lovingly smooth your child's path to Slumberland. So rest easy — you're doing the right thing, and everyone (including your little night owl) will be better off!

Chapter 2

Understanding the Importance and Stages of Slumber

. . . .

In This Chapter

▶ Understanding sleep and what makes it tick

▶ Checking out the stages of sleep

▶ Recognizing the patterns and amounts of baby and toddler sleep

. . . .

*P*icture yourself, head on your pillow, happily dreaming away. As you're traipsing along in dreamland, your heart is pumping blood, your lungs are breathing, and everything else is chugging along — a little more slowly than in the day, but not by much. Your brain, which labors so hard during the day, is also working away.

Even though people tend to think of sleep as rest, the body doesn't really quit. In fact, nearly every organ in the body works just as hard during sleep. So what good is it, and why do people need it so much if nothing's really resting?

Although the pros still don't know *exactly* why people need sleep, they do know that the brain, more than any other part of the human body, needs it. Your skin works whether you sleep or not and so does your heart, bones, and kidneys. But skip a single night of snoozing, and your brain starts to go on the fritz. Skip two nights, and you're a complete mess — you don't remember what you had for breakfast, you get cranky and angry, and bright lights and noise hit you like a sledge hammer. If you try to stay awake, you eventually keel over into a deep sleep or suffer more serious harm. So whatever sleep is, it's a big deal for the brain.

In this chapter we take a peek into the hidden world of slumber and explain why quiet slumber is really a busy and important time, especially for babies and toddlers. We also take an in-depth look at those funny sleep stages, where everything from wacky dreams to sleepwalking and sleep-talking can occur. Finally, we explain how your tot is busy growing into the sleep pattern he'll have for the rest of his life.

The Poetry of a Good Night's Snooze

No look at sleep is complete without talking about its *poetry* — and nobody's better at that than Shakespeare. The following sections point to his genius on the subject.

Sleep is break time for the mind

When Shakespeare called sleep "the death of each day's life," he was right on the money. Your active, waking day comes to a complete and crashing halt when you call it a night. Whether you spent your day stuck in freeway traffic or figuring out where the triangle piece fits in the shape-sorter toy — when the lights go out, it's over.

At this finish line of each day, a big or little person's mind can shift from working on the outside world's problems to doing its own thing, free from worries and obligations. Of course, outer and inner worlds are connected, so dreams often reflect waking experiences. But in the world of sleep, you can think whatever you want — any thought can come true. And it's a welcome break from the outside world, where humans big and small face a less flexible reality. (Thanks to Mother Nature, though, the brain has a little alarm that wakes you when anything *too* exciting happens in that outside world!)

Sleep soothes the troubled soul

What about getting a rest from the *mental* pains of the day? Shakespeare called sleep the "balm of hurt minds," and again he was right on target. Life's a joy, but it's also full of dashed desires. For your tot, those frustrations can include getting a dumb breakfast cereal instead of his favorite one, Daddy being too busy to play ball, a rivalry with a playmate, or a broken toy. These disappointments can leave a little mind in turmoil. The solution? A good night's sleep.

In addition, sleep seems to do the following:

✔ Builds memories through brain connections so you can file away everyday facts and figures like how to say "Mama" or count to three. (More on this process in the sections "The Brain's High Heaven: Sleeping through Stages" and "Taking a detour into Dreamland: REM.")

✔ Lets you make sense of the emotional swirls that went along with these memories. (See "Taking a detour into Dreamland: REM" later in this chapter.)

✔ Helps you come to terms with disappointments and frustrations and come out stronger the next day.

✔ Cuts you off from the troublesome world, letting you put a personal stamp on the events of the day and see events solely in your mind's eye.

As you do this, you retell the story in your own way and put setbacks in perspective. Even those hard-to-explain dreams can prepare you for new and better approaches to your nagging problems.

✔ Lets you use dreams to rewrite the ending of a daily story and create new memories in the process.

Unfortunately sleep can't accomplish these goals if you can't get to Sleepyland in the first place. So parents need to set the stage for good sleep — especially when a child's in turmoil — and get him into the routine. (We cover this topic more in Chapters 5 and 6.)

Sleep is food for body, mind, and soul

Shakespeare also called sleep "great nature's second course, chief nourisher in life's feast." In other words, sleep is the glorious last course of the day's marvelous banquet.

Perhaps the most compelling proof of how sleep nourishes the brain comes from studies of the brain when sleep is interrupted. Studies show that in children as young as 2 years of age even a minor disruption (like their own heavy snoring) leads to severe problems in brain function. These problems include irritability, aggression, emotional instability, attention deficits, and loss of memory function and overall intelligence. When doctors fix the snoring problem and good sleep returns, these important functions return to normal.

In animal studies, a three-hour interruption of sleep sharply reduced the ability of the *hippocampus* (an important center for memory function in the brain) to make new memories. In addition, the animals became extremely irritable. A nine-hour interruption wiped out the measured memory function altogether! (See the section on Stage 2 and REM sleep later in this chapter for the types of memory that sleep helps create.)

It's easy to understand why food gives a boost of energy — food is fuel. But, studies show that sleep clearly provides energy too. The question is: How is this possible when sleep doesn't give the body actual fuel? The answer appears to lie in the brain. Food may *give* your body the fuel, but sleep allows your brain to *use* that fuel to order your mind, memories, and moods. End result: You have the mental energy to tackle the big job of life.

By allowing the brain to make new connections, file away precious memories, and spin the lessons of the day into the story of one's life (see the bullets in the previous section), sleep helps a person to

✔ Emerge better-rested and more able to tackle another day in the real world

✔ Be less irritable about life's little disappointments, less sad about the big ones

✔ Think more clearly after sweeping away the debris of the previous day.

Not surprisingly, little tykes, just like grown-ups, can go to bed fussy or sad or exhausted and pop out of bed the next day rarin' to go again. That last course in the banquet — sleep — makes the next day seem new, fresh, and full of opportunity.

Sleep trivia: Lions and tigers and bears, oh . . . zzzzz

From a survival standpoint, sleep seems like a weird idea. After all, there you are, totally out of it for hours at a time, and anybody can whack you with a rock or steal your stereo. So why does Mother Nature program you to do something that seems so dangerous?

One unusual explanation stems from the old, old days when people roamed the savannah and their biggest worry wasn't burglars or bad people but animals. When you think about it, sleep's a mighty good form of camouflage because most predators spot their dinner by watching for motion, and nothing stops us from moving like a good long snooze.

Interestingly, if you line up all the mammals according to who's most vulnerable to predators, they line up in the same order as who's the most sleepy. So the more hunted the mammal (at least historically), the more sleep it needs!

Understanding Your Internal Clock

The first and most dramatic moment of sleep is the big leap from being awake to being asleep. If you've ever tried to spot the exact moment when you go from sleeping to waking, you know it's impossible; one minute you're thinking, "I need to get celery at the store . . ." and the next you're out like a light.

As it turns out, that line between waking and sleeping marks a huge chasm between two very different states of being. Consider these three steps:

- ✔ When scientists look at brain wave patterns of a wide-awake person, they see a whole bunch of varying waves.

- ✔ If they ask the person to meditate (or simply enter that trance world of television-watching), these waves slow down and become more regular.

- ✔ When the person falls asleep, the waves slow much more dramatically and start marching in parade-drill sync.

 Keeping this sleep-wake cycle under control is a major task, so a big chunk of the brain's work involves managing when, how often, and how long a person sleeps each day. And although nearly every part of the brain pitches in to keep the sleep-wake cycle on track, one part in particular does the heavy lifting to summon the sandman. Read on.

The arbiter of sleepy time

People are wired to be awake when it's sunny and asleep when it's dark, thanks to the *suprachiasmatic nucleus* (SCN — but we promise you won't be tested on that!). The SCN is a small group of cells deep in your brain's *hypothalamus,* the control center for lots of body functions like sleeping, eating, and breathing.

Of course, the SCN doesn't manage the brain's clock all on its own. Input from every part of the body helps, and the *pineal gland* (which makes a sleep-related hormone called *melatonin*) plays an especially important role. In some animals, in fact, the pineal gland continues to make melatonin according to the animal's clock even after the gland is removed!

Nevertheless, the SCN appears to be command central for clock operations, and the coolest part is its extraordinary ability to keep time. When your eyes tell your brain that it's light or dark outside, this information goes straight to the SCN. (See Chapter 4 for info on this day/night pattern, called the *circadian rhythm.*)

Sleep trivia: What a piece of work is man (and woman and child)!

The wonderful design of the human brain lets people engage in two activities that most living things can't — being awake and being asleep.

Little one-celled animals, which make up most life on the planet, zip around without any minds at all, so sleep is out of the question. Plants also lack brains; they simply react to chemical changes without switching between being awake or asleep. At a casual glance, fish and reptiles appear to sleep, but scientists say these creatures don't have clear states of asleep and awake. (The waking state of a lizard, for example, looks pretty much like a human's deep sleep.)

In reality, only birds and mammals have sleeping and waking states. And most interestingly, the more complex the brain (from bird brain to human brain), the more conscious — awake — it is. Deep sleep, even *rapid eye movement* (REM) sleep, goes way back in evolution, but being wide-awake is *the* new concept on the planet.

This consciousness both complicates and enriches human life with infinite choices, desires, and possibilities — and, in turn, elevates sleep from mere instinct to a powerful tool for managing thoughts and memories. So sleep is a big chapter in the amazing story of how human minds live in, craft, and create the world around them!

One of the great properties of the SCN — and the body's internal clock as a whole — is its adaptability. If you've ever experienced jet lag, you may wonder how good your brain is at adapting. But jet lag actually demonstrates how solid your clock is and how quickly it can adapt. The body's clock resists changes (which is why that first day in a new time zone is sheer misery), but when it has to change, it can shift the whole body onto a new schedule in just a day or two.

Grasping what makes your own clock tick

The SCN doesn't run on batteries or plug into the wall. Instead, it uses chemical *vibes* — molecules that actually vibrate on a microscopic level — that tell you to open your eyes and say "Good morning!" or hit the pillow and snore.

This clever little clock calculates your bedtime based on

- ✔ The cycle of light and dark
- ✔ The times you eat

✔ Your daily routine

✔ Your emotions (which explains why there's nothing like a big
scare or upset to chase away sleep).

If you don't throw your day/night schedule out of kilter (say, by
flying cross-country), and you eat regularly, follow your usual routines, and stay on an even keel emotionally, this tiny internal clock
keeps humming away right on schedule. And each night around
bedtime, it sends out a signal that says, "Shut those eyes!" so you
can enter the very exciting world of slumber.

Each person's internal clock is unique, of course; everything from
tiny biochemical variations to different personality traits and
lifestyles can influence whether a person's an early riser or night
owl, and whether he likes six, eight, or ten hours of sleep each
night. These variations are just one reason why getting your tot
to sleep on your schedule is a bit of an adventure.

Sleeping through Stages

Because sleep is mainly about the brain, the brain naturally controls the most striking aspect of sleep: its stages. These stages are
a fascinating part of Slumberland, and knowing a little about them
can help you manage your infant and toddler's sleep better. In fact,
getting a handle on sleep stages can help you to

✔ Know when your tot is ready for sleep scheduling (see
"Getting Used to a Sleep Pattern: The Early Days of Life"
later in this chapter).

✔ Understand why your child sleeps lightly at some times
and soundly at others.

✔ Know what's going on when nightmares, sleepwalking,
or night terrors crop up (see Chapter 7 for more on
these issues).

Your brain can be in five different states while you're sleeping.
Four of these states are called the *stages* of sleep (which tend to
flow from one to another in an orderly sequence), and one state
is called *rapid eye movement* sleep (REM — see the later section
"Taking a detour into Dreamland: REM"). In the following sections,
we look at how people enter the kingdom of Sleepyland and then
cycle through its stages.

Stage 1: On the border between wake and sleep

When you enter Stage 1 sleep, you're on the boundary between waking and sleeping. These are the facts:

- ✔ It's the shortest stage of sleep; you spend about 5 percent of your time there.

- ✔ It's easier to rouse you in this stage than any other, which is why a creaking floor or a flapping curtain can snap you back into the land of the waking.

- ✔ You can sometimes experience a very brief, strong muscle twitch.

  Sometimes it's so powerful that you actually wake up; it often goes hand-in-hand with a sensation of falling.

  This *hypnic jerk* is perfectly normal for tots and adults (but don't yell out "hypnic jerk!" when your partner does it in bed or you may be in trouble).

Even though you barely have one foot in the land of sleep when you enter Stage 1, your brain's electrical patterns are already changing to a lower voltage and your eyes are starting to roll. The sleep game's already afoot.

Stage 2: The biggest territory in Sleepyland

Although tots have to grow into it (see "Getting Used to a Sleep Pattern: The Early Days of Life" later in this chapter), grownups spend most sack time in Stage 2.

When you hit Stage 2,

- ✔ You're not in deep sleep, but you're much more soundly asleep than in Stage 1.

- ✔ Your eyes don't move any more.

- ✔ There may be some dreaming, but most dreams appear to occur in REM sleep, not during the four sleep stages. (See the section on REM sleep later in this section.)

- ✔ Your brain starts to create bursts of electrical activity that may help it move *away from* the hectic electrical activity of being awake and *toward* the slower, more orderly rhythms of being asleep. Each burst lasts just a few seconds, but that's a long time in your brain's world.

What happens to a person during these bursts? The sleeping person has no way of knowing because she can't remember anything from Stage 2 sleep.

But thanks to hard-working scientists — who never seem to snooze themselves — some exciting clues about the brain's secret world are beginning to surface. For instance, research shows that a key reason for sleep is to help each day's memories settle into images that can last a lifetime. (See the section "Sleep is food for body, mind, and soul," earlier in this chapter for more on how sleep affects memory.)

In addition, scientists believe different types of memories get cast in stone in different stages of sleep. Stage 2 sleep seems to sort out and preserve facts, figures, and other dry bits of information — like 2 + 2 = 4 and the capital of Montana (these are *declarative memories*). In fact, the more sleep *spindles* (a type of electrical burst peculiar to Stage 2 sleep) that your brain creates at night, the better you can remember the facts from the day before; the more you can learn in the day, the more spindles you can generate at night! So if you *can* remember the capital of Montana, thank your Stage 2 sleep. (It's Helena — you can put that on your spindle!)

Stage 3: Ahh, deep sleep

When you head into Stage 3, you're entering the world of deep sleep — a very different place from Stages 1 and 2 (light sleep) and from REM — the sleep of dreams, which we discuss later in "Taking a detour into Dreamland: REM"). In Stage 3, those funny bursts of electrical energy from Stage 2 disappear, replaced by a very slow wave pattern called the *delta wave*.

Just as Stage 2 sleep is a bridge to Stage 3, Stage 3 is a staircase — to Stage 4, the basement of the sleep cellar. The further your tot climbs down these steps, the more soundly he sleeps. (But that sound sleep can only take place after these stages fully develop, which explains your tot's deeper, uninterrupted sleep as he gets older. See "Getting Used to a Sleep Pattern: The Early Days of Life," later in this chapter, for more info.)

Deep sleep, which kicks in at Stage 3 and accounts for roughly one-quarter of total sleep time, is one of life's greatest mysteries. It hides more secrets than even the deepest seas because no one ever returns from deep sleep with any memory of the experience.

When you reach this stage,

✔ You have a pretty hard time climbing back to the waking world.

✔ People can't easily rouse you.

✔ You're likely to be a bit dazed and confused if you do wake up.

Stage 4: The mystery realm

In Stage 4, the deepest of deep sleep, those slow delta brainwaves that enter the picture in Stage 3 now dominate the brain's activity. (That's why sleep specialists call Stages 3 and 4 *slow wave sleep.*)

Stages 3 and 4 are very much alike, but the really rock-solid deep sleep occurs in Stage 4. Many of the most interesting events in deep sleep (night terrors, bed-wetting, sleep-talking and walking) also occur in Stage 4 sleep.

As babies get older, even in toddlerhood, they spend lots of time in Stage 4 sleep in the first part of the night and less and less as the morning grows near. As Stage 4 sleep gets shorter in each sleep cycle, REM sleep (see the next section) gets longer. This expanding REM sleep may shorten the Stage 4 phase.

Because Stage 4 is the deepest level of sleep, you may suspect that not much happens. However, research shows that, in fact, a whole lot's going on. Here's the evidence:

✔ **People grow — especially at night!**

The human body makes a substance called *growth hormone,* which — you guessed it — stimulates and controls growth. The pituitary gland cranks more of this hormone out at night than in the daytime, and it really revs up in Stage 3 or Stage 4 sleep.

✔ **People are moved to, well, move.**

A visible clue that something's going on in deep sleep is *sleep arousal.* These arousals are

- An odd mixture of some waking brain functions and very deep sleep. (We delve into these events in Chapter 7 but bring them up here because they happen in the deepest depths of Stage 4 slumber.)

- Generally very short — just long enough to roll over in bed (important so you don't get bedsores) without waking up or even leaving deep sleep.

- Sometimes alarming. Occasionally, sleep arousals last much longer than a simple rollover, and kids can wet the bed, sleepwalk, or experience night terrors (see Chapter 7 for details).

Detouring into Dreamland: REM

All night long, a person cycles through the stages of sleep, sliding from Stage 1 to 2 to 3, all the way down to Stage 4, and then climbing way up from 4 to 3 to 2 to start all over again (see Figure 2-1). For adults this cycle happens four or five times a night, with each cycle taking about 1 ½ hours. (We talk about tots and their cycle that eventually relaxes into the adult REM in "Getting Used to a Sleep Pattern: The Early Days of Life" later in this chapter.)

At regular intervals during this cycle, however, a person can jump off the path and into the wild overgrowth of REM sleep, the state in which most dreams occur. During the first few hours of sleep, the detour into REM sleep is brief, but toward morning the dreamer spends much more time exploring this strange land. At the end of each REM state, after you're back in Stage 2, you choose whether to go toward deeper sleep or to wake up.

The reasoning for REM: Some speculations

One theory about REM sleep is that it helps people manage desire. According to this idea, humans store up frustrations and unmet desires each day; at night all of those frustrated dreams come true in the realm of REM. This theory suggests that people couldn't live without dreams and still keep their sanity because those desires would pile up and become overwhelming.

Although people store facts during Stage 2 sleep, they don't need to create a whole scene to remember that 12 + 36 = 48! In contrast, memories about a special time or place — like the excitement of a birthday party or the highlights of a road trip — seem to enter the memory only in REM sleep. So another theory about REM sleep is that it etches the more interesting memories involving emotions or events in a person's memory so he can find them later. People seem to need a narrative to understand and remember their important emotional memories; dreams are the stage that allows them to write these plays.

These dreams, then, help a person understand, explain, and remember these emotional kinds of information — like why you love one special person or can't stand to be in the same room with an archenemy!

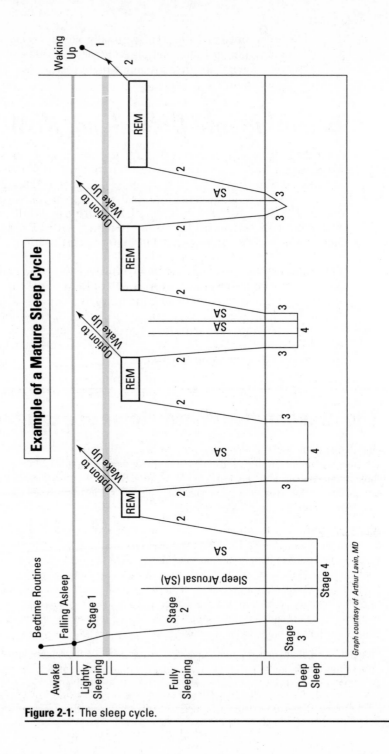

Example of a Mature Sleep Cycle

Figure 2-1: The sleep cycle.

Graph courtesy of Arthur Lavin, MD

We know that REM sleep is a prime time for dreaming because sleepers who awaken when REM patterns occur on a monitor often report vivid dreams. Dreamlike episodes do occur at other times, but they appear to be more business-like — that is, brief and rational. REM dreams, in contrast, are typically a crazy quilt of illogical events and wild emotions.

Although REM sleep usually starts only in Stage 2 sleep, it's very different from all four regular stages of sleep in four ways:

- ✔ **REM is the wild land where the most interesting dreams occur.** It's where you're most likely to encounter dragons, flying cars, or your first-grade teacher doing the hula.

- ✔ **REM *looks* different.** You can tell when people are in REM sleep because their eyes dart about furiously. (Strangely, the eyes move about more frantically during this dream phase than they do when people are wide awake!)

- ✔ **REM sleep disconnects the body.** When REM sleep begins, the brainstem suddenly cuts off communication between your brain and your spinal cord, leaving the muscles of your body (except for the ones you need to stay alive) unconnected to the brain. It's exactly like being paralyzed, but you snap out of it as soon as REM sleep ends. (Babies, however, don't have this shut-off switch yet, so they move during REM sleep.)

- ✔ **REM is a wild brain-wave ride.** When REM sleep starts, the slow waves of brain electrical activity in sleep suddenly burst into the irregular, unpredictable, more rapid, more energetic patterns seen during waking. And that's not all; your heart rate, breathing, and body temperature all start acting like you're awake. A male's penis can become erect, and a female's clitoris can become engorged. These events are very rare during other stages of sleep.

Why do babies need so much REM sleep? A look at the animal kingdom offers a clue. Platypus babies are some of the most immature of nature's newborns, and they spend almost all their time in REM sleep. Dolphin babies, on the other hand, arrive on the scene ready to swim, eat, and do lots of other grownup stuff — and they spend close to zero time in REM sleep. This hints that REM sleep plays a big role in mental development, including exercising a child's brain when she's too immature to get lots of stimulation from the outside world.

But why, then, do *adults* spend so much time in REM sleep? Think about the range of thoughts, wishes, and ambitions humans have and the scope of human imagination to invent new technologies, create music and books, and establish complex relationships. Humans may grow up, but the mind is never done dreaming and trying to make those dreams come true.

Getting Used to a Sleep Pattern: The Early Days of Life

The different stages of sleep occur in kids just as they do in grownups, but tots need to grow into a mature sleep pattern. Sleep, just like walking and talking, develops over time.

This section covers how sleep begins and evolves from Day 1 in the womb up through the toddler years.

Snoozing before birth

The fertilized egg doesn't know beans about being awake or asleep because it doesn't have a brain yet. Even when an unborn baby starts moving (at about 10 weeks of pregnancy), he shows no signs of being awake or asleep.

However, between Week 20 and Week 28, your unborn baby wakes up — and as a result, he also starts to sleep. (Ultrasounds of fetuses as well as visual observations of very premature babies confirm this.) At this point, your baby snoozes about half the day in snatches of sleep lasting minutes to hours and often doesn't breathe when he's dozing. (**Note:** When he's awake, a baby whose lungs are developed breathes amniotic fluid in and out.)

At this point, your baby even has two kinds of sleep: *quiet* and *active*. Eventually, his quiet sleep turns into the four stages of sleep we outline earlier in this chapter, and his active sleep becomes REM sleep.

Although grownups (and toddlers, as we discuss later) spend about 25 percent of their time in REM sleep, unborn babies at Week 30 spend a whopping 90 percent of their time in the active sleep that later turns into REM. We have no idea what their little brains are doing during these times — but it certainly would be fun to know!

Sleeping after birth

When she first arrives, your sweetie spends an average of 16 to 17 hours a day sleeping — and still manages to work in six to eight feedings a day! In fact, many newborns wake up just long enough for a meal and then conk right out again. Your cherub's immature sleep patterns explain why she can fascinate you one hour with her wiggling and grimacing and alarm you the next by being too zonked to wake up for a meal.

Newborn babies spend half of their slumber in active sleep, and they're quite a sight: Eyes roll and wink, faces grimace, mouths suck, hands and arms quiver, and little limbs stretch and wave about. *Note:* Although grownups are essentially paralyzed from the neck down during their equivalent of active sleep (refer back to "Taking a detour into Dreamland: REM" for more on this), babies don't have this disconnect switch yet.

During quiet sleep, newborns simply lie there looking like angels. Quiet sleep is *really* quiet because a baby's brain isn't creating the type of electrical activity that yours does when you're sleeping (check back to "Stage 2: The biggest territory in Sleepyland").

Many people wonder why newborn babies sleep so much. The answer is that these little gumdrops just don't know how to be fully asleep or awake — their mature sleep stages and wakefulness are the last brain states to fully develop. So babies spend much of their time in the more primitive stages of active and quiet sleep. But as the early weeks and months pass by, babies slowly but surely become more awake and alert. (See our sidebar "Sleep Trivia: What a Piece of Work is Man (and woman and child)" for related info.)

Establishing mature sleep cycles

As she grows, your tot's sleep patterns also develop. Here's how they change:

- ✔ **The electricity starts a-churning.** When your baby's about 4 weeks old, she starts experiencing the electrical bursts during sleep that will become a mature Stage 2 of sleep when she's 18 to 24 months old (see "Stage 2: The biggest territory in Sleepyland"). When she's about 4 months old, this electrical activity becomes more regular, putting the pieces in place for all-night sleeping. By the time she's 6 months old, the electrical activity is helping her brain develop the slower, more organized patterns that bring her closer to a solid night's sleep.

- ✔ **REM sleep grows up.** By 4 months, your baby's active sleep looks much more like grown-up REM sleep and consumes 40 percent of her total sleep time. (Remember that all fetal sleep begins as active sleep; it evolves in time into REM sleep, where most dreams occur.) By 6 months of age, the percentage drops to 30, and by 3 years of age, it levels off (with minor blips) to about 20 percent, where it remains for the rest of her life.

✔ **Deep sleep enters the picture.** The deep-sleep brainwave patterns of Stages 3 and 4 are in full swing by 6 to 8 months of age. As we note earlier, the electrical activity of brain waves is at its slowest and the waves are most synchronized in these stages; the person is also in deepest sleep and very hard to awaken. During Stage 4 in particular, all deep sleep events — sleep-talking, bed-wetting, and night terrors — occur. (See Chapter 7 for more on this.)

✔ **Cycling starts.** Newborns cycle through their active and quiet sleep states in 30 to 70 minutes.

By 3 months of age, she'll cycle every 75 minutes or so.

When your little snuggle-bunny hits the 4-month mark, the beginnings of a more grownup sleep cycle emerge.

She'll need another four or five years to reach the 90-minute cycles of a grownup.

Getting in step with nature's rhythm

About the time that sleep stages and REM sleep begin to mature (4 weeks to 4 months of age), your sweetie's body is preparing to make a major shift in her sleeping pattern:

✔ She starts falling into a sunrise/sunset cycle by about 6 weeks of age. (More on this in Chapter 4.)

✔ Her sleep stages start to repeat and she may start dozing four to five hours straight.

✔ Her need for food drops a bit, allowing her to skip one or two nighttime feedings — yes!

With a little luck and lots of help from the sleep strategies we describe in later chapters, you can stretch these periods to 6 to 8 hours, and then — keep your fingers crossed — maybe even to 12 hours of unbroken nighttime sleep. Hallelujah!

Of all 2-month-old babies in the United States, 44 percent sleep all night and stay up all day, except for napping.

Those naps, too, fall by the wayside over time:

✔ At 2 months, babies typically nap one to four times a day

✔ By the time they're 1 year old, they're down to one or two naps a day.

   ✔ Between the ages of 3 and 5 years, the child skips those little rest stops altogether.

In short, your tyke sleeps less and less as time goes by — but you sleep more and more because the two of you are finally on the same wavelength. When that happens, you can both happily cycle through the world of Sleepyland together.

Knowing How Much Your Wee One May Sleep

If we could, we'd put the next paragraph in big red letters, surrounded by flashing lights. (You'll just have to use your imagination!)

Here's our very important message: We can tell you the *average* amount of time that babies and toddlers sleep, but we can't tell you what's *normal* — there's no such thing as normal amounts of sleep. So don't fret if your child sleeps a few hours more or less each night than the averages we talk about here; if he's happy and healthy, that amount is perfectly fine!

With that caution in mind, we provide a chart and figure (see Table 2-1 and Figure 2-2) showing the average number of sack-time hours (both daytime and nighttime) for babies and toddlers.

Table 2-1	Average Hours of Sleep for Babies and Toddlers	
Age	*Nap Time (Hours)*	*Nighttime Sleep (Hours)*
1 week	8	8
1 month	7	8.5
3 months	5	9
6 months	4	10
1 year	2	11
2 years	1	12
3 years	0.5	11

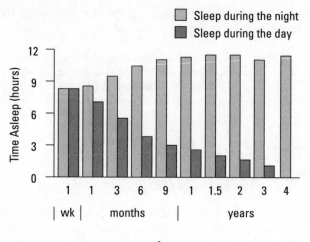

Figure 2-2: Average nighttime and daytime sleep for babies and toddlers.

Chapter 3

Personality: A Big Piece of the Puzzle

In This Chapter

▶ What is *personality*?

▶ How do children's personalities affect their sleep?

▶ Can your personality and your baby's get along at bedtime?

▶ What role does parenting style play in baby's sleep?

▶ Do you know your style of parenting?

*A*long with ten toes and ten fingers, each baby comes into the world with a personality that's all his own. One baby nurses with vigor, and another needs to be prodded and prompted. One baby barely moves an inch in the crib; another wiggles into the corner and gets stuck. One is super-sensitive to noise, but another can sleep through a *Terminator* marathon without stirring.

So what gives? To find out more about personality, you need to revisit that old debate about nature-or-nurture, which we take you through in the first section. We also offer lots of advice in this chapter that may seem a little overwhelming at this point. Getting your tot's personality, your own personality, and your parenting style to mesh smoothly can seem like a mighty big task — and at first, it will be.

But remember those last days before your baby's arrival, when you wondered how on earth you'd handle the huge job of becoming a parent? It probably seemed overwhelming — which is why so many soon-to-be parents get the urge to say, "Wait, I changed my mind!" Yet in no time, you got the hang of bottles, diapers, and burping. In fact, you probably started handing out advice to new parents yourself.

Understanding personalities is just like that: If you try to figure out what makes your baby tick and recognize how your own personality and parenting style fit in, you quickly find ways to help your new family live in harmony. Your house becomes calmer, your bed-time routines are vastly smoother, and you spend much less time asking that familiar question, "*Why* is he doing that?"

Understanding the Role of Personality in Sleep

Experts used to think of babies as blank slates, waiting for life's ups and downs to write their personalities. Now, however, science has shown that genes play a big role in whether your tot is a shy violet, a comedian, an adventurer, or a quiet and contemplative type. The importance of genes helps explain why two kids raised in the same household, by the same rules, often have completely different personalities (something that's even true for twins!).

But, back up. What does *personality* actually mean? The simple version is that each person has a different pattern for reacting to the world around her — her own style of thinking, behaving, and feeling. The sum of those styles is her personality.

You're probably starting to spot clues about your own tot's person-ality already, even if she's still a baby. Does she lie in her crib think-ing deep thoughts when she first awakes, or does she holler to be picked up instantly? Does she sit happily in the restaurant high chair gumming her key ring or flirt outrageously with every person who passes by? As time goes by, those small signs blossom into full flower, and you start to understand your one-of-a-kind kid.

 Personality affects both daytime and nighttime, and it plays a big part in how easily your baby gets to sleep at night. But if you understand your little individualist and where she's coming from, you can more easily base your decisions on what's best for her — and in this case, one size does not fit all! When you combine the info in Chapter 1 about your baby's wants and needs with info in this chapter about her personality, you're fully prepared for the bedtime battles ahead.

Homing In on Your Baby's Personality Type

Before you get far into this book, you need to know that personal-ity traits, even those of your freshly baked bun, are largely hard-wired by Mother Nature. Your child's personality will play a big role in how he reacts to other people, how he tackles his world, and even how he sleeps. And no, you can't do a whole lot to change his personality — only his outward behavior.

Luckily, you *do* have a big say in how your child *manages* his personality as he grows — one of life's greatest opportunities and challenges. And you can start right now by discovering how to factor your tot's personality into the bedtime equation.

In this section, we look at four different types of tykes — active, quiet, sensitive, and mellow — and show how each type typically reacts at bedtime. In the process, we offer tips to help you tailor sleep strategies (we explain these strategies in detail in Chapters 4 through 8) to suit your angel's personality type.

The active child

If your sweetie's a perpetual motion machine, you probably had a clue — in the form of constant kicking — even before she arrived! Your active baby came into the world squirming and squawking, and she can get so excited about feeding that she has a hard time calming down enough to nurse or take a bottle. She may gulp her food or eat in short spurts because she can't stay still for long periods of time. Her motto is, "I move, therefore I am."

Active tots exhaust themselves in the daytime and often sleep soundly — but not for long. A very active baby often awakens with a start and begins crying heartily as soon as she opens her eyes.

Naps are short and hard to come by if your angel is the active type, and she's likely to drop them altogether before she hits the one-year mark. Also, don't be surprised if she doesn't melt into your arms when you try to cuddle — she maybe more interested in trying to wiggle away so she can continue her explorations.

Parents of active kids typically have two reactions. One is pride: "Wow, look at her go!" The other is exhaustion: "You get her down from the bookcase. I've had it." Amazingly, these tots don't slow down as the evening progresses. Instead, the closer to bedtime, the more wide-awake they become.

A tot who's stuck in hyper-drive often needs more help snuggling down and conking out than her calmer peers. If you're the parent of a kid who's set permanently to *On*, these tips can help:

> ✔ **Think *calm*.** As you read through the chapters that follow, zero in on the calming strategies we describe (for instance, nix evening roughhousing; instead use calming music to soothe your savage beast). You need these strategies to an even greater degree than other parents do.

✓ **Talk — even if your tot doesn't!** Little whirlwinds are so busy honing their motor skills that they sometimes put their language skills on hold. As a result, parents of non-stop kids tend to forego words and instead rely on actions to pave the path to Sleepyland. But your sweetie understands much more than she lets on, so give her lots of verbal hints that it's time to quiet down.

✓ **Try swaddling.** One trick that can work well for an active child, at least during the first few months of infancy, is to wrap her tightly in a blanket, a technique called *swaddling*. (Techniques for swaddling along with illustrations are in Chapter 12.) *Note:* Although swaddling calms some active tots, it only makes others angry. So if it helps, use it; if it doesn't help, stop.

The quiet or cautious child

Quiet children are the easy babies, content to watch the world from the safety of Mommy's or Daddy's arms. As they grow up, however, they create a different set of worries.

Quiet babies often sleep like rocks and occasionally scare their parents when they need to be roused for a meal. As they grow, they can lag a bit in gross motor skills (big movements), but they frequently have well-developed fine motor skills (small and precise movements like picking up a piece of cereal). Their forte, however, is language, and they often talk circles around their play-group peers.

✓ **Keep life predictable.** Even more than other babies, these little ones need a routine. They're very sensitive to changes; a new caregiver or even a new night light may cause fretting. As you read through the sleep strategies in upcoming chapters, focus on creating and following a very structured routine. Also, when changes occur, be sure to talk your tot through them.

✓ **Think *motion*.** If your quiet baby loves to just sit for long periods of time, take a few minutes each day to challenge him physically. If he thinks that tummy time is torture time, make it as fun as possible (for instance, offer enticing toys) so he's more eager to move about. Give him a good workout at least once a day; you'll tire him out and make sleep a sweet release.

✓ **Watch for early mental milestones.** The quiet or cautious tyke often hits the separation anxiety stage early. (See Chapter 6 for an explanation of this stage.) If your quiet little mouse clings to you when you're in a crowd — even if it's a crowd of friends or relatives — be sensitive to his needs. Don't pass him around like a plate of tasty hors d'oeuvres, or he's likely to be too stressed to sleep.

✔ **If your baby is premature or isn't gaining weight, you may need to do the unthinkable: Wake him up in the middle of the night for a feeding even if he's willing to sleep through.** Your health care provider can help you decide when to let sleeping babies lie. (See Chapter 12 for a discussion of premature infants.)

The child with sensory sensitivity

Do you cut the tags off every garment you own, get sick at the smell of some household cleaners, or find it impossible to concentrate at a party because of the background noise? Almost all of us are touchy about some sounds, aromas, textures, tastes, or types of lighting, and that's true of kids as well.

Adults try to avoid the situations that make them uncomfortable, but tots don't have that luxury. Your baby can't say, "Get this shirt off me — it scratches like crazy," or "The vacuum noise is hurting my head." So she does the next-best thing — she cries.

Some babies do a whole lot of crying because they're extra-sensitive to *sensory input* —the info from the outside world that comes through our eyes, ears, mouth, nose, skin, and internal motion and gravity detectors.

For the hypersensitive tot, the world is just too much of a good thing. Even a trip to the playground can bring on sensory overload with accompanying tears and tantrums. Suspect sensory issues if your child has any of these challenges:

✔ Has trouble with changes. Transitions — like leaving a fun time in the park — are hard for many kids, but the sensitive child may balk at any change of venue (for instance, moving from indoors to outdoors or from the car to the store). Shifting gears may prompt an infuriating slowdown or a complete meltdown.

✔ Fusses a lot at her clothes and complains about tags or seams.

✔ Reacts strongly to sights, sounds, smells, or textures that don't bother other kids her age (for instance, she often covers her ears when she hears music or the television or refuses to touch finger paints).

✔ Doesn't like being touched.

✔ Goes bonkers more easily than other tots (for instance, at every trip to the mall).

Other clues that can point to sensory issues (although they also pop up in other personality types) include a strong startle reaction and trouble calming down after an upsetting or exciting event.

The good news is that when you spot clues that your child is sensory sensitive, you can change her little world in ways that make her happier — and sleepier at bedtime. And that means more peace and quiet for you — a good thing even for a parent who's *not* sensitive to noise!

Here are a few adjustments that can make a big difference:

- ✔ **Lower the volume.** We talk in Chapters 5 and 15 about keeping your home quiet at bedtime. That advice goes triple for the touchy tot because a dropped pan or the laugh track from a television show can set off an hour-long crying jag. If necessary, supplement the tips in the other chapters with two simple but effective ideas: Buy a CD of white noise to block out household sounds and install a set of blackout curtains in your little snuggle-bunny's room.

- ✔ **Stay away from scents.** The fragrances in detergents, soaps, and cleaning products can set a hypersensitive poppet's teeth on edge. Try fragrance-free products to see whether they make a difference.

- ✔ **Test the temp.** Your baby may need to be a little cooler or warmer than most people in order to sleep well. Try adjusting the thermostat — but be careful not to make a young baby's room too hot. Over-heating is a possible risk for sudden infant death syndrome (SIDS; see Chapter 4).

- ✔ **Think inside the bag.** Tags, collars, and jammie feet can drive a sensory-sensitive tot wild. Consider using bag-style pajamas instead.

- ✔ **Rub away the tension.** Avoid rough-and-tumble play right before lights-out time, and substitute a massage. Apply firm pressure as you massage because sensory-sensitive kids can find a light touch almost maddening. As your child reaches the preschool years, she may love a firm back rub before bedtime.

In some cases, signs that suggest sensory issues are so powerful or complex that do-it-yourself approaches aren't enough. If that's the case with your child, be sure to meet with your pediatrician and establish a plan to determine why your child is having so much trouble. When you know the nature of the difficulty, you and your pediatrician can more easily create an approach that helps your sweetie cope successfully.

The mellow child

Mellow babies are a joy both day and (usually) night. They nurse or take their bottles with no fuss. They hit milestones so perfectly that parents wonder whether they're sneaking peeks at the baby books. ("Let's see, today I mastered peek-a-boo, so I'll shoot for gumming finger foods tomorrow.") And early on, some of these babies often just start sleeping through the night — without even a hint of encouragement from Mom or Dad.

However, saying "Goodnight" may turn out to be the only step some of these mellow children don't do by the book. If your normally tranquil tot throws you a curve ball at sunset, it's perplexing and easy to assume something's wrong. But the good news is that laid-back personalities are more likely to fall into an acceptable routine and offer less resistance than feistier kids.

Even if your mellow lad or lass is a great sleeper, we have some words of wisdom: Enjoy it while it lasts! The first few years of a child's life are like the stock market — lots of ups and downs — and even a child with a sunny disposition experiences a few setbacks now and then. So if a life change (like divorce or a move to a new house) throws your placid little pumpkin into a tizzy, check out Chapter 14 for advice. If a cold or flu bug turns your love-bug's happy mood to a sour one, see Chapter 13. Otherwise, savor the peace and quiet . . . and consider loaning this book to the parents of the screaming tot next door.

Meshing Your Personality Type with Your Wee One's

Just like your baby, you're one-of-a-kind. You have your own way of acting and your own likes and dislikes. Maybe your idea of heaven is cuddling on the couch with a good book and a cup of chai tea. Maybe it's hosting a dinner party for 50 or climbing Mount Everest. You may love jazz, heavy metal, or Mozart.

And that's just *you*. If you have a partner, this means another unique grownup lives in your house — two adult personalities that need to mesh with your baby's personality. Maybe you luck out and you're all on the same wavelength. (You probably know families where everyone's quiet and bookish and others where Mom, Dad, and all the kids love sports and tailgate parties.) If not, your child can benefit greatly from your two different perspectives on life, and parents with different personalities often complement each other well. For instance, maybe Dad's a quiet night owl who loves the 2 a.m. feeding, and Mom's a social butterfly who can't wait for morning play-group.

But even if you and your partner have your personality duet down pat, you still need to harmonize with that little person in the crib. In the following sections, we look at some examples of the issues that can arise when Mommy or Daddy is a very different type of person than Junior.

Laid-back parent and raring-to-go baby

Are you a relaxed and quiet type who's raising an active baby? If so, the wild child bouncing off your walls from morn to night may seem like a total mystery to you. You probably interpret your baby's vigorous crying and her resistance to the usual calming measures as a sign that you're flunking Parenting 101. In reality, however, you only need one bit of parenting advice: Relax!

When your sweetie wakes up screaming, do you rush in to save her from her obvious distress? If you're the type who displays emotions only with really important issues, you can easily misinterpret your drama queen's hysterics for the real deal. The result? Many months after your baby is ready to sleep on her own, you're still dashing into her room like an Olympic sprinter each time she shrieks.

The key is to recognize that your little dumpling isn't in distress at all. She just wakes up ready to rock 'n' roll — even at 2 in the morning — and she knows that screaming like an actress in a budget horror flick brings you running pronto.

In Chapter 5, we describe how to break this parent-on-demand pattern — a lesson that's especially important for quiet parents of tornado tots. As you follow our guidelines, remember these two clear possibilities:

   ✔ Your active tot will squawk louder and longer than babies with calmer temperaments, so steel your nerves.

   ✔ Because you treasure calm and quiet, you're more sensitive to those screams than other parents may be.

By recognizing these personality traits in yourself and your baby, you can more easily keep your sleep strategies on track and resist the urge to give in. What's more, your response teaches your busy bee very early in life that she can't always take advantage of your powerful desire for peace and quiet, and that's a win-win!

Red-hot parent and thoughtful tot

If you're the life of the party and make friends easily, winding up with a tyke who inches his way cautiously through the world is a real surprise. We meet many outgoing parents who mistake their sweeties' quiet, thoughtful natures for a sign of serious emotional problems. In reality, though, the only problem these families have is a major personality mismatch.

A hale-and-hearty parent who's raising a quiet and thoughtful tot can err on the side of over-attentiveness. So the best bet with a contemplative tot is to let him explore the world and figure it out in his own time and his own way. Step back, be patient, and don't force the issue.

The same is true about sleep. You may feel the urge to run to your tyke when he cries because he's so quiet other times. You think, "He must really need me if he's making so much noise." But the truth is that he simply needs a chance to figure out sleep time (just like day time) on his own.

Sensible parent and sensory-sensitive child

Are you the kind of person who doesn't care whether you're wearing cotton or nylon, who boogies to loud radio music when you dust, and couldn't care less about a dripping faucet? So how'd you wind up with a kid who screams if the lights are too bright, the music's too loud, or the underwear label is scratchy?

Because you're not hypersensitive to your own senses, you may think your tot's just spoiled when she overreacts to the world around her. But she's not! Many children enter the world not-quite-ready for its exciting sights, sounds, smells, and textures, and they need time to begin to cope.

The biggest challenge for these tots is to let Mommy or Daddy know that they're not faking it — so listen to your baby's cues and then make adjustments where you can (we cover the specifics in "The child with sensory sensitivity" earlier in this chapter).

REAL WORLD

Stories from the crib: The high-maintenance sister

Nita had two daughters, Ruchira (age 4) and Sari (age 2), and she saw differences in their behavior from the moment Sari arrived on the scene. Sari was fussier, needed to be carried more, and never fell into a regular sleep pattern. Just when Nita thought she had a schedule down, Sari changed the rules.

When Ruchira reached the toddler years, Nita could take her to a family party and park her in her stroller for a quick nap. Sari, on the other hand, sobbed piteously if Nita tried this trick. When they came home, she made life miserable for everyone the rest of the day and night. Nita quickly realized that she needed to either forego social events or leave Sari home with a sitter. Eventually, Nita realized that she needed to parent Ruchira and Sari differently.

Nita also found out the hard way that she had to make other changes to keep Sari calm. When dressing Sari brought on tears, Nita switched to 100 percent cotton clothing and started using scent-free detergents. She kept the house extra-quiet at night and watched Sari closely in noisy settings to see whether she needed a break. Over time, Sari grew less tense in the day; tuck-in time became much more relaxed for everyone.

As Nita told her friends, Ruchira was like polyester — go anywhere and never get crumpled. But Sari was like fine linen — the smallest disruption caused her to crinkle!

The anxious parent and the tranquil tot

As we mention earlier, you've hit the jackpot if your tot is mellow and easygoing. But there's a hitch: If you're a worrier by nature — and especially if Little Mister Mellow is your first child — you may have trouble recognizing that your sweetie's doing just fine.

If you fuss, fret, and worry too much about your good-natured little guy, you can actually create problems where none exist (especially at bedtime!). So keep your cool. If your pediatrician says your child's right on track, try not to complicate your life — or your baby's — by being a Nervous Nellie. And if you can't take the doctor's word for it, talk with your partner or friends or relatives. You probably can't bother your laidback tot by worrying excessively, but you can drive yourself or your partner nuts.

The Final Piece of the Puzzle: Your Parenting Style

When we say *style,* we're not talking about whether you wear your old sweats or a pair of Armani jeans when you take your sweetie to the playground. In parenting, *style* refers to your typical response to your sweetie's actions. Your parenting style affects how you approach daytime discipline, nighttime sleep issues, and everything in between.

In the previous sections, we show how parents' and kids' personalities can be out of sync. Just the *awareness* that differences can exist often gives parents the insight and the confidence to make the changes that promote positive, peaceful solutions. The same is true for parenting style: When you spot patterns in your reactions to your child's behaviors, you can replace knee-jerk responses with well-designed actions that promote the behavior you want to see.

Your parenting style stems largely from these sources:

- ✔ **Your own personality:** For instance, if you're quiet by nature, you may give in to your tyke's demands just to restore calm. If you don't mind racket, on the other hand, you may just let her squawk.

- ✔ **The way your parents raised you:** Do you want to follow in their footsteps or avoid their mistakes? Your answer plays a big role in your reactions to tears, tantrums, and bedtime issues.

- ✔ **The tips you pick up:** The knowledge you gain from other parents, parenting classes, and books can give you insights into good parenting and steer you away from mistakes.

- ✔ **The feedback loop:** Your little darling's responses to you affect how you respond to her. In fact, babies train their parents as much as parents train their babies!

All of these ingredients blend to create your own recipe for parenting.

Examining the three main styles

Typically, your style falls into one of three broad categories: permissive, authoritarian, and authoritative. Of course, you may act one way on Tuesday and a different way on Thursday — but over time you establish a pattern for discipline and other parenting issues.

Permissive parents

Permissive parents — their motto is *All you need is love* — avoid punishing their tot or inhibiting his impulses, desires, and actions. As their sweetie grows up, these parents make few demands regarding chores or house rules. They see themselves more as resources than role models and tend to let their child regulate his own activities as much as possible.

Permissive parents are willing to reason with their kids or even manipulate them, but they draw the line at using parent power to achieve a goal like sleeping through the night.

Authoritarian parents

Authoritarian parents — the drill sergeants of the parenting world — live by a firm set of rules; they value obedience, manners, and a ship-shape house. A drill-sergeant parent's home has strict schedules, a challenging list of weekly chore assignments, and little or no discussion about what Junior wants to eat, wear, or do over the weekend.

A drill sergeant's house has no flexibility and little concern for how a tot's feelings may affect his behavior. If he asks why he needs to eat spinach or wear a jacket, the only explanation he gets is, "Because I say so." And if he looks for a shoulder to cry on, he's likely to get a lecture instead.

Authoritative parents

Authoritative parents — gentle bosses — offer guidance and direction while still valuing their little cubs' thoughts and wishes. These parents welcome discussion and they love sharing ideas with their tots, but they take a firm stand when it's time to resolve a conflict.

The child of a gentle boss may snooze in bed with Mom and Dad during a thunderstorm or get to stay up a half hour later on a holiday. However, he doesn't sass a neighbor, throw a hissy fit in the toy store, or wake Mom or Dad up six times a night on a whim.

His gentle bosses know when a firm rein is needed and when they can relax the rules. They enjoy his quirks and funny ways, but they also look toward the future and understand that the better he behaves, the better he'll do in life.

Recognizing how parenting styles affect tots' sleep

A famous study by Diana Baumrind, whose research on parenting styles published in 1966 and revisited in 1991 is a cornerstone of child development, looked at kids raised with different parenting styles. Just about all the kids grew up to be fine, but the children of permissive or drill-sergeant parents did have some specific issues that didn't affect kids of gentle-boss parents. Here are some examples from her research following these kids through adulthood:

- ✔ Kids of permissive parents had trouble regulating their emotions and tended to talk back or act defiantly when their wishes weren't met. In addition, they didn't persist as much as other people when they faced a difficult task. Why? Kids who don't get a gentle nudge to attempt age-appropriate tasks can get the message that they're not capable. This assumption discourages them from plugging away until they solve a problem.

- ✔ Kids with drill-sergeant parents, on the other hand, typically did well in school and didn't talk back or have trouble sharing. But more than other kids, they tended to be anxious and unhappy as they grew up. And just like the kids of permissive parents, they had trouble solving problems on their own. Because Mom or Dad always told them what to do, they didn't know how to cope without that familial compass.

And how about the kids with the gentle-boss parents? These kids typically grew up happy, able to get along well with other people, and capable of solving problems without needing their parents to either bail them out or impose a solution.

What do all these characteristics have to do with sleep? A great deal, as it turns out! Here's why:

- ✔ **Bedtime is decision time.** At tuck-in time or during a middle-of-the-night waking, your angel needs to decide: Do I go to sleep or stay awake? The parents who acknowledge that saying "Nighty-night" is hard but still establish firm and reasonable expectations set the stage for a good night's sleep and help Junior become an effective problem solver later.

- ✔ **Stress equals sleeplessness.** The anxiety of kids raised by my-way-or-the-highway parents can set in early. These tots may be so worried about their parents' reactions that they have trouble falling and staying asleep, which keeps them from being wide-eyed and ready for daytime activities.

- ✔ **Emotional issues sabotage sleep**. Kids raised by permissive parents aren't allowed to feel responsible for their own actions. So in the middle of the night, they call for an adult to *fix* their problem of getting back to sleep. Early on, these kids discover that they can just let Mom or Dad do it — they don't need to figure out the solution for themselves.

✔ **Drill sergeants expect the impossible.** Parents who demand unquestioning obedience often have unrealistic expectations. For instance, a parent may expect a 3-month-old to sleep through the night, not realizing that newborn tummies need frequent fill-ups. The result is frustration for everyone.

By now you can see that gentle-boss parents have the best luck getting their tots to fall asleep and stay in bed. These parents encourage their tots to take big steps toward independence (like sleeping through the night or moving from the crib to a big bed). They can be flexible when life demands it — for instance, when a big life change keeps a tot wide-awake — but gentle bosses know that sometimes Mom and Dad need to call the shots.

Evaluating your parenting style

If you're one of the gentle-boss parents, you're already on the right track and our only advice is to stay on it. You'll still have your share of frustrations — because even the easiest kid on the block can't get through life without a few bumps in the road — but problems should pass quickly if you keep responding with firm guidance, flexibility when necessary, and a loving touch.

If you're not a gentle-boss type, take a look at your current parenting style and see whether it needs some tinkering. Of course, as we note earlier in this chapter, your parenting style stems in part from your own personality. That's a core part of who you are, so we don't want you to change it (and you couldn't if you tried).

Luckily, however, you do have a big say in how you *express* that personality. If your parenting style isn't working out as well as you'd like — especially at nighty-night time — consider the following questions. They may lead you to refine your style and solve some big sleepy-time issues along the way.

Are you too permissive?

If you're a softie who's starting to realize that love *isn't* all your sweetie needs to stay on the right track, start offering her some guidance with these steps:

1. **Define the rules that matter to you and decide on limits.** You can explain the new rules to an older toddler, and your calm follow-through can help a non-verbal tot get the message as well.

2. **Set a routine.** See Chapter 5 for a detailed explanation of establishing routines. Understand that your child's wails in the middle of the night aren't a sign of trauma — no matter

how loud and insistent they are. No doubt your little one is mad as a wet hen, but by the next morning she doesn't have any hard feelings — just a well rested, ready-to-go attitude.

3. **Follow through. Be kind and flexible, but be in charge.** Consistency is the key to solving bedtime puzzles. For example, if you decide that it's time for her to stop middle-of-the-night visits to your bed, then each time your little one makes the trek, you need to calmly take her back to her room — and even gate her in if that's the only way she'll stay. Your own exhaustion may tempt you to give in, but just two or three days of standing firm can change your world of sleep!

Are you too demanding?

If you fall into the drill-sergeant category, lighten up! You're an authority figure to your child, but that doesn't mean your house needs to run like a military school. Try these changes:

1. **Set reasonable rules and decide on the consequences for breaking them.** Talk to your pediatrician or consult baby books first to make sure you're being realistic.

2. **Let your rules do the talking.** If you child decides to break a rule, kindly but firmly impose the consequence — without yelling or threatening.

When you let your child take the responsibility for making decisions about her behavior, you do her and yourself a favor in the long run. You also lower her stress level and keep sleepy-time calm because your little angel isn't lying awake at night, worrying about your anger.

Are you on the same page as your partner?

If you and your partner are on the same wavelength for discipline, bedtimes, and all the parenting decisions, great! But what if you aren't? Presenting a united front is awfully hard to do when you can't agree.

If that's the case, you and your partner need to sit down and have a serious talk. Lay out your ideas about parenting, figure out where you're on common ground and where you disagree, and then hash out compromises that you both can accept. To help with these steps, try these suggestions:

✔ Find a time when you and your partner can talk without interruptions. Getting a sitter may be worth the effort so the two of you can head to the local coffee shop for an honest conversation.

✔ Bring paper and pencils. Separately, write down the biggest sleep issues you're facing and how you want to resolve them. (For example, Mom thinks it's okay to let Junior wander into the master bedroom in the middle of the night, but Dad misses his privacy.)

✔ Compare lists to see areas of overlap and areas of possible compromise. Create a common list of goals.

✔ Discuss strategies for reaching these goals and decide who will implement them. If Mom is the pushover, then maybe Dad needs to be the middle-of-the-night enforcer.

✔ If you're so far apart that you can't reach a compromise, consider reaching out to a community parenting program or an individual mediator who can help arbitrate the process. In most cases, sleep is just the most pressing of several issues. Getting on the same page as your partner will impact your parenting styles through the years and through lots of different stages.

The more you stray toward being permissive or authoritarian in your decisions, the more bedtime battles you can anticipate. And if that prediction isn't an argument for meeting in the middle at the gentle-boss style, we don't know what is!

Part II
I Have a Dream: Winning Sleep Strategies for Every Age

The 5th Wave   By Rich Tennant

"Y'know, I think some oil and a little soothing music are all we need."

In this part . . .

*D*ealing with a newborn who cries non-stop? A 1-year-old who's teething? A preschooler with night terrors? In this part, you discover how to handle these issues and many others as we outline the best sleep strategies for each age and stage of your little one's early years. In Chapter 4, you get the inside scoop on why your baby wakes you up so often plus facts about the dreaded colic (and why it's not so scary any more) and crucial info about preventing SIDS. Chapter 5 talks about sleep from six months to one year and tells you how to take advantage of a golden opportunity: your baby's new ability to understand a routine.

Chapter 6 describes what happens to sleep patterns when your baby starts standing and walking and why separation anxiety can mean sleepless nights. In Chapter 7, you find out what to expect sleep-wise when your little one starts talking, and we give you tips on how to handle nightmares, night terrors, and sleepwalking. In addition, you find out how to handle that big life change: the move from the crib to a grownup bed. And Chapter 8 covers two major life events — preschool and potty training — and how these changes affect both daytime naps and nighttime sleep.

Chapter 4

Growing and Changing: Sleep from Birth to 6 Months

Congratulations! As a brand-new parent, you're enjoying one of life's most joyous experiences: holding your precious new little son or daughter in your arms after so many long months of waiting. Nothing can prepare you for the mixture of love and awe you feel when you look into that little face and realize what an amazing gift you've been given.

If you're like most new parents, you'll spend a large part of these early months walking on clouds. Of course, no matter how blissful you are, you're also dragging around like a zombie, realizing that a good night's sleep is a luxury of the past (at least for now).

Whichever condition you're in, blissful or zombified — or both! — keep one word in mind throughout these first six months: *change.*

In this chapter, we describe the remarkable transformations that occur over the first six months of your baby's life and how they relate to sleep. You also discover why some little ones think daytime is for sleeping and nighttime is for partying — a pattern that can have already-frazzled parents pulling their hair out. (Don't worry, it's only temporary!) In addition, you get the inside story on cures for colic, the pros and cons of pacifiers, and the crucial steps to keeping your little one safe and sound.

The Ride of Life: Baby's Early Development

No other time in life is as full of change as a baby's first six months. During some spurts, the rate of weight gain equals fifty pounds per year, and the rate of growth equals 24 inches a year. (Fortunately that's just temporary or you'd need a bigger crib!)

Parallel to this astonishing physical growth, your little one rapidly develops new abilities and interests. She has no idea how to talk, move from one spot, or imagine anything beyond the present. And yet, within a year, she's taking her first steps, trying out sounds or even words, and developing an active, conscious imagination. During that time, she moves from total dependence toward a remarkable little person with a flowering mind and a personality of her own.

As these exciting first months go by, something else changes: your baby's ability to sleep. Each week she figures out this strange business of snoozing and waking a little bit better, and — slowly but surely — she gets it right.

The first two months: Baby meets world

It's amazing how much time a newborn spends sleeping — and, at the same time, how often he rousts you out of bed. To understand how your newborn sleeps and why he needs to wake up so often, consider his waking life:

- ✔ **The newness of it all:** Imagine going from the warm, cozy predictability of the womb to a big, bright, noisy, chaotic world. By comparison, the changes that grownups face, like moving to a new town or changing jobs, seem tiny.

- ✔ **The total lack of routine:** The newborn doesn't have a clue what's going to occur in the next two days, two hours, or even two minutes. Even his own poops can surprise the heck out of him! From his point of view, the world is utterly new and unpredictable.

Knowing what time it is: Baby meets circadian rhythm

Many little creatures know just what to do with their lives from the get-go. Fish start swimming; spiders start spinning. Human babies, however, haven't the foggiest idea what to do next because they greet the world at a much earlier stage of development than most other animals. They're born with innate personalities and Dad's hair color or Aunt Jane's dimple, but a sense of daily activities? They're clueless.

This lack of programming makes your baby remarkably adaptable — he can fall into just about any routine or lifestyle that life hands him — and the exciting potential to do anything and become anyone is one of life's greatest miracles. But starting life brand new has its drawbacks when daily routines are involved.

The flip side of your baby's talent for adapting is that he has to start from scratch with a biological clock that isn't set yet. As a result, the tiny time-telling molecules in his body simply make a wild guess as to day and night — and that means that he can be hungry, sleepy, or wide awake at any hour of the day or night. About one-third of babies get it right, another third are in the ball-park, and one-third are way off-base (so having a newborn with a correctly-set inner alarm clock is probably pure luck). As a result, most new moms and dads find their baby's sleeplessness the biggest challenge of the first six months.

However, even infants *got rhythm,* their own sense of the day/night cycle. Just like all humans, babies have a *circadian* rhythm — a pow-erful internal clock that helps create a daily cycle. (See Chapter 2 for more details.) By the time they're about 6 weeks old, most little ones feel tired at night, become more alert in the day, feel hungrier in the daylight hours than after dark, and even want to cuddle a little more at night. They start to figure out that daytime is for play, exploration, and eating, but night is the time to take it easy.

The one-third of babies that get this cycle backwards develop a very strong day-and-night reversal. They're as hungry as truckers in the middle of the night, and a hurricane can't rouse them during the day. That's good evidence of the strength of circadian rhythm, even if it's set to the wrong time zone!

Recognizing Baby's big surprise: The feel of hunger

For his first six months in the womb, your little dumpling spent nearly his whole life sound asleep. Even in the third trimester, he snoozed almost constantly. Sleeping all day and all night was just the ticket.

So why doesn't he sleep now? Good question. Before he reached the outside world, Mom's body offered up all the food he needed. But now he wakes up with this peculiar sensation in his tummy — hunger. He's not sure what it is, but he instinctively knows what to do about it — cry! It's his only way of saying, "Feed me."

Stories from the crib: Three strategies, three winning families

At 5 months of age, little Keiko still woke up every four or five hours. As it turned out, in the middle of her fifth month, Keiko started sleeping through the night all on her own — and she's been doing it ever since.

Molly and Jack, on the other hand, felt a sense of urgency to sleep all night. When Billy was 4 months old, Molly and Jack started using the strategies we outline in Chapter 5 to help him figure out how to sleep through the night.

Laura, the oldest of three kids, had watched her mother matter-of-factly plunk her siblings in their cribs, shut the door, and wait for them to quiet down. She knew this technique worked fast and tried it with her infant Sarah. By the third night, Sarah snuggled down with barely a whimper. By the fourth, she was asleep almost before Laura shut the door.

Which parents made the right choice? All of them — because they picked the solutions that worked best for their lifestyles and their babies.

And boy, does he need to eat! Newborns require an astonishing amount of food to fuel their rapid growth. If you calculate their calorie intake per pound, the numbers works out to five times your normal intake. Your little one is wolfing down food like a lumberjack, and he can't do it all at once or he'd explode.

So he uses a smart strategy: He sucks down as much as his tummy can hold and drops off to sleep again for two or three hours (three to four if you're really lucky) till his tummy signals him again. Then he hollers for more. He needs to eat this often, around the clock, for at least the first few weeks. And your best strategy for these first two months? Total surrender.

Right now, your newborn has an ironclad excuse for rousting you out of bed every few hours: He really needs to eat that often. So let him call the shots for the first two months. This means feeding him every time he yells and resigning yourself to lose lots of sleep. Bid a fond farewell to long, luxurious slumbers. Seek out and be happy with opportunities to catnap for a few hours at a stretch while your baby rests.

There's a bright side in all this chaos: As you wait on your infant hand and foot, you begin to find surprising joy in caring for this little human being. The total change in your own routine shocks your system into focusing totally and intensely on your cherub. You're physically forced to attend to who he is, what he wants, and when he wants it. This round-the-clock connection, although stressful at times when you're short on shuteye, draws you even closer to your little one — perhaps as close as you can be.

Catching a ray of hope: 2 to 4 months

One night, when your baby is between 6 and 16 weeks old, something astonishing will happen: You'll wake up to your little one's cries, look at your clock, and think, "Wow! I've been asleep six whole hours!" Of course, the very fact that this surprises you means that those frequent feedings aren't history yet.

This magic moment is a big deal, however, because it signals your baby's first step toward being civilized. She's getting in the groove — falling into synch with her world — and she's doing it all by herself.

Until now, your baby's life was a swirl of unpredictable, frequent interruptions of sleep at all hours of the day and night. But suddenly your sweetie is staying awake for longer stretches during the day. With no planning, preparation, or charts (without even reading this book!), she begins to master the key element of being human — the ability to stay awake long enough to learn, work and play. She's truly awake and aware for much of the day — and you're truly out like a light for more of the night.

More order, less chaos: 4 to 6 months

By the time they reach the 4-month mark (give or take a few weeks), nearly all babies tease their parents with the occasional surprise night off. But these clever babes have a secret they usually don't reveal: Most of them are now able to routinely sleep through the night without a meal or a visit from Mom or Dad.

Some babies do let their parents in on this secret and start sleeping through the night all by themselves. These little ones go from sleeping three hours at a stretch to five, seven, and then nine hours nonstop. If this doesn't happen in your household, check out the next section, "Guiding Your Baby on the Path to Mature Sleep," for some solutions to your nighttime woes.

Guiding Your Baby on the Path to Mature Sleep

If you're like lots of parents, you probably feel a little conflicted right now. On the one hand, you *really* want to sleep like a normal human being again. On the other, the realization that your tot's ready to snooze all night on his own — his first big step into the big-kid world — can make you think, "My baby's growing up too soon!"

And that's why you may have mixed feelings about his sleeping through the night at the 4-month mark without a meal or a cuddle. But when he starts settling into an all-night sleep schedule, you still have plenty of time for hugs and cuddles in the daytime. What's more, you have lots of extra energy for playtime. So take heart, and don't fear this step into the future — the fun is just beginning!

Setting your baby's internal clock

As we discuss earlier in this chapter, many babies need help falling in sync with their circadian rhythms — and who better to help than their loving parents? The happy news is that, eventually, even little night owls shift into a very regular pattern of being awake in the day and asleep at night, and this change usually doesn't take more than six to eight weeks. These are long, long, *long* weeks, but you can help your baby's little clock reset more quickly by letting her get Mother Nature's signals loud and clear. Here's how:

- ✔ During the day, throw open the windows and let the light stream in. Play music, generate lots of hustle and bustle, and schedule a little outdoor activity if the weather is fine.

- ✔ Do just the opposite as night approaches. Turn down the lights, make as little noise as possible, and turn off the television and radio. Also, for the most part, avoid talking. (Even that "quiet old lady whispering hush" in *Goodnight Moon* needs to keep her lips sealed!) Feed, cuddle, massage, and hold your baby as quietly as possible.

These simple tricks help remove distracting influences and allow your baby's body to pay attention to the ultimate clock-setters, your local sunrise and sunset. In time, the sun's rhythm can trigger chemical reactions that reset your baby's inner timepiece. And with that goal accomplished, day and night flip-flops become a ghost of the past . . . at least until the teenage years!

Homing in on the sleepy-time bandit: You

If you're still getting up at all hours of the night after your baby reaches the 4-month mark, you can be heartened by the news that your situation is temporary. At this point, most babies are physically ready to sleep through the night. They've plumped up nicely — you'll be surprised when you compare pictures of your tiny, wiry newborn to the roly-poly bambino you're holding today — and they're growing much more slowly. Their tummies don't really need middle-of-the-night fill-ups any more, and most of them can comfort themselves to sleep. These two skills — eating enough during the day and getting to sleep — are all a baby needs to doze all night long.

So, if your baby's still waking up when he reaches these milestones, only one reason stands out — you. As he sleeps, your baby cycles in and out of deep sleep (more on this in Chapter 2). When he hits that moment of near-waking, he has a decision to make: Wake up or head back to sleep? If he chooses Door Number One, it's usually because you're still hopping out of bed to give him a snack and a snuggle.

To address this situation, you first need to make a decision:

- ✔ Are you desperate to get past the sleepless stage?
- ✔ Are you willing to wait a few more months before encouraging your little one to drop his middle-of-the-night demands?

Either choice is perfectly fine, but you need to decide what works best for your lifestyle, your work schedule, and your sanity. If you feel fully ready to proceed with helping your infant sleep all night, Chapter 5 walks you through the steps. If not, the next section helps you weigh your options and make a decision.

Knowing when you're ready to give up the late-night snuggles

Just as your 4-month-old emerges from the newborn phase expecting you to be on call 24/7, you too have acquired certain expectations — the key one being to hustle when your baby screams. As a result, you each have a pattern going. Hers is, "Wake up, cry, wait for Mom or Dad to show up." Yours is, "Wake up, hear cry, respond."

The call-and-response pattern made perfect sense a few months ago, but now it's just a habit for both you and Baby. You can start changing that habit now or wait as long as you like. Here are three ways to approach this stage (there's no right or wrong decision here):

✔ **You can keep going to your baby whenever she calls for you.** You'll be tired for a few extra weeks, but you can't spoil your baby or even set irreversible patterns by giving in to her demands at this stage. If you're lucky, your baby may decide on her own to start sleeping through the night. If so, you'll be off the hook.

✔ **You can simply stop responding to your baby's cries if you're sure she's okay.** You can expect your baby to scream bloody murder for two nights and then start sleeping angelically. This is the quickest road to a good night's sleep, but it's also one that many parents can't face. This approach doesn't traumatize your baby, but, if it makes you uncomfortable, don't try it.

✔ **You can employ the strategies we outline in Chapter 5 for gently but firmly easing your baby into an all-night sleep routine.** These strategies work for nearly all babies over the age of 4 months. (Although babies are generally ready for this approach at the 4-month mark, many parents aren't!)

Whichever option you pick, be sure you follow this all-important rule: Don't change your mind midstream! Weigh your options, make your best choice, and then stick with it for at least a week or two to give your baby the best chance to adapt. Otherwise, you confuse your baby, and she spends many nights testing you in an attempt to figure out what game you're playing. Sticking to your guns is far easier on both of you.

Safety First, but Also Comfort

No matter which sleep strategy you choose, two topics are all-important: keeping your angel safe and ensuring that he's comfy. Here are our top tips on both fronts.

Keeping your baby safe while she sleeps

When it comes to babies and sleep, no topic is more important than safety — and for babies under 1 year of age, no safety topic is more important than sudden infant death syndrome (SIDS). For an excellent review of the subject, see the American Academy of

Pediatrics' recent statement on SIDS at http://pediatrics. aappublications.org/cgi/reprint/116/5/1245. This section provides a summary of SIDS and how to keep your tot safe.

Understanding what SIDS is

SIDS is one of life's greatest tragedies. Fortunately, it's rare and getting rarer. In 1991, SIDS struck more than 1 in 1,000 infants. Thanks to new safety measures, that rate dropped by 50 percent by 2001; SIDS now strikes slightly more than 1 in 2,000 babies. To put that number in perspective for worried parents, nearly 1,999 of every 2,000 babies *don't* fall victim to SIDS.

Doctors use the term *SIDS* to describe any sudden, unexplained death during a baby's first year of life. Most cases of SIDS (about 75 percent) occur between the ages of 1 and 4 months, and the risk drops rapidly after that period. SIDS is more common (but still rare) in premature infants and babies exposed to cigarette smoke. For premature infants, the risk goes up with the severity of prematurity (see Chapter 12 for details about prematurity). For infants born at 28-32 weeks of pregnancy, the SIDS risk is roughly double that for full-term babies, rising with increasing prematurity and dropping closer to term. Some studies suggest that the risk of SIDS is as much as five times higher for a baby exposed to tobacco smoke (more in the next section).

SIDS rates are dropping for two reasons:

- ✔ SIDS, by definition, are *only* unexplained deaths. As doctors continue to identify more medical problems that can lead to SIDS, fewer cases go unexplained.

- ✔ A few years ago, doctors reported this wonderful discovery: Simply putting a baby to sleep on his back rather than on his tummy can cut the risk of SIDS in half! Parents are reducing the risk by following this advice.

Protecting your kid from SIDS

If you remember nothing else that we tell you about bedtime safety, remember this: Back to Sleep! Simply put, your baby should *always* sleep on his back. **Note:** This also means no sleeping on his side. It's not as risky as being on his tummy, but it's not as safe as being on his back. We illustrate a good sleep setup for Baby in Figure 4-1a and a dangerous one in Figure 4-1b.

What if your baby rolls from his back to his tummy? The accepted belief is that babies who are mobile enough to roll over have a lower risk of SIDS because they can get themselves out of an uncomfortable or stressful position. So put your baby on his back, but don't fret too much if you find him on his tummy later.

Figure 4-1: Crib safety: a) A good setup; b) A bad setup.

Following the back-to-sleep rule is just one way to protect your little one against the threat of SIDS. In the following list we identify more guidelines that can help keep him safe. (This list features the most powerful approaches first, but be sure to read them all.)

- ✔ **Smoking is a *very* strong risk factor for SIDS.** In fact, some studies show that a baby's risk is five times higher if the baby is exposed to tobacco smoke during pregnancy or after birth. Because this is one of the most powerful risk factors for SIDS, be very careful not to expose your baby to tobacco smoke!

  If you're a smoker who's reading this book before your baby arrives, do your best to quit. If your little one is already here, make his entire home a smoke-free zone. Even second-hand smoke a floor away increases the risk of SIDS.

- ✔ **Some studies show a strong link between SIDS and soft bedding, pillows, and face-covering blankets.** We don't know why, but soft bedding is dangerous even if your baby sleeps on his back. The risk of SIDS can go up as much as five-fold if Baby has a soft mattress, fluffy pillows, or blankets that can cover his face.

- ✔ **Sofas, couches, and waterbeds are not good sleeping spots.** All of these can increase the risk of SIDS, so nix them and put your sweetie to sleep on a real bed with a firm mattress.

- ✔ **Pacifiers may reduce the risk of SIDS** (see the following section "The Power of the Pacifier"). The extent to which they may reduce this risk is still unclear, but many studies state that using a pacifier can cut the risk of SIDS by more than 50 percent.

- ✔ **Baby's room should be at a comfy but not-too-warm temperature (65 to 72 degrees F).** This small change may help to reduce the risk of SIDS, so avoid cranking up the thermostat.

✔ **Breastfeeding is** *associated* **with less chance of SIDS.** The incidence of SIDS appears lower in breast-fed infants, but studies link this protection to the fact that mothers who breastfeed tend to smoke less. Breastfeeding itself doesn't appear to offer special protection against SIDS. So if you bottle-feed your infant, don't fret about raising the risk of SIDS. (Of course, breastfeeding offers many other health advantages.)

✔ **Though it's a controversial issue, co-sleeping may increase the risk of SIDS.** In Chapter 9, we look at the controversy over co-sleeping and whether it increases or decreases the risk of SIDS. If you co-sleep, be sure to read and follow the bed safety rules (as well as the taboos on smoking or drinking alcohol) we list in that chapter.

✔ **Gadgets and gimmicks have no proof of working.** The evidence is clear-cut: Products that claim to prevent or reduce SIDS aren't proven to be effective or even safe, including home monitors and even prescribed units. (However, these monitors do have their place in protecting against a different breathing problem in premature infants — see Chapter 12.)

Employing the power of the pacifier

When you're bored or fretful, you have plenty of ways to do something about it — e-mail a friend, go for a bike ride, read a good book, curl up on the couch and watch television, and so on.

Your little one, on the other hand, has a pretty short list of entertainment options. She can't move from one spot to another, she's too young to read a novel, and even the plotline of *Days of Our Lives* is a little over her head (thank goodness!). So she does what she knows best — she sucks on stuff.

Sucking is at the top of every baby's top-ten list of favorite activities (right up there with cuddling and gazing at the wallpaper patterns) because eating is one of the very few activities that your baby has down pat even just after birth. In fact, her very survival depends on feeding, so the urge to suck is a powerful one. Many babies become frantic if they go for very long without something to suck on.

Enter the pacifier — with lots of big advantages:

✔ **It's a great comfort when your baby's discovering how to get herself to sleep.**

✔ **It's safe** (in fact, sucking on a pacifier may lower your baby's risk of SIDS — see the previous section).

✔ **It's easy to wash.**

However, pacifiers do have a few drawbacks:

- ✔ **A few newborns resist nursing if they use a pacifier.** Typically this happens within the first three weeks, when a baby begins to nurse. When your baby has nursing all figured out, pacifiers are much less likely to cause any feeding problems.

- ✔ **Pacifiers get lost in the middle of the night**. However, most parents think the occasional squawk from a baby who's lost her binkie is a fair trade-off for the hours of peace that a pacifier brings. Also, as you begin to use the sleep strategies in this book, your baby learns to comfort herself when her beloved piece of plastic vanishes.

- ✔ **Pacifiers can cause a baby's teeth to shift forward.** Luckily, pacifiers only affect the teeth that are already in, not the adult teeth. So if you can get rid of that pacifier before your little one turns 5 years old — and we certainly recommend that you do! — her next set of teeth will come in just fine.

Another complaint is that they're hard to quit. In most cases, this isn't true. If you decide to get rid of the pacifier in the first year or two, eliminating it can be surprisingly easy. If your toddler is older and has some grasp of language, discuss the change ahead of time. (One ploy: If another little one is joining your family, see whether your toddler is willing to give the pacifier to your new arrival as a gift.)

Overall, pacifiers are more of a blessing than a curse, and they save you and your baby lots of grief — especially on those nights when your sweetie finds sleep to be a challenge. We think they're a very reasonable choice.

The Greatest Common Obstacle: Myths and Facts about Colic

Ask a doctor, "What's *colic?*" and you get an answer like this, "A state of sustained and strong crying lasting more than three hours a day, which has no known cause and does not respond to the usual comforts like eating, massages, being held, or getting a diaper change."

Ask a parent, however, and you probably hear, "It's a nightmare — an eternity of shrill cries that can sand the ears off an elephant; a form of torture that makes bamboo splints under the fingernails sound like sissy stuff; a horrible experience of listening to your baby suffer at decibel levels that can shatter glass!"

Both definitions seem pretty clear, but this common and upsetting problem was the center of uncommon controversy for years. The biggest question was: Is colic a real condition, or are babies with colic in pain from a painful medical problem that makes them unhappy?

Until recently, doctors had few clues to go on. They did know:

✔ Babies with colic typically show no signs of a problem at birth.

✔ They have lots of problems starting around 1 month of age.

✔ They get back to normal around 3 months of age.

✔ Setting colicky babies on a vibrating surface often makes them feel better.

These facts weren't a lot to go on, so until the 1990s (and even a bit beyond), colic remained a mystery.

The myths about colic

Over the years, doctors spun many theories about the roots of colic. They were all wrong, but we're going to describe a couple of them so you're ready in case someone inflicts them on you.

The worst theory was that tense parents caused colicky babies, an idea that caused zillions of parents unnecessary guilt. Fortunately, this theory got the boot before you became a parent — but you may still hear it from one of your relatives.

More recently, doctors thought that a colicky baby hadn't grown up enough to handle emotions. As a result, so this theory went, babies who didn't know how to manage their feelings fell into fits of crying and couldn't stop. This theory, however, failed to answer a key question: Why do babies with colic seem to be in so much *physical* pain?

The facts about colic

Thanks to recent medical findings, doctors now know that two minor (although painful) conditions underlie most cases of colic: allergies and stomach acid. This discovery is very good news for parents because both problems have safe, fast, and simple remedies. Here's the scoop on each culprit and its remedy:

Villain #1: Allergies

Doctors used to think babies couldn't have allergies before 2 years of age. Recently, however, doctors discovered that many newborns who scream in terrible pain have inflamed intestines as the result of food allergies. These babies almost instantly recover from colic and start having normal poops when their parents stop feeding them the foods to which they're allergic.

In addition, the proteins in a mom's diet can pass unchanged right into her breast milk. So, if you eat yogurt for lunch and then breast-feed a baby who's allergic to milk, you can expect trouble ahead.

Add up these two facts — little tykes can be allergic, and even moms who breastfeed can deliver the foods that make them suffer — and you have one very good answer to the question, "What causes colic?"

If this is your baby's problem, work with your pediatrician to figure out which foods cause the reaction and then eliminate them:

- ✔ If Mom is breastfeeding, the bad guys usually are proteins from cow's milk, soy, or other foods, and the answer is to have Mom stop all intake of the troublesome foods.

- ✔ If Baby takes a bottle, the soy or cow's milk in infant formulas can cause the problem, and the solution is to feed your baby an *elemental* formula (all of the proteins are broken down; it's still nutritious but no longer causes allergies). Your pediatrician can tell you whether this approach makes sense for your tot.

Villain #2: Tummy acid

For years, doctors failed to consider stomach acid as a cause for colic for the same reason that they ignored allergies: They thought babies were too young for this problem.

Recently, however, research proved otherwise. Studies show that heartburn (also called *reflux* or *gastroesophageal reflux disease, GERD*) can make babies just as miserable as it makes grownups.

Heartburn occurs when acid from your stomach burns the lining of your esophagus or intestine (the parts right before or after the stomach). Most people have stomach acid capable of causing this problem, but they also have protective linings — like oven mitts — that keep the acid from reaching sensitive spots. If the lining develops a gap, the acid can seep through and burn . . . Ouch! But, you ask, nearly everyone has stomach acid and nearly all babies have acid that washes up into their esophagus (do you know any babies who *never* spit up?), so why do only some babies suffer from heartburn? We don't know — but we *do* know that a whole lot of babies have this problem.

When adults feel the pain of heartburn, they usually grab an antacid. But babies have only one way of saying they hurt — they cry their hearts out. Luckily, if heartburn is causing your baby's pain and tears, these solutions can help:

- ✔ Your pediatrician can recommend safe and simple medications that actually stop production of stomach acid altogether.

  Stomach acid appears to have little benefit and stopping its production does little harm — at least for a few months, until your sweetie outgrows the risk of heartburn.

- ✔ Keep your baby upright after a meal to reduce the chance for that burning stomach acid to splash up into his esophagus.

- ✔ Elevate the head of your baby's crib a little bit, which also helps to keep stomach acid in the tummy.

- ✔ If you bottle-feed your baby, thicken the feeding by adding just a little bit of rice cereal. Again, this helps to keep acid in the stomach, where it belongs.

Many, many babies with colic have treatable problems, but a few don't. These infants cry their little hearts out for the first few months even when doctors eliminate every known culprit. The cause probably has a good explanation . . . but medical science needs to discover it. The good news is that even in this situation, the crying jags usually stop after the 3-month mark. So hang in there — there's a light at the end of the tunnel!

Chapter 5

Getting the Hang of It: Sleep from 6 to 12 Months

. . . .

In This Chapter

▶ Choosing to sleep through the night

▶ Encouraging a full night's sleep

▶ Making it easier: Lovies, naps, and occasional setbacks

. . . .

Are you the only parent at playgroup who's still wearing sunglasses to hide under-eye circles? If so, don't despair. Babies have a wide range of personalities and sleep requirements, and some just need a little extra time and encouragement to develop a sleep routine.

In this chapter, you discover the tricks to getting your little cutie to follow a routine: creating your own beddy-bye ritual; changing the menu at mealtimes in ways that encourage longer sleep; and gently and kindly setting limits on the nighttime demands she makes on you. All these techniques add up to more hours of sleep (and more energetic days) for you and your little one.

Your baby's sleep habits don't change overnight (no pun intended); it takes days or even weeks. But with patience, you'll finally experience the nirvana of sleeping until the alarm clock rings. And with a little time, this stretch becomes the rule, not the exception.

Knowing When You and Baby Are Ready to Sleep All Night

Sleeping through the night is a milestone on the road to independence, and deciding whether or not to sleep is the first real choice your little one makes in her young life. Meanwhile, you'll earn a gold star in parenting for helping her take that first baby step toward being a big kid.

The question, "Can my little one make it through a whole night alone?" doesn't have a one-size-fits-all answer. As a rule, however, most babies are physically ready to sleep through the night when they reach 4 months of age. (See Chapter 4 for more about this readiness.) Object permanence may help one sleep all night without calling for parents and develops at about 9 months of age — we discuss this topic in greater detail in Chapter 6.

So why are we talking about this issue in a chapter on babies 6 to 12 months old? Good question! This is the time when most *parents* feel comfortable setting some limits for their little ones. Although some parents may start trying a little earlier (with good reason), many choose to wait until the six-month mark before taking active steps to change the bedtime rules. The plan is good because it virtually guarantees that your angel is ready — and that you've had enough midnight cuddles.

Because each family is unique, factor in both your baby's readiness *and* your own needs and feelings when deciding whether now is the right moment for your baby to take this big step.

Knowing when Baby is set to sleep the night away

How can you feel confident that your sweetheart is ready to be alone in that crib all night? Ask yourself these questions to make that decision:

- ✔ **Can your baby fall asleep on his own?** In other words, if you put him down in his crib before he's fully asleep, can he take the last step to the Land of Nod all by himself?

  If your baby falls asleep on his own and doesn't need his nighttime snacks but still rousts you at 1 or 2 a.m., he's probably more interested in a little face time with Mom or Dad than a meal. Waking up every few hours has become a desire, not a need, and he's ready to sleep through the night. (See Chapter 1 for more on needs versus desires.)

- ✔ **Can your baby consume all the calories he needs during the daylight hours?** The answer is yes, unless your tot arrived prematurely (see Chapter 12 for info on early-birds' feeding needs). Babies as young as 4 months of age are big enough — and their growth is slow enough — that they don't need a midnight snack. (See the later section "Using Calorie Shifting to Reset Your Baby's Clock" for specific suggestions on how to eliminate nighttime feedings.)

✔ **Is your baby healthy and not dealing with a chronic issue that can interfere with sleep?** A health problem can complicate feeding and sleep issues, so check with your pediatrician about any health issues before you assume that the runway is clear for all-night slumber. (See Chapter 13 for details on dealing with sleep and health problems.)

Some babies do have legitimate nighttime needs at this age. Babies who were born early, are ill, or are able to eat only a little at a single feeding may still need to wake at night to feed. In these cases, the techniques in this chapter are still helpful — but you need to wait a few extra weeks or months before trying them.

This leaves only one question: Are *you* ready?

Making sure you're on your mark

If your baby has the skills and maturity to sleep all night, that's half the battle. The other half is making sure your own heart is in the game.

If you're like most parents, you're torn between the guilt that comes with not satisfying your baby's every wish and the desire of wanting a good night's sleep so you can feel human again. Maybe you're secretly reluctant to give up that little late-night cuddle, but you're also more and more grouchy, exhausted, and (admit it) resentful each time a loud shriek drags you out of bed.

These conflicting emotions can make your decisions about all-night sleeping a little complicated. But at this stage, the ball is in your court and not your baby's. There's no right or wrong decision, so you need to find the balance that works for you and your tot. What follows are a few guideposts to help you along the way:

✔ **Don't confuse *helping your baby get to sleep* with *letting your baby cry.*** Crying is the sideshow (and you may hear lots of it in upcoming weeks!), but it's not really the main issue. Instead, stay focused on this point: Are *you* still getting your baby to sleep, or is your baby figuring out how to get *herself* to sleep? Your goal is to help her reach independence in this big life-skill, so don't let her distract you with those tears. If she manipulates you into feeling guilty, you both have lots of sleepless nights ahead.

✔ **If you're making this decision with a partner, be sure you're both totally committed to this step.** If one partner is prepared and the other isn't, you can't be consistent and your tot will play the more reluctant parent like a violin. Better to wait a few weeks (or even months) than to apply your sleepy-time strategies halfheartedly.

When you've decided the time is right, give yourself a quick reality check with these reminders before you set the dreams in motion:

- ✔ **Understand that sleeping through the night means different things to different people.** Ideally, sleeping through the night means you and your baby feel rested and ready to take on the day. For some families that means a full ten hours of beauty rest for their little one, but other families are just fine with a quick 2 a.m. feeding or an early human alarm clock.

- ✔ **Be prepared for a little frustration.** Don't be surprised, for example, if your little angel sleeps blissfully through the night for weeks and then goes back to screaming like a banshee at 2 a.m. A baby's rest is often disturbed right before important developmental surges, and many of those developments occur during the 6-to-12-month stage.

Establishing a Bedtime Routine

At this point in your baby's life, *routine* is the key word. (By this we mean a *predictable schedule* for day and night activities.) At this age your baby is ready to get into the habit of eating and sleeping on a fairly regular timetable. If he doesn't quite have that schedule thing down, don't fret — this section offers effective approaches to help your wee one adjust his timetable to yours.

Some simple pointers to get you started

By the time your baby is 6 months old, she starts to associate familiar routines with bedtime. The goal of these rituals is to gradually ease her from the busyness of daytime into the relaxation of evening, preparing her both mentally and physically for bed. In time, you'll have your own favorite nighty-night rituals, but these guidelines work well for many parents:

- ✔ **Set a bedtime.** This time can be flexible, but try to keep it fairly consistent. Babies vary in their need for sleep, and typical bedtimes range from as early as 7 p.m. to as late as 9 p.m. Of course, your work schedule and your preferences factor into your decision.

Don't fall for the idea that keeping your baby up until she's absolutely exhausted encourages her to sleep in. That ploy usually doesn't work — and likely leads to a major meltdown when she's overtired.

✔ **Consider the day she's had and be somewhat flexible.** For instance, if your child just paid her first visit to Chuck E. Cheese, she's probably over-stimulated (and possibly still getting over the trauma of being hugged by a giant rat), so keep the bedtime ritual as calm and quiet as possible. On the other hand, if she had a lazy day indoors, she may not be tired enough to sleep well. If that's the case, see whether you can work in a little activity before you start your bedtime routine.

✔ **Get a head start.** Start setting the mood for bedtime 30 to 45 minutes before you want to put your baby down for the night. Do this by turning off lights, putting on soft music, and turning off the television.

If your child is an infant, feed her before bedtime, stopping when she's drowsy but not yet fully asleep. You may need to rouse her gently to make sure she doesn't conk out too early. As we note earlier, much of the work in getting your baby to snooze all night centers on teaching her how to get herself to sleep — so you don't want to do the job for her.

✔ **Dress for success.** Change your baby into comfy jammies with no frills, buttons, or tags that can poke, bind, or itch. One of the most common mistakes is overdoing bedtime warmth. Babies can control their body temperatures just as well as adults, so dress your baby in the same weight of clothing that you're comfortable wearing.

✔ **Keep the lights down low.** Some babies fall asleep easily in the dark, and others like a little bit of light. If your little one falls into the second category, invest in a dimmer switch and turn the lights down low at crib time. After your baby falls asleep, turn the light off.

Over time, this step accustoms her to sleeping in a totally dark room (which can help keep sleep schedules on track). If your infant gets used to sleeping in a dark room, the issue is less likely to be a problem during toddler years.

Activities to help your baby wind down

Grownups like to read a book, watch a little television, eat a snack, or take a leisurely walk to relax before bedtime. These rituals say, "Forget the pressures of the day — it's time to relax." Your baby can't do any of these on his own, so you need to provide a little quiet entertainment before sleepytime.

✔ **Try a tubby-time.** A little trial-and-error is necessary here because some babies find baths restful and other babies rev up in the tub. If a bath helps your baby calm down, give him one before you change him into his jammies. If baths make him wired, schedule them earlier in the day.

✔ **Give your baby your magic touch.** A gentle rubdown can help melt tension away, and it's a nice way to bond with your baby. Rub a little oil (regular olive oil or baby oil works great!) on your hands and give your little one a slow, relaxing head-to-toe massage. For more information on massaging your little one, pick up a copy of *Baby Massage For Dummies* by Joanne Bagshaw and Ilene Fox (Wiley). Figure 5-1 shows a good calming massage technique — just run your hand along each side of your baby's body to lull him into dreamland (or at least sooth his nerves!).

✔ **Read a good book.** One of the best bedtime activities is story time; simple, rhyming stories that have a sing-song verse or pattern are particularly soothing. Besides helping your baby to wind down, stories are a prime way to stimulate language skills. Flip to Chapter 17 for a whole host of suggestions.

✔ **Sing a little tune.** Babies love singing, too, and a soft lullaby while rocking can mellow out even the most wide-awake little one.

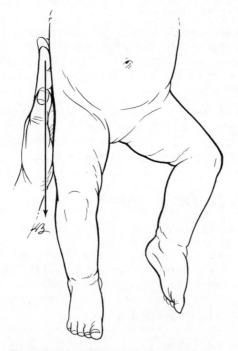

Figure 5-1: A soothing massage technique.

Lulling Baby beyond the yawns

When your baby is hovering on the edge of sleep, make your move. Place her in her crib and quietly say something like, "Good night, I love you, see you in the morning." (And quietly pray that it *is* morning before you see her again!)

Many babies like to hear soft music when they're dozing off. Musical patterns are powerfully pleasing to the brain and can mask household sounds that disturb your little one's sleep (especially if other kids are in the house — sibs have a tough time turning down the volume when a little one is trying to sleep). If you play the same songs each night, the music also signals to your baby that sleep is approaching.

Using Calorie Shifting to Reset Your Baby's Clock

One of the best ways to help your baby sleep through the night is to reset his tummy clock. The goal here is *calorie shifting*, gradually decreasing your baby's nighttime food without letting him get hungry.

Calorie shifting works because the human body remembers when it's been fed. As a result, people fall into patterns based on when they eat. For instance, people who regularly eat dinner at 10 p.m. typically aren't very hungry at 6 p.m. and vice versa.

The same is true of your baby. If you regularly give him a meal at 2 a.m., his tummy says, "Feed me!" at 2 a.m. each day. If you want to banish the middle-of-the-night bottle or breastfeeding, you need to reset his internal clock — and it's actually pretty easy.

When you use the calorie shifting technique, don't fret about starving your little one. (If Grandma says you are, she's wrong.) At any given age, most babies take in a fairly constant number of calories each 24 hours. If you cut down on the midnight snack, your baby simply eats more during the day.

In effect, the calorie-shifting step we describe in the next few paragraphs is the last step in a process you started when you introduced cereals, fruits, and vegetables into your baby's diet. That change shifted your baby's eating heavily toward the daytime. To ensure a sound sleep, however, you want to tweak that balance even more.

If you're breastfeeding

Moms who breastfeed can still reduce the number of nightly feedings their babies need. When your little one wakes up during the night,

- ✔ Rub her back or sing to her to see whether you can comfort her back to sleep without feeding her.

- ✔ Try to figure out which night feeding is of least interest to her; try skipping that one each night.

- ✔ Send in Dad or anyone else capable of handling the baby instead of Mom. The aroma of breast milk can stimulate your baby to want to nurse.

- ✔ If you're comfortable using bottles, consider giving your baby a bottle of breast milk for night feedings, slowly diluting them more each night until they're basically water. (See the next section.) Again, Dads may have more luck with this step.

   By this age, *nipple confusion* (trouble returning to breastfeeding after switching to a bottle) is no longer an issue. More information on this topic is available in *Your Baby's First Year For Dummies* by James Gaylord and Michelle Hagan (Wiley).

If you're bottle-feeding

If you're bottle-feeding, use the following dilution strategy to induce calorie-shifting:

- ✔ Choose the first night feeding that you want to eliminate, and make the formula for that feeding ⅞ or ¾ strength.

- ✔ If your baby takes this bottle well and is satisfied, gradually decrease the strength of the formula by ⅛ or ¼ until only water is in the bottle.

Repeat this process for each nighttime feeding; before long, your baby won't be hungry at all during the night. At this point, he's waking you up for only one reason: It's just so darned much fun! And this is when you need to gently and lovingly change the rules of the game.

Setting Limits with Love

When you know your little one is getting plenty of calories during the day, you can be pretty sure that her primary reason for waking is to see you. This is a powerful desire and one that your baby expects to have satisfied.

The key, however, is that it's a *desire,* and not a *need.* Much of your life as a parent will involve helping your child see the difference between *want* and *need,* and the bedtime issue is your first big test. (Believe it or not, it's also one of the easiest. Wait until you explain to your 13-year-old that she doesn't need to wear eyeliner or tell your 16-year-old that he doesn't need his own car!)

Beginning to change your little one's habits

Changing this appear-on-demand pattern starts not with your baby, but with you. Your first step is to realize that your child will be just fine if you change the pattern. You don't traumatize him a bit (if you have any concerns, see our discussion of disappointment versus trauma in Chapter 1) when you give him the chance, gently and lovingly, to adapt to new expectations. The more power you give your tot to discover that *he* can solve problems, the more confidence he gains in his own strengths and abilities.

Of course, you're biologically wired to react to those piteous shrieks, so you need to recognize this situation as a chance for your angel to learn. You're not just being tough; you're being wise.

Considering strategies to guide your way

Now that you know why your child needs to fall asleep on her own, it's time for specifics. Here's an effective way to hand your love-bug the keys to Sleepyland:

- ✔ **Wait a minute or two when you hear your baby cry.** She'll cycle between deep and light sleep stages three to four times each night and may wake up for just a moment. If you run to her at the first sign that she's awake, she doesn't have time to make a natural transition back to a deep-sleep stage.

- ✔ **Remember that crying isn't a pick-up line.** If your tot's cry sounds normal and you're sure she's fine, avoid picking her up. This is a possible signal for play or even a feeding. Instead, wait a bit to let her find her own way back to sleep.

If you're ready to make the change to all-night sleeping, remember this motto: If at first you don't succeed, try again . . . and again . . . and again! The best approach is setting a bedtime and a wake-up time and not going into your child's room in between — and consistency is the biggest key to success. If she sees you even once during this time, you reinforce her sense that you appear when she cries. Typically, you need only two to four nights for your child to change her expectations, give up the crying game, and sleep the whole night.

Safety valves for high-pressure times

Even under the best of circumstance, you need to bend the rules a little. Here are a couple of ideas:

- **Know when your baby means business.** If your sweetie's wide awake and his cry sounds different — really a howl — then a visit is in order. Check to make sure that he isn't sick, stuck, or soaking wet. If all is fine, put him back in his crib, rub his back, and let him know in a soothing voice that you're there. Some babies need Mom or Dad to stay until they drift back to sleep, but others calm down quickly and can be left while they're still awake.

- **Bring in reinforcements.** We mention in the earlier section "If you're breastfeeding" how the scent of breast milk can make your baby work up an appetite. Obviously this problem doesn't occur if a guy takes over the night shift! For this and other reasons — including those deep, rumbling male voices — men seem to have especially good luck getting babies to conk out. But any substitute can help, so ask a nanny, a mature teenaged child, or a grandparent to take over the night duty if you're lucky enough to have one of them on hand at 2 a.m.

- **Don't beat yourself up if you aren't as firm as you'd like to be.** This may sound like a contradiction of the *consistency-is-key* rule, but being at your beloved little tyrant's beck and call is a hard habit to break. Picking your little one up now and then doesn't cause a major setback — but try to resist the urge.

Handling Logistical Matters

Lots of factors, large and small, play a role in creating a successful sleep routine. In this section we look at three of them: safety, comfort, and those all-important naps.

Making sure your nursery is safe for an escape artist

Your baby's safety as she sleeps is a primary concern. To feel comfortable establishing a routine, you need to be sure your baby's crib is truly a safe place — even when she's on her own.

In the early months, safety-proofing your baby's bedroom was easy. Now, however, the rules are changing because your baby is on the move in every direction — including up!

When your baby starts pulling up into a standing position:

- ✔ Remove bumper pads so she can't climb up on them and tumble out of the crib.

- ✔ Get rid of low-hanging mobiles.

- ✔ Make sure she can't reach curtain pulls, pictures hanging on the wall, or other potential dangers.

- ✔ Double-check the crib hardware to make sure everything's holding firm.

- ✔ Make sure all electrical outlets have safety plugs, even if you think they're too high for your baby to reach.

You'll be amazed at what she can get into and climb up to during the months to come.

Dealing with blankies and other treasures

You'll probably notice that your baby becomes attached to certain items — a cloth diaper, receiving blanket, or soft doll — as he moves into the second half of his first year. If you ask your mom or dad about your own baby days, you'll probably find out that you too had a *lovie* that comforted you and helped you feel safe.

 These items are known as *transitional objects* because they remind children of the love and nurturing they receive from their parents. In effect, the beloved blankie or dolly acts as a bridge between being with Mommy and Daddy and wanting to be with them.

A lovie can be a definite help at sleep time after your child hits the 12-month mark and is old enough to sleep with a stuffed toy or blanket. A child who wakes during the night can embrace his special lovie and use it as a tool to recall Mom's or Dad's presence and be comforted back to sleep. *Note:* Don't worry if your child doesn't have a favorite blanket or doll. Many babies don't, and they get to sleep just fine.

 One trick with your baby's lovie is to rub it against your own skin before putting it in the crib. This idea sounds gross, but leaving a little *eau-de-you* on the lovie can make it even more comforting at nighttime.

Parents tend to have a love-hate relationship with one particular lovie, the pacifier. Babies who fall asleep while sucking on one may be at a loss when they can't locate it in the middle of the night; then, of course, they scream for help — a particularly vexing problem between 4 and 8 months of age. (After that, they seem to employ baby sonar and find the hidden prize themselves.)

To avoid the middle-of-the-night pacifier hunt, try trading it for another lovie like a doll or blanket and see whether your baby accepts the switch. However, keep in mind that recent studies suggest that pacifiers can help protect against sudden infant death syndrome (SIDS). (For more information on pacifiers in general and preventing SIDS in particular, see Chapter 4.)

A note about naps at this age

For a weary parent, a baby's nap is like a life preserver to a drowning person. Babies' naps provide the crucial breaks parents need to relax and recharge — and, of course, to read great parenting books. Naps typically take place in the middle of the morning or the middle of the afternoon.

Children between 6 and 12 months of age typically sleep 10 to 12 hours at night and take two naps that last about an hour each. (Naps may taper off to just one toward the end of the year.) Of course, that's the average amount of sleep — and as everybody knows, no one has an average child! In reality, sleep needs can vary a great deal, and you have little control over the total number of hours your baby needs each 24 hours.

The good news is that you can use the same strategies for naps that you use for nighttime (check the earlier sections of this chapter for a review of these strategies). Consistency is the ticket. In addition, these tips can promote a peaceful naptime:

✔ **Timing:** Stick as closely to a schedule as you can, but you don't need to bring your life to a screeching halt in order to put your baby down at exactly the same times each day. Consider these tips:

- Plan a nap for half an hour after lunch or a snack to ensure that your baby's tummy is full; this helps her sleep more soundly.

- Move naptime up a bit if you notice that your darling is getting drowsy a little ahead of schedule. Otherwise she's likely to get overtired and be too wound up to sleep.

- Time your baby's second nap for early afternoon to give her plenty of time to get sleepy again before bedtime.

 ✔ **Sounds:** Keep the noise level in your house low during
  naptime and put some soft music on in the background.

 ✔ **Lighting:** Consider buying blackout shades for the nursery
  because young babies sleep better in a dark room.

 ✔ **Toys:** When your tot reaches the 12-month mark and crib toys
  are no longer taboo, place some safe toys in the crib. They
  can buy you a few precious minutes of peace and quiet by
  amusing your baby when she first opens her eyes.

No matter how inviting you make naptime, be ready for an occasional struggle. At bedtime, you hold all the cards because biology
eventually forces your baby to fall asleep — even if it seems to take
forever. At naptime, however, your baby has an ace hidden in her
diaper; she's physically capable of refusing to fall asleep. To her,
the world has such exciting appeal that she may very well insist on
staying awake, no matter how cranky she gets.

However, you don't need to give in completely. Even if you can't make
your baby fall asleep, you can place her in her crib and keep her
there. She may fuss the first few times you do this, but she eventually
takes the hint — and gives you a much-needed hour or so of freedom.

Identifying and Combating Difficulties due to Milestones

Developmental milestones can have a big effect on your baby's
sleep. Think of each developmental surge as a huge ocean wave
coming up behind you. As you sense the water coming, you tense
up to brace yourself for the wave. When babies are nearing a big
milestone, they too sense the tension, and this tension often spills
over into the sleep cycle.

Sitting up, crawling, and pulling up to a stand are perhaps the most
common developmental leaps that change sleepytime. Sometimes, a
tot is so excited by a new skill that he can't sleep. Other times, a tyke
learns a new skill like sitting or standing up in his crib but hasn't mastered the fine art of getting back down; he squawks for help because
he wants to plop back down on his bed but can't figure out how. (For
ways to help a tot who gets stuck this way, see Chapter 6.)

You may find it interesting to keep a chart of your child's sleep-cycle
fluctuations to see whether the disruptions precede the appearance
of a new skill. Of course, this charting can't make any difference in
your child's sleep, but your understanding of this temporary change
can be comforting to you. Typically, sleep returns to normal after
your baby masters the new skill.

To chart your baby's sleep, simply use the forms in the appendix of this book to record the number of hours that your baby sleeps each night and nap. Then look for patterns. For instance, five good nights of sleep followed by four crabby nights or three missed afternoon naps in a row may be signaling a big change like learning to sit up or crawl. Charting can also help you spot trends and see how well your sleep strategies are working.

Figure 5-2 shows an example of a completed two-week hour-by-hour sleep log of a 10-month-old who learned to pull himself to standing at the beginning of Week Two. You can see how this sleep log highlights the pattern: His picture-perfect sleep routine briefly turns to chaos before settling down again. The parent of this tot can use this data to figure out what happened during that brief wild ride — for instance, company arriving, a major developmental milestone, a flu bug, or a change in sitters.

We provide a blank daily sleep log for you in the appendix.

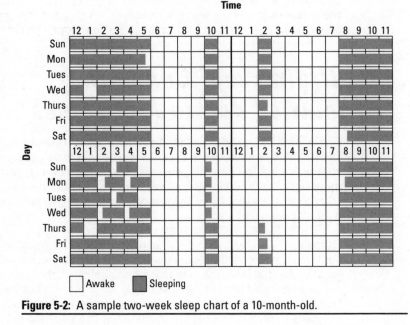

Figure 5-2: A sample two-week sleep chart of a 10-month-old.

Chapter 6

Baby on the Move: Sleep from 12 to 18 Months

*I*magine how it feels to master a new skill every few weeks. In your adult world, that's like becoming an expert guitar player, great golfer, and gourmet cook — all in a couple of months. And that's what life is like now for your child, who's mastering amazing skills at a rapid rate. What an exciting time the second year of life is for your little one!

Two of the biggest skills are crawling and walking. Although there's plenty of variation, most children start crawling around 9 months of age and graduate to walking near the 1-year mark. These transitions lead to some big psychological changes that typically kick in shortly after the 12-month milestone.

Crawling and walking are important events because they expand your child's physical and mental horizons. But they also affect your little one's daytime and nighttime sleep. So just when you thought you were home free, you may be faced with the sleepless nights that haunted you during your baby's first few months.

In addition to the crawling, standing, and walking, a problem called *separation anxiety* can wreak havoc on your little one's sleep. Luckily, sleep problems at this stage tend to be temporary, but in this chapter we show how you can handle them with a few tried-and-true techniques. We also talk about standing in the crib, why it can be a problem for a toddler, and how you can help your baby quickly solve it.

Gaining Independence: The Joy — and the Scare!

In addition to the heady feeling your 1-year-old gets from beginning to make big decisions (which toys to grab, what sights to explore), his new freedom has another side: He realizes he can move away from you . . . and you can leave him. Up to now he's viewed you as a permanent fixture, sort of like the sofa or the coffee table. But now he knows that — unlike the furniture — you can take off for parts unknown. Initially, it's alarming news, and he responds to impending separations by clinging to your leg like a suckerfish, weeping . . . well, like a baby, or even throwing full-fledged hissy fits.

Your child's panicky responses to your departures — a reaction that child psychologists call *separation anxiety* — is actually a normal developmental milestone. In fact, it shows that your toddler is gaining these important new skills:

- ✔ He sees the difference between familiar people and strangers.

- ✔ He realizes how very important you are in his life.

- ✔ He has the awareness to *anticipate* the sad feeling of missing you when you're gone.

However, he can't understand that partings are temporary, so he sees them, even at bedtime, as threatening.

Parting is such sweet sorrow: The beginning of separation anxiety

You can't predict when separation anxiety will enter the picture, but it's a natural outgrowth of *object permanence,* the knowledge that you don't just vanish when you're out of sight. Object permanence usually develops around 8 months of age, and separation anxiety arrives on the scene a bit later, typically between 12 and 20 months. Separation anxiety slowly fades as your child understands that you come back after each parting.

When separation anxiety takes center stage, your child — even if she's always been a people person — suddenly balks when you introduce her to strangers. The arrival of a sitter (even a familiar one) is also likely to trigger tears or tantrums. And because the line between friend and stranger is still a little blurry to your angel, even Grandma and Grandpa may suddenly get the cold shoulder.

Each child reacts to separation anxiety in a unique way. Some kids can barely let their parents out of sight, and other toddlers breeze through this stage with only occasional clinginess. Personality plays a big role in how children deal with the partings. Shy tots often suffer the most, but even the most carefree and outgoing tykes can surprise their parents by developing a raging case of separation anxiety. Major life changes, such as a move or the arrival of a sibling, can also trigger an intense fear of separation from Mom or Dad.

Understanding why separation anxiety affects sleep

When separation anxiety issues crop up, sleep problems are often part of the package because sleep is a very big separation for your toddler. At this stage he can anticipate how he'll feel when he's all alone in his crib, and he lets you know — at the top of his lungs — that he's not looking forward to your absence.

The message he's sending with these blood-curdling shrieks is that he's powerfully attached to you and counts on you to keep him safe and secure. Realizing that your baby has such a strong bond with you can give you the warm fuzzies. But that warm feeling quickly turns to heartburn when you realize *it's back* . . . the nightly bedtime struggle.

Taking Back the Night: Battling Common Sleep Struggles

Your child's developmental road may seem a bit bumpy right now because she's literally taking two steps forward and then plopping down on her bottom. The same is true for her psychological development. The more she understands, the more she thinks about even the simplest tasks. Your tot's consternation can lead to some rough nights and tough decisions for you, too, as you adapt to her growing needs and desires.

You can't avoid these developmental growth spurts (and you don't want to!), so this section offers some strategies that can help your toddler chill out.

Relieving nighttime separation anxiety

Routine is particularly important to children mastering the exciting but potentially scary skill of separating from their parents because predictable patterns ease their anxieties at this stressful stage. This means toddlers thrive on consistency, so if you didn't establish a routine during the second half of your child's first year (see our advice in Chapter 5), now's a good time to create one and stick to it.

Although you want predictability, your bedtime rituals also need to reflect your child's changes. This flexibility means that the books you read, the songs you sing, or your child's pre-bedtime snack will change. However, if your general routine is firmly established, the small tweaks you make won't interfere with the bedtime process.

TIP

When you spot the first signs of separation anxiety, put all the pieces of your sleepy-time drill back in place (we explain the basics of the routine in Chapter 5). In this section we add some new components and modifications now that your child is older.

- ✔ **Stick to a script.** Take advantage of your child's growing verbal skills when you're preparing him for bedtime or other transition times. Using short, clear sentences (think of Jane talking to Tarzan), say the same words to your baby each night as bedtime approaches. For instance, a few minutes before your targeted bedtime, you can say, "Look at the clock — it's almost time for bed!" Your child can understand a surprising amount of this message, and he'll find the repetition reassuring.

- ✔ **Keep the bath solo.** At this age, a warm bath is a wonderful way to usher in the sandman. However, if you have more than one child, avoid popping everybody in the tub together. Two or more kids in a bathtub full of toys, suds, and water is not a recipe for relaxation for anyone! If separate baths are impossible to fit in every night, let the cleanest kid skip a day.

- ✔ **Cuddle up with a book.** Even though you add new books as your child ages, keep going back to the originals — especially during stressful times like the separation-anxiety phase.

- ✔ **Resist the urge to fudge on bedtime.** Keeping a child up just a little longer can be very tempting (especially if Mommy or Daddy gets home from work late), but this switch only overstimulates your wee one and disrupts the bedtime routine. Instead, try to schedule family time for a few extra minutes in the morning, after everyone's had a good night's sleep.

✔ **Let Teddy take the night shift.** Now that your sweetie is past the 1-year mark, he can safely take a doll or stuffed animal to bed (see the safety tips at the end of this chapter). You can make this *lovie* a part of the bedtime ritual. For instance, have Teddy join you during story time and then tuck him in and tell him "Night-night" too.

Squelching separation anxiety while the sun is up

Leftover stress from a hectic day can cause anyone to toss and turn, and that's just as true for little people as it is for grownups. If you want to avoid fussy nights, try smoothing your child's path during the daytime hours, particularly when separation anxiety reaches its peak.

Powering up predictability

One key to achieving peace and quiet is to keep changes to a minimum. The following tips can help you minimize your baby's daytime stress:

✔ At home, let your child approach strangers, friends, and relatives on her own terms. This stage is definitely not the time to scoop her up and say, "Give Nana a big kiss!" (unless Nana handles rejection well). Instead, let your child observe people quietly; let her decide when she's ready to be more friendly.

✔ Try to stick to consistent nap times; prepare your little angel for naps by offering quiet games, lullabies, a story, and a cuddle.

✔ If possible, avoid switching sitters or day care during this time in your child's life.

✔ If you need to leave an anxious toddler with a friend or sitter, be sure to make your parting cheerful. Say "Bye-bye, I'll see you soon," offer a quick kiss, and scoot. Even if you're nervous about parting from your sweetie, don't let your smile slip until you're safely out of sight.

✔ If you have a choice, don't take an extended vacation away from your child during this time in her life. A toddler's sense of time is vague, and even a long weekend can seem like eternity. You may have earned a little time off, but the price tag — in terms of sleepless nights — can be awfully steep.

Making a conscientious preschool decision

To help ease your child's separation anxiety, hold off preschool until your little one is closer to 2 — when her verbal skills and her understanding that you *do* come back can help her cope. Children under 3 often react strongly to being separated from a beloved caregiver. But if preschool is a necessity, a tot over 2 can make this transition with only temporary fussing. You can ease the way by choosing a preschool that allows time for your child to transition slowly. This means you get to stay with your little darling until she feels comfortable with her teachers and new surroundings. For more information on sleep solutions involving day care, flip ahead to Chapter 11.

Dealing with setbacks in your routine

Even if your bedtime routine is polished to perfection, it isn't always enough. Lots of big and little adjustments — a change in babysitters or a new tooth coming in — can cause a bump in the road, and sometimes you feel like you've made a U-turn. When this problem occurs, take a step back and reintroduce some of the strategies we outline in Chapter 5.

Giving Baby a refresher course: Revisiting the basics

If your little one is backsliding, get firm about your bedtime drill so you can get the basics back in place:

- ✔ **When your child cries or bangs on the crib rails as you leave the room, calmly say, "I love you. It's bedtime, and I will see you in the morning." Then calmly and cheerfully walk out and close the door.**

- ✔ **Be prepared for your baby to cry probably 30 to 60 minutes.**

  Your child is disappointed but not traumatized; he *wants* you but doesn't *need* you. (See Chapter 3 for an explanation of these very important distinctions.) Try — really, really try! — to resist the urge to go back into his room even if he uses those new power words: "Mama!" and "Dada!"

- ✔ **If you can't stop yourself, then go in briefly, pat him on the back, tell him once again that you love him, and say you'll see him in the morning.**

  Don't be too hard on yourself if you give in and pay him a visit. But remember, every time your sweetie wins the game, he wants to win again. He's like a gambler in Vegas, and you're the payoff that keeps him pulling the lever.

Striking a compromise at midnight

If your child falls asleep but then wakes during the night, you really want to have a plan in place (after all, who wants to start deep-thinking at midnight!). Here are some strategies that can help you compromise between tough love and all-out surrender.

- ✔ **Keep it simple.** Analyze your baby's cries and decide whether he's really in need or just seeking attention. If you're sure it's nothing serious, steel yourself to wait him out.

  This stall technique gives you (and your little Paul Revere) a chance to find out whether he can get back to sleep on his own. Giving him a chance to cry it out and comfort himself is the best approach, but it's definitely hard to do. If you absolutely must go into his room, give him a quick pat and a reassuring word, and then leave. Don't pick him up, or you'll signal playtime. (Yikes!)

- ✔ **Keep your cool.** If several minutes seem like several hours and you can't fight the desire to comfort your little howler, strike a deal with your softer side:

  - If you hear your little one sobbing around midnight, tell yourself: "It's 12:02 now. If he's still screaming at 12:15, I'll go in."

  - At 12:15, re-evaluate his cries. If they're just as loud or louder and you can't take any more, go to him. However, if you sense that he's winding down, set another target time and see whether he falls asleep before that new time.

- ✔ **Keep increasing the intervals.** If he wakes you up again and again, make him wait a little longer each time. If you wait 10 minutes the first time, make it 20 the next, and so on. Parents who use this technique often find that about 45 minutes is the longest they can wait until going in. However, after going in three or four times in ever-lengthening intervals, you may just want to say, "That's all, folks" and not go in until morning — even if your pride and joy cries for another hour.

  This technique makes Mom and Dad feel better, but it takes longer than if you stay out of your tot's room altogether. If the slower plan's okay with you and your family, then it's a workable compromise.

Stick to this drill each time problems arise in the middle of the night so you can nip those buggers in the bud. Over time, your child's wake-up calls will become fewer and farther between — and you'll gain more confidence as you discover that setting limits works for both of you.

When Problems Stick Around: Monitoring Your Child's Sleep Patterns

The combination of separation anxiety, big new skills like walking and talking, and more independence can make sleep issues harder than ever to sort out at this stage. To help make sense of the chaos, try replacing your hour-by-hour sleep chart with the version in Table 6-1, which allows you to track clues like life changes, the effects of new people in your tot's life, and major milestones.

Table 6-1	Sleep Log and Milestones		
Date	*Duration of Sleep and/or Sleep Problems Spotted*	*What's New? (Company Visiting, New Sitter, and So On)*	*Milestone Reached*
January 15 (4 m/o)	Night - 10 hrs; woke up twice during the night; nap - 3 hrs	Visit from Grandma	
March 23	Night - 9 hrs; up at night 2-3x; nap - 2 hrs	Back from vacation trip	
May 3	Night - 10 hrs; up twice crying, clearly uncomfortable; nap - 2 hrs		Learning to stand
July 19 (10 m/o)	Night - 10 hrs; had trouble falling asleep, very clingy; nap - 2 hrs	Visit from Grandma	
August 12	Night - 10 hours; up once, fussy; nap - 2 hours		Took first step!
November 16	Night - 3 hours; nap - none	A bad cold	

Three More Steps to Success: Safety, Naps, and Substitutes

When you've fine-tuned your bedtime drill and handled separation anxiety, your nights should be full of sweet dreams again. But you're not quite done until you take three more steps to ensure a safe and quiet sleepytime for everyone: Update your safety rules; adjust those naps, and offer age-appropriate lovies and soothing substitutes for Mommy or Daddy.

Safety check: Mattress down, bumpers out, lovie in!

Young toddlers have a powerful case of wanderlust, so make sure your little explorer can't find a way to get into trouble during the night. When he reaches the standing stage, be sure to lower the crib mattress so his head comes just above the crib rail when he's standing. This height keeps him from pulling himself up and over the top rail and taking a nasty tumble. Also, if you haven't already removed the bumpers in the crib, take them out now so they don't give him a leg up . . . and out.

Note: Excellent news on the safety front! The risk of sudden infant death syndrome (SIDS) is incredibly small after the first year, so you can breathe a sigh of relief and put your little one's beloved blankie or stuffed monkey in the crib with him. Just make sure the toys don't have hard edges and — of course — are safe for children under 2 years old. (Also make sure his toys don't have loose parts he can put in his mouth or any holes where stuffing can fall out.)

Morphing two naps into one

Sometime during the second year of life, most kiddies begin to give up their morning snooze in favor of a longer afternoon nap. As you can probably guess, this change doesn't happen suddenly — and it may require some work from you!

The first clue is when your toddler resists going down for her nap in the morning or holds out until late morning and then doesn't sleep well in the afternoon. These are signs that your baby's world is changing; she's now able to stay alert for longer periods, taking in all the new sight and sounds. You may miss that morning break (perfect for a quick shower) at first, but you soon realize that a longer afternoon nap gives you and your angel a much-needed respite from a busy day.

Some toddlers figure out this switch all by themselves, but most need a little help:

- ✔ Lots of babies seem to want to nod off right at lunchtime — it's not uncommon to find a young toddler asleep with her head resting in her macaroni and cheese! To avoid this, feed your toddler a bit earlier, moving up the schedule by 15 or 30 minutes (although some kids don't eat as well because breakfast is still a vivid memory). If you don't feed her before the nap, her tummy wakes her up and she can't sleep as long as she should.

- ✔ As your child grows, try to feed her later and later until her lunch occurs at more convenient times. Give her a little break before beddy-bye so nature can take its course (diaper-wise, that is) and her tummy can settle down.

- ✔ Some parents find that a child is so ready for an afternoon nap that she sleeps for more than two hours. Figure out how much sleep your child needs, and if a lengthy nap doesn't interfere with a regular bedtime — go for it. But you may find that you need to wake your sleeping beauty to insure a decent bedtime hour.

Updating your lovies for a separation-shy sweetie

In Chapter 5, we talk about *transitional* objects or *lovies* — items like photos or articles of clothing that remind your cherub of you when you're not around. These can be powerful tools during the separation anxiety stage, and you can be more creative now that your angel's a little older.

For instance, some parents buy nontoxic ink stamps and make a little design — a butterfly, flower, or dinosaur, for example — on their little one's arm and say, "That's right where I'll give you a big kiss when I pick you up today." This idea's great because, unlike lovies, an ink stamp can't get lost (put the stamp where it can't wash off —not on a hand!). Let your child pick different stamps to add to the fun — and maybe let her put a stamp on you, too.

Chapter 7

The Wake-Up Call: Sleep from 18 Months to 2 Years

. . . .

In This Chapter

▶ Observing your toddler in her exciting new world

▶ Understanding a child's nighttime imagination

▶ Getting off the nighttime bottle and out of the crib

. . . .

*I*f toddlers had an official motto as their second birthday approached, it'd be: "Watch out world, here I am — but where am I!?" After spending their first year and a half in a cocoon of contentment with every need met by Mommy or Daddy, they're now at a new level of awareness. Like butterflies, they're emerging to see their world in different ways.

Not surprisingly, this big transition and the many other physical and mental changes of this age (like giving up the nighttime bottle and moving from crib to big bed, which we discuss near the end of this chapter) can affect your tot's sleep cycle in new and interesting ways. In this chapter, we also talk about some common sleep problems that occur around this time: nightmares, night terrors, sleep-talking and sleepwalking. In addition, we describe two alarming but generally harmless bedtime behaviors: rocking and head-banging. (No, it's not a toddler rave — just a normal stage!) We also take a quick look at tooth-grinding, an annoying but usually temporary issue.

Underlying Changes for the 1½-Year-Old

The age of 1½ is a time of big changes. Your 12-month-old and your 20-month-old may look about the same on the outside, but *inside* it's a different story.

Only adolescence creates so dramatic a change, and parents usually know what to expect (and dread!) when puberty hits. The great changes that take place in an 18-month old tot, however, usually take families by surprise. So, knowing what to expect can keep you a step ahead of the game — especially when sleep's at stake.

Expanding awareness

Consciousness — call it the *awareness of awareness* — is the most remarkable aspect of being human, and it begins at this age. Before this point, your baby was aware of a hungry tummy or a wet diaper, but now she *realizes* that she's aware. She's developing a life of the mind, which means she can ponder big questions like "What am I really hungry for?" This is a major milestone — the biggest one since birth.

The power of this new consciousness is also its challenge. For the rest of your child's life, every situation will be an opportunity to think, "How can this be better?" Your well-established sleep routines, for example, become targets when she realizes that bedtime doesn't have to be the way it always was.

Awakening desire and imagination

Before now, your child was pretty satisfied with life. Now, however, his eyes are open to the rich and exciting world around him, and that awareness feeds a growing imagination and a powerful new emotion: desire. But he doesn't know how to make sense of these feelings or express them in words because of his limited communication skills.

Take a look at these three feelings and how they set up new challenges:

> ✔ **The budding imagination:** *Imagination* is the ability to form a mental image of something that isn't actually present. Your toddler is no longer always content with the toy in his hand, the storybook on the couch, or the box of cookies in the kitchen.

✔ **The power of desire:** This little person realizes a whole lot of wonderful and amazing stuff is out there, and he wants it all — now, now, *now*. This flood of desire can be simply overwhelming, especially the new and gnawing feeling that the here-and-now isn't good enough. He knows that he wants something to be different, but he's not sure exactly what he wants or how to get it.

✔ **Limited communication skills:** In time, as your toddler's vocabulary grows, he'll more easily describe his thoughts and longings. But not at 18 months of age! Right now, he's a bundle of fiery desires that he can't explain — either to himself or to you. That's why you're getting the first glimpses of the *terrible twos* that are just around the corner.

These overwhelming feelings lead to some pretty heavy sleep disturbances, which we cover in the next section. They explain why you're encountering some new sleep issues at this age, too.

What to Expect from the Active Mind during Sleepy Time

Once upon a time (in fact, just a few weeks ago), your baby snoozed without much drama. The path to dreamland was a little rocky, but when she got there, your sweetie slept contentedly. Now she's changing, and her new awareness and imagination can turn the once-peaceful Land of Nod into wild terrain.

At this stage, several behaviors you may have spotted in earlier months can become more frequent or intense. They include:

✔ Rocking and head-banging before sleep

✔ Tooth-grinding during sleep

✔ Nightmares and night terrors

✔ Sleepwalking and sleep-talking

Some of these behaviors seem a little scary, but in the toddler years, nighttime thrills and chills are almost always normal. As long as your toddler is happy and well-adjusted during the daytime, you don't need to worry about her or feel guilty — the vast majority of these problems have nothing to do with home, school, or you.

If you want to get a good handle on the *hows* and *whys* of the sleep events we discuss in the next sections, we recommend you check out Chapter 2 first. Then again, if you'd rather cut to the chase and get some quick answers on how to cope with each behavior, read on.

A whole lotta shakin' goin' on! Rocking and head-banging

Finding your little angel whacking his head against the crib bars or headboard a little after tuck-in time can be scary. But don't panic if this happens — both head-banging and its close cousin, crib-rocking, are common and normal behaviors in this age range. In fact, about one in six toddlers rocks or head-bangs. *Note:* The actions can appear earlier or later than the age of 18 months, but they tend to fade away by the age of two.

The explanation for rocking and head-banging is simple: Both actions actually have a calming effect. There's a world of difference between the exciting, action-packed daytime hours of a toddler and the quiet state of just lying there. For some little nippers, this is a way to discharge their batteries so they can snuggle down for the night.

Both behaviors can be very alarming to parents, who typically ask four questions. We cover these questions in the following list, along with our answers and explanations:

- ✔ **Can my child hurt himself when he head-bangs?** No. Rocking and even head-banging stop far short of causing harm. Protecting those little noggins is very important, but head-banging in the bed doesn't hurt them.

- ✔ **Is he doing it because he's upset about something?** If your child seems happy and well-adjusted during the day, then no, rocking and head-banging aren't signs of emotional troubles.

  However, if your toddler does seem unhappy or distressed during waking hours, be sure to talk to his pediatrician. The point of concern is the daytime issues, not the rocking and head-banging in bed.

- ✔ **Is this an early warning that something may be wrong with him?** Rocking and head-banging can raise a parent's fears that a child has developmental issues, but the deciding factor is the quality of interaction during the day, not the rocking and head-banging before bedtime.

- ✔ **Should parents do something to stop a toddler from head-banging in the bed?** The answer is *No* for two very good reasons. One: You can't do much to stop this behavior. Two: No harm is being done, so why stop it?

  If your toddler is sociable, makes eye contact easily, responds when you talk to him, and is pretty much on track with major development milestones, then don't waste time worrying about these common-as-dirt bedtime behaviors.

The tooth fairy's pet peeve: Grinding the chompers

The sound of a toddler grinding her teeth in her sleep (also called *bruxism*) is like fingernails on a chalkboard — only worse, because it raises the fear that she'll wear her pearly whites down to a nubbin. Fortunately, these worries are groundless. As it turns out, tooth-grinding is a normal and harmless behavior at this age.

Doctors don't really have a clue why some tots grind their teeth and others don't. Some experts guess that it has something to do with moving the teeth into good position, and others think it's a way to express feelings.

Roughly one in five children is a tooth-grinder, but the behavior tends to disappear as children grow beyond early childhood. In adults or older children, it's cause for some worry — but for toddlers, it's no big deal.

If you're worried about damage to your child's teeth, ask her dentist to check whether the enamel is wearing down or whether the teeth have any chips or cracks. Also, ask your child whether her jaw hurts. Most likely, neither the dentist nor your child will report any problems.

Our suggestion? Reassure yourself that this behavior, although rough on your ears, isn't hurting your toddler's teeth at all. Cross this worry off your list . . . and pop on your MP3 player so you don't have to hear that awful noise!

Different problems, different cures: Nightmares and night terrors

You hear blood-curdling shrieks at 3 a.m., leap out of bed, and race to your toddler's bedside. He's sitting up in bed, screaming hysterically, and you wonder, "What can I do to help?"

This question has two answers, and to pick the right one, you need to know which scenario you're viewing. Is it a nightmare or a night terror? They look and sound alike, but they're actually as different as night and day — and so are the strategies for dealing with them. In the next few sections, we explain why.

Nightmares: The dark side of dreaming

In Chapter 2, we talk about rapid-eye-movement (REM) sleep, the stage in which people have vivid dreams. A nightmare is just a dream, but one loaded with bad feelings like fear and sadness. Like any other dream, it has two interesting features:

- ✔ It feels completely real.

- ✔ People often remember it after waking up.

In fact, dreams (both good and bad) appear to be all about memory. Dreams are created from the building blocks of our waking memories; in turn, they create their own memories that can carry over into the day. But bad memories have added punch because

- ✔ **Fear and sadness are so terribly powerful.** Life holds many joys, but hurt and loss are realities as well. Unfortunately, as consciousness awakens at age 18 months, so does a tot's awareness of what can go wrong. That adds some scary new plotlines to your tot's bad dreams.

- ✔ **The nightmares of young children can be even bigger and scarier than an adult's.** At this age, toddlers become conscious of the world's dangers — people get hurt, flowers die, Mommy and Daddy can get sick. As a result, a child's bad memories are often very vivid. Even the happiest little tykes head off to bed with heavy baggage (memories) of real and imagined worries, and those worries can wind up in their dreams.

What can you do when your child wakes up screaming after a bad dream? Remember these suggestions:

1. **Make sure he's really in the grip of a nightmare and not a night terror (see the next section).**

   If it's a nightmare, he'll be awake but will try to figure out which world is real — the realm of nightmares or his safe bedroom.

2. **Help him get back to reality by calming him, talking to him about how nightmares aren't real, and staying with him until he knows that everything's hunky-dory.**

   Your touch, your voice, the sight of your face, and even your familiar aroma all help him get over his big scare.

Night terrors: The wild ride of deep sleep

Night terrors are one of the most alarming events a parent can witness, but they're also perfectly normal — a fact that may reassure a mom or dad who's watching the scary episode. They occur most often in children between the ages of 1½ and 3, and affect as many as 5 percent of tots in this age range.

To understand night terrors, you need to know how their underlying causes and symptoms differ from nightmares:

- ✔ **When they occur:** Night terrors strike during *sleep arousals* — brief moments of awareness during deep sleep, the Stage 4 we discuss in Chapter 2. Nightmares, on the other hand, occur at the edge of waking during REM sleep.

- ✔ **How they affect your toddler's actions while sleeping:** Night terrors allow a sleeper's body to act as if he's awake; during nightmares, however, a person's body doesn't move.

  A toddler in the grip of a night terror can act out the drama that's going on in his sound-asleep brain. For instance, he may jump up and down in his crib and howl at the top of his lungs.

- ✔ **How they affect the ability to wake up:** The child who's having a night terror is sound asleep and often virtually impossible to awaken (due to being in Stage 4 sleep), but a parent can rouse a tot from a nightmare — and a bad dream may even jolt him right out of sleep.

- ✔ **How they affect your toddler's waking life:** People with night terrors often have no awareness or memory of the event, but nightmares are frequently remembered.

To sleep, perchance to dream . . . but why?

When we dream, our brains create scenarios that feel like flesh-and-blood events. But what's the point of this? What possible benefit is there to winning the lottery or sinking a three-pointer in the NBA finals if it's only happening in our imagination?

Freud, that most famous of dream analysts, believed that dreams allow our brains to break free from the rules and restrictions of our wide-awake hours so we can experience life without limits. In the process, he speculated, we get the chance to try out different approaches to challenges without the trouble that real-life decisions can cause.

A very different theory derives from modern neuroscience, which proposes that dreams help to repair the wear-and-tear that daily life inflicts on our brains. According to this line of thought, dreams build or repair the circuits that allow us to remember the important life-lessons of each day. If this theory is true, then dreams give our brains a chance to have dress rehearsals, allowing our memories to get firmly established. And in the case of toddlers, who are building thousands of new brain circuits each minute, establishing these memories is a very important job!

If you mistake a night terror for a nightmare, you expect your screaming toddler to leap into your arms for comfort when you reach his bedside. In reality, however, he has no clue that you're there, even if his eyes are wide open and you're standing right in front of him! This situation is highly distressing to a loving parent trying to rescue a toddler from a terrifying event.

In a night terror, your child is just as asleep as when he's dozing blissfully. As a result, your reassuring words and hugs have absolutely zero effect.

So what should you do about your shrieking, crib-rattling, can't-be-woken-up toddler? Our recommendation is that you do nothing at all for the following reasons:

✔ You can't rouse your sweetie during a night terror.

✔ In a short while, the episode ends, and your little one snuggles right back down to snooze peacefully once again.

✔ In the morning, when you're bleary-eyed, he won't have a clue that anything happened at all. Night terrors typically leave no trace when they're over.

When you recognize a night terror for what it really is, you'll be able to relax even if your little bedbug is screaming bloody murder. You'll know that this is a harmless phenomenon of very deep sleep, and it doesn't carry over into waking.

The only exception to the do-nothing plan involves children who have regular night terrors about the same time nearly every night. If that's the case in your household, you can try disrupting the sleep cycle by waking your little one up half an hour or an hour before the night-terror hour rolls around.

Variations on a theme: Sleepwalking and sleep-talking

It's the basis of many favorite stories: Mom or Dad hears a funny noise in the night and wanders out to see Junior raiding the refrigerator or pooping on the potty while totally asleep. In other versions, parents find their little tykes mumbling away in their sleep or even speaking in sentences.

These behaviors, known as *sleepwalking* and *sleep-talking*, occur during sleep arousals, just like the night terrors we discuss in the previous section. During these arousals, toddlers' brains are sound asleep, but their bodies can still move — and sometimes take off on their own adventures in the middle of the night.

Sleep-talking is very common — about ⅓ of toddlers do it — and it's even more common as children reach the preteen years. Sleepwalking, on the other hand, is rarer, affecting about ⅒ of children by age 10. Neither behavior is a reason for concern as long as you can keep a sleepwalker safely corralled.

Knowing how long these disturbances last

Many sleepwalking episodes and nearly all bouts of sleep-talking are brief. For instance, your little cuddle-bunny may murmur a few syllables of gibberish while snoozing or stand up next to the bed for just a few seconds before keeling over again.

In some cases, toddlers' sleep-talking or sleepwalking episodes last for several minutes. Sleepwalking toddlers may perform several very complex steps and then do something totally off-the-wall. For example, a child may get out of bed with a purposeful expression, walk confidently to the closet, pull down her pants, pee on the floor, and march efficiently back to bed.

Reacting appropriately

If your little sweet cake is a sleep-talker, don't bother trying to translate what she's saying. Sleep-talking, far from being a child's attempt to communicate some form of deeply felt emotion, is typically just meaningless strings of nonsense. The old belief that sleep-talking offers a window into the soul is baseless unless your child's soul is trying to say, "Wubba tubba gicky boo!"

The dangers of sleepwalking, on the other hand, are no laughing matter and neither is the distress it can cause for parents. When a little sleepwalker starts to take some steps, all sorts of trouble can occur. Many parents, for instance, tell horror stories about their tots opening the front door and going for a stroll around the neighborhood in their jammies. A single, brief episode of sleepwalking isn't anything to worry about, however — so just keep the following tips in mind:

> ✔ **Don't try waking your child when she's sleepwalking.** Just as with night terrors, she's in very deep sleep and is nearly impossible to arouse. If she doesn't resist, you can gently steer her back to bed — but don't try to force the issue.

> ✔ **Don't discuss your child's sleepwalking with her when she's awake.** She has no control over it and typically will have no memory of it when she awakens, so you'll simply worry her and make it harder for her to get to sleep. ·

If sleepwalking is a habit for your toddler, see the next section for our advice.

Keeping a sleepwalker safe

If you see repeat sleepwalking performances, you need to take extra precautions to keep your little sugar plum safe. Before you adapt your home in general, first confine your child to her bedroom and make sure her immediate surroundings are safe:

- ✔ Put a toddler gate at the bedroom door to keep your roaming toddler confined. The gate provides a barrier without cutting your child off from the rest of the house and family.

- ✔ Make sure all bedroom floor coverings are slip-proof (and washable in case of a pee incident!).

- ✔ Pad sharp corners.

- ✔ Make sure all outlets are childproof, preferably with a back plate that blocks access by anything except a plug.

- ✔ Look at the room each night from a child's viewpoint, and spot everything your child may run into when moving unpredictably. Move toys off the floor so she can't trip over them, and remove breakables from her reach.

After you're sure the bedroom is safe, safeguard entrances throughout the rest of your house:

- ✔ Lock doors leading to stairs and put up baby gates where stairs don't have doors.

- ✔ Put locks out of your toddler's reach on exterior doors.

- ✔ Consider installing an alarm that goes off when an exterior door opens.

Smoothing Two Important Transitions at This Age

Between the ages of 1½ and 2, toddlers begin the march toward preschool age. Your toddler leaves more and more of his infant ways behind as he reaches for greater maturity and independence.

Two major steps in that direction include:

- ✔ Moving away from bottles or even regular nursing to a cup.

- ✔ Moving from a crib or your bed into a big kid bed.

The switch to a cup can cause a glitch in your sleepy-time routine if your tot is accustomed to a nighttime bottle. The move to a big bed can rock the beddy-bye boat a bit and raise important safety issues.

Saying bye-bye to the bedtime bottle

If your infant uses a bottle (breastfeeding parents can skip this section), the day will come when you decide to switch from bottle to cup. You'll probably ditch the daytime bottles first and then the nighttime bottle.

At this stage, the bedtime bottle is one of your child's favorites, and until now it's been a big part of the bedtime ritual. So, when you're ready to bid it farewell, be prepared for some sleepy-time fallout.

Before you withdraw the nighttime bottle, you need to divert your wee one's interest in what the bottle has to offer. Simply put, you want to make the contents of the bottle less interesting. This preliminary phase guarantees that your toddler won't be hungry when the bottle goes bye-bye. Follow these steps:

1. **Make sure your infant can drink from a cup.** You don't want to ask your sweetie to do something she can't do. (See the previous section "Knowing when to give it up.")

2. **Gradually start diluting the contents of the bottle with water.** For instance, switch to ⅛ water for two to three days, then to ¼ water for another two to three days, and then to a 50-50 mix of water and formula or breast milk for two to three days.

3. **Continue the dilution strategy until the bottle contains only water.** *Note:* We don't recommend introducing juice because it can cause excessive weight gain.

Now, simply wait for the right moment to stop providing the bedtime bottle altogether — preferably a time when no other major life-changes are occurring and your child's sleep patterns are well under control. (Giving up the bedtime bottle leaves a big hole in your toddler's nighty-night routine, so you want the other pieces of the ritual firmly in place.) If you don't already have a bedtime routine, see Chapter 5 for ideas on creating one.

When the nighttime bottle is gone, your child misses it, is sad or angry for a little while, and fusses the first few nights. In response, you can be understanding, kind, and loving — but whatever you do, don't give the bottle back! As an alternative, offer a cup of water. After all, if you stay firm, this little cloudburst will pass in a day or two.

Movin' on up: The switch from crib to big bed

Just as nobody keeps drinking from a baby bottle forever, no one stays in a crib forever. The case of cribs versus beds, however, has a big safety issue: Jumping out of a crib can cause broken bones. So be sure you make the change before that risk becomes reality.

In this section we help you make this switch safely and successfully.

Figuring out when to make the switch

The first priority is to make sure your toddler doesn't get hurt. So if your little one is bouncing around the crib, hanging on the bars like a monkey, or — worse yet — trying to somersault over the top rail, think about moving him from the crib to a grownup bed. And if your toddler is actually getting out of the crib, make that move quickly — before he takes a dangerous tumble.

On the other hand, if your toddler happily stays put in the crib (and you're *really* sure he can't jump out), the timing is a bit more flexible. In any case, we recommend that you begin the transition by 18 months of age. If you choose to wait much beyond this age, make the crib-to-bed switch before you start toilet training. The big bed acts as a signal that your tot's growing up and prepares him for other big steps like using the potty.

The right timing for the crib-to-bed switch depends not just on your toddler's climbing ability but also on what's happening in his world. Two questions that can factor into your decision are

- ✔ **Are you expecting a new baby who will need the crib?** If the stork will be visiting soon, move your toddler to a big bed at least six to eight weeks before your new baby arrives. Consider taking the crib down completely, with your child's help, and storing it until you're ready for your new arrival. This way, your child is less likely to think that he's getting the boot just so his new sibling can take over his territory.

- ✔ **Are other big changes going on in your child's life?** Try to make this transition during a calm time in your toddler's life. Leaving his secure little crib can be too much to handle if he's also coping with big life-changes — for instance an illness or a move to a new house. Also hold off on the crib-to-bed move if your child is in the middle of toilet-training. A good motto is: One big change at a time.

Introducing the bed

When the new bed enters the picture, prepare your toddler for this big change. Talk about how exciting it is that he's ready for this grownup step, and take him to the store where he can help pick out new sheets and pillows. You can even create a picture book about this big change (see Chapter 14 for ideas). Also, if you start out by putting the crib mattress on the floor (see the later section "Making the move" for this), the change is so subtle that your sweetie may not protest at all.

Getting the room ready

When the crib is history, your toddler has free run of his room at night. At this point, a careful safety inspection is a must! The following childproofing steps should already be in place when your tot starts moving around (crawling or walking), but now's a good time to review them:

1. **Make sure all wall sockets have secure covers — not the little plastic ones that your child can pull out and swallow.**

2. **Remove any furniture that a child can knock over (or secure it to the wall).**

3. **Put locks on dresser drawers so your little wanderer can't use them as stepping-stones.**

4. **Put a latch on the closet door.**

5. **Move drapery pulls, pictures, or mobiles out of reach.**

6. **Teach your child to put his toys away before bedtime so he doesn't trip over them if he wakes during the night.**

In addition, take these steps when the crib no longer limits nighttime journeys:

✔ **Install a door gate.**

This basically converts the room to a crib and keeps your little one from walking all over the house at night. Make sure the gate is sturdy enough that your toddler can't push it open.

✔ **Add a nightlight so your little munchkin can navigate safely in the dark.**

Making the move

When you're ready to introduce your baby to the big bed, follow these steps for a successful transition:

1. **Start with the crib-mattress-on-the-floor approach.**

   Starting your baby out on his crib mattress offers two big advantages. First, he's safe because crib mattresses are only a few inches high; falling can't cause injury or even much of a scare. Second, this mattress is the one your child knows and loves, and its familiar feel and smell reduce the drama of this big change.

   Initially, put the crib mattress on the floor for daytime naps, and then pop it back into the crib for nighttime. When your child gets familiar with sleeping outside the crib bars, leave the mattress on the floor at night as well. At this point, take down the crib. (Let your angel watch and even help a little, so he doesn't think it just disappeared into thin air!)

2. **After your sweetie gets a good feel for his new boundaries, go ahead and switch the crib mattress for the bed mattress you plan to use long-term.**

   Again, simply set the new mattress flat on the floor. It's easy to know when to do this; just wait until your child stays on the crib mattress without rolling off onto the floor for a straight one to two weeks.

3. **When your child seems very at ease on the new mattress and goes for one to two weeks with no spills onto the floor, add the box frame.**

4. **When your child goes for another one to two weeks without falls, complete the ensemble by adding the bed frame.**

Fortunately, the risk of SIDS ended completely on your tot's first birthday, so he can go to sleep on his back, stomach, or even his head! Also, he can have any assortment of sheets, blankets, pillows, and stuffed animals. Toddler beds can also go anywhere in the room, so feel free to use a wall as a barrier to keep falls from happening.

Handling free-roaming tots

A funny thing happens at the toddler stage: Parents who *didn't* co-sleep with their baby start hearing the sound of freedom — the pitter-patter of little feet heading straight for the master bedroom. If your toddler starts invading your territory when he transitions from crib to bed, see Chapter 8 for ideas about helping him stay in his own room. Another option, of course, is to scoot over and let him join you. Whichever you decide, be consistent! If you opt to start co-sleeping at this stage, make sure it's your choice, not just your toddler pulling one over on you.

Chapter 8

The Big Tug of War: Sleep from 2 through 3 Years

• •

In This Chapter

▶ Taking a look at your child's changing emotions

▶ Prepping for bedtime and your reluctant sleeper

▶ Saying *Goodbye* to naps

▶ Dealing with the nighttime potty and your child's fears

• •

*O*ne stage of childhood, more than any other, calls for the patience of a saint and nerves of steel — the phase parents affectionately call the *Terrible Twos*. At this stage, your little one isn't really a baby any more and his new abilities are becoming more complex each day. To him, these changes are both exciting and disturbing. And what a toddler feels on the inside, he shows on the outside.

Despite the strain these 12 months can cause, we like to refer to them as *tumultuous* rather than *terrible*. As your child's world expands in the most exciting ways, he rides a roller coaster of emotions — and you get to go along for the ride. As a result, both of you will have plenty of ups and downs, but overall it'll be a wonderful time of growing, discovering, and maturing.

In the course of this ride, you'll have a number of sleepless nights as your toddler tries to cope with real and imaginary fears, gives up naps, and handles the art of peeing and pooping in the night hours. However, by using the tips in this chapter, you can prepare him for these changes as you help reduce his fears and anxieties. With luck, you'll discover that sleep is *not* the impossible dream!

Getting a Glimpse of Your Child's Issues at this Age

Lots of changes are going on inside your little one as she evolves from babyhood to childhood, and her ever-growing brain is giving her a more sophisticated outlook on life. For example, she has a rough understanding of time, and she knows you haven't totally disappeared even when you're not right next to her. In some ways she's like a *tween* — no longer a baby but not really a big kid yet. She struggles with giving up her baby ways, not 100-percent convinced that *big* is all it's cracked up to be. (Diapers do seem a whole lot more convenient than having to remember to use the potty!)

Children at this age truly understand that they're separate from their parents, but this awareness doesn't make them Gandhi or Mother Theresa. On the contrary, this age's theme song can be "I've Gotta be Me!" with the subtitle "It's All about Me." Although *egocentric* isn't a complimentary term for an adult, it's a perfect (and perfectly normal) description of a toddler.

Understanding your toddler's internal tug of war

Do the following scenarios sound familiar?

✔ On the days you're in a big hurry, your toddler insists on putting his own shoes on. On other days when you have all the time in the world, your darling lies on the floor and cries, "You do it!"

✔ You're at a friend's birthday party and your toddler clings to you like lint. Just a few hours later at the mall, he's slippery as an eel.

No wonder this age gets such a bad rap! To understand this stage of development and how it affects your toddler's sleep habits, you need to understand what your toddler is thinking and feeling when he bounces from one mood to another.

Picture your child as being in a tug of war with himself. Pulling on one side of the rope is the baby inside him, and tugging on the other is the big boy. Eventually, the big-boy side is going to win, but right now the momentum in this tug of war shifts from moment to moment.

This contradictory behavior can confuse and confound a parent because adults are looking at the situations rationally — something your toddler can't do just yet. For example, your child may say "No" even to something he usually likes or looks forward to. Why? It's his way of asserting his *self* and his need for independence — while still wanting you to be in charge.

Seeing how a 2-year-old's emotions affect sleep

The conflict between baby and big person affects every aspect of your toddler's life, and sleep is no exception. That's why a toddler who snoozed peacefully for months may now be popping up like a Jack-in-the-Box each night.

But what makes a 2-year-old fight a nap when she's so tired she can hardly stand? (You'd *love* it if someone told you to go lie down!) Here are a few insights:

- ✔ **To your tot, the world is more magical than logical.** This mixture of real and not-so-real can cause mixed-up feelings that can easily interfere with letting go and falling asleep.

- ✔ **Your little one worries, too.** Your toddler may understand *just enough* about a situation or life change to keep her up. In toddlers' eyes, the world revolves around them — so naturally, anything that happens in that world is due to them. If Mommy and Daddy have a fight or Grandma gets sick, for instance, they must be the cause. This type of thinking can easily gum up the sleep works.

- ✔ **Kids this age still see you as omnipotent and able to fix anything.** We know one child who was furious at her mom because she couldn't stop the rain! As the world becomes more logical to your child, it can leave her feeling a bit uncertain: "How can everything be okay if Mom and Dad really can't make everything all better all the time?" This new concern can creep into little minds and interfere with sleep.

- ✔ **Your toddler has trouble seeing the world from your point of view.** When she calls you in the middle of the night, she fully expects you to come and fix everything. Even though she's smart as a whip, she doesn't realize how disruptive her actions are to your sleep; she just knows that she wants you when she wants you.

- ✔ **At this age, your little one is full of desires and not too savvy about limits.** If one cookie is good, then six cookies with ice cream are even better! All the logic in the world can't rock this belief, and so it is with wake-up calls: She can never have too many.

In short, your tot is just doing her job — growing up! And 2-year-olds, just like teens, go through a stage where contradictions, uncontrolled desires, and negativity are perfectly normal. (Of course, we didn't say *fun* — we said *normal.*)

In reality, your child's real reason for waking up and calling for you have nothing to do with her requests. Yes, people get thirsty in the middle of the night, and teddy bears get lost — but it's a good bet that your toddler wants only *you* and is willing to push all of your buttons to get her wish!

If you fall into this trap, sleepytime comes later each night and those middle-of-the-night demands become more and more insistent. Even little tykes have a knack for wielding power, and when she sees the effect that her words have on you, she'll keep thinking up new ways to get you out of bed. Understanding your child's emotional merry-go-round may give you insight into sleep issues, but those issues shouldn't give your angel *carte blanche* over the routine. You can still be in charge of the sleep situation.

Lovingly Promoting Sleep While Standing Your Ground

Luckily, you have some tools in your own bedtime toolbox. By using them — firmly, lovingly, and consistently — you can put the lid on nighttime demands and regain control of your sleepy-time routine. Although you can't force your child to go to sleep, you can prepare him for bed, provide a comfortable and safe place for sleep, *and* expect him to stay in his room. Achieving that last goal, of course, is more easily said than done! But have no fear — in this section, we tell you how to respond effectively to your little escape artist.

Preparing for bedtime with your toddler's help

Bedtime is the perfect time for parents to help a child with that internal tug of war (see the previous section). A 2-year old is hungry to master the universe, and parents can help by tugging on the big-kid end of the rope and leaving the baby end alone. Set up your nighttime rituals so that your child knows exactly what to expect and what part she plays.

Giving your child a sense of control

Children at this age love a routine so much that if you miss a step, your tot surely points it out! Clearly defined steps each night help wind your babe down and get her ready for sleep — both physically and emotionally. In addition, by letting your child take charge of some bedtime routines, you give her a sense of control over it.

For instance, parents can allow a child to make a few decisions like what to wear, which book to read, or which toothpaste to use. These simple tasks send a powerful message: It's time for bed, and you're big enough to get ready yourself! In addition, get a digital clock for your toddler so you can step back from saying, "It's time for bed" and give your toddler the opportunity to tell *you* when sleepy-time arrives. This technique often makes toddlers comply more easily at tuck-in time and allows them to take another step toward independent problem-solving — a very important life skill.

Appealing to your child's learning style

As you help your toddler adjust to a healthy sleep schedule, consider your method. Adults have a variety of learning styles, and so do children. Some toddlers respond best to verbal cues (speech) and follow along well if their parents talk them through the bedtime routine. Others respond to visual cues or tactile cues (touch).

For children who are visual or tactile learners, one of the most effective approaches is a schedule strip. Here's how to create one:

- ✔ **Make sure you have a consistent routine for bedtime: bathing, tooth brushing, putting jammies on, reading a bedtime story, and going to sleep.**

- ✔ **Break this routine into four to six parts. Then draw a picture, cut out a magazine photo, or use a photo of your own child to represent each activity.** (See example in Figure 8-1.)

- ✔ **Give the strip to your child in the evening, and ask her to tell you what activity comes next.** This changes the dynamics because she's telling you what she does next instead of you telling her.

Jenny Goes to Bed

Brush teeth.

Take bath.

Put on PJs.

Read book.

Go to sleep.

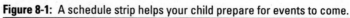

Figure 8-1: A schedule strip helps your child prepare for events to come.

Maintaining the upper hand when your child doesn't stay down

A big challenge in helping older toddlers get to sleep is managing their interest in leaving their room. (See Chapter 7 for how to make the change from crib to bed if this hasn't happened yet.) If your toddler doesn't stay put when you tuck him in, you have several choices:

- ✔ **Put up a sturdy gate, which in essence turns his entire room into a big crib.** Learn to ignore your child's pleas to get out, and don't be surprised if he falls asleep on the floor instead of in his bed for the first few days.

- ✔ **If a gate doesn't hold your little wanderer (for example, he's nimble enough to climb over it or can undo the latch), take him back to his room each time he leaves and tell him that you'll close the door if he doesn't stay there.**

  Note: This only works if he likes to sleep with the door open. If he keeps opening the door, hold it shut, let him know that you're on the other side, and show him that you mean business. Leave it open only when he's able to stay in the room. This ploy often works, but it may backfire if he thinks he's winning because you're still close by. (When this happens, abandon this approach.)

- ✔ **Put some books and quiet toys in the room.** Tell your toddler, "I know you don't feel like sleeping, but it's bedtime and you can play by yourself until you do feel sleepy." Again, this gives him a bit of control over when he falls asleep, which can make him more cooperative.

Some families choose an entirely different route, giving their toddlers access to their room and letting them sleep in the grownup bed or in a sleeping bag or blanket on the floor. This arrangement works if you don't mind having your bedroom resemble a youth hostel, but it can cause dissension in the ranks if you have a partner who likes privacy. Also, if you or your partner feels a little angry or resentful about sharing your space, your toddler is likely to pick up on those negative vibes.

If you choose this arrangement, be prepared for your child to remain your roommate until you take steps to change the situation. Under these circumstances, children rarely return to their own room without a little nudge from Mom and Pop.

If your child is rapidly nearing the 3-year-old mark and he's still in his crib, you need to help him move to a big kid bed. Of course, as soon as your child is *capable* of jumping out of a crib (even if he seems uninterested), safety demands a move to a bed. Check out Chapter 7 for more on this major move.

Managing a 2-Year-Old's Transitions

So many changes! So little time! When your baby was a newborn, the changes were physical and oh-so-visible. They may not be so easy to see when your baby becomes a toddler, but they're just as real. Change is difficult — even for adults — so no wonder giving up the crib or diapers can send your pumpkin into a loop-de-loop.

Choosing which transition comes first: Crib-to-bed or diapers-to-underpants?

If your toddler's still in the crib when potty-training time arrives, you need to figure out which change to make first. The easy answer is to move your toddler from the crib to a bed first, because the crib represents babyhood and potty training is a move into a more grownup phase.

Baby books typically suggest the same progression. (In fact, that's why we cover the crib transition in Chapter 7.) The problem is, however, that toddlers don't read baby books. So you may wind up with a toddler who's making great progress in toilet training but isn't willing to leave those crib bars behind.

If your child is more interested in the potty than in having a big girl bed, make sure her potty skills are firmly established before changing her sleeping arrangements. Saying "Goodbye" to diapers and giving up the crib are two big changes; doing both at the same time can be overwhelming. Again, safety trumps all, so if she's able to climb out of the crib, get her out of the crib first. (See Chapter 7 for details.)

Solving nap issues: When your napster sings his own tune

If your little one falls asleep in the afternoon (for instance, in the car seat coming home from the store), his little catnap can completely disrupt his sleep at night; even a 15-minute doze can keep him going at whirling-dervish speeds well past his usual bedtime. On the other hand, if you keep him awake in the late afternoon, he may fall asleep around dinner time and then be ready to party in the middle of the night.

To help you combat these less-than-desirable situations, this section guides you through the nap transition.

Knowing when to phase out the napping routine

Some toddlers nap right up until kindergarten, but children often start giving up their naps between the ages of 2 and 3. This adjustment is often gradual but not always easy.

In fact, at some point you're likely to have an exhausted toddler who ferociously battles sleep and winds up cranky as a wet mule by the end of the day.

There's no one right answer to when your child should give up a nap. A child who resists napping but seems to fall apart by late afternoon can probably benefit from a *rest time* (see the next section for some ideas on how to structure one). You may want to nix daytime dozes, however, if your child's long afternoon nap has disastrous effects on nighttime sleep, keeping him awake until 9, 10, or later. In this case, you may be willing to put up with a cranky, demanding toddler for a few hours in the afternoon in exchange for a decent bedtime hour.

Helping your tot with the transition

Toddlers are bound to have some rocky days when they're giving up naps, and you may feel helpless in preventing them. However, here are some tips that may work:

- ✔ **Avoid car rides and other soothing situations in the late afternoon.** Road trips (even little ones!) and watching television on a soft couch make a child particularly vulnerable to a late-afternoon nap, so avoid these activities if you're trying to keep your toddler awake.

- ✔ **Plan an interesting activity in the late afternoon.** Try baking cookies, creating an art masterpiece, or whipping up a batch of homemade play dough.

- ✔ **Feed your child earlier than usual in the evening, even if this means not eating together as a family.** Family mealtime is important, but during this brief transitional stage you're wise to be flexible.

✔ **Move up your child's bedtime.** A toddler who's giving up his nap may go to bed as early as 7 p.m. and sleep straight through till morning.

If you have a nanny or other care provider in your home, let your caregiver do the preliminaries — bathing, tooth-brushing, and so on — while you handle other family responsibilities. Then you can take over for story-time and a snuggle. This plan allows you to move up the bedtime routine and still get plenty of quality time with your sweetie. (See Chapter 10 for other ideas on how to handle this situation.)

Don't fret too much when these tricks don't work (and we can pretty much guarantee that they won't work every time). Even if you try your hardest to keep your toddler up until bedtime, he'll probably conk out early and wake up too early at least a few times a week. Inconsistent sleeping patterns at this stage aren't a setback; they're merely a stage — and this too shall pass.

Starting a quiet time so you can get a break

Even when naptime is history, you can still insist on a little down time — and it's a very good idea. In day-care settings, children who don't feel like sleeping still spend quiet time on their cots. If you follow the same plan at home, you get a much-needed break and your little one develops the valuable skill of quietly entertaining himself.

To create a quiet time, choose a time early in the afternoon. If it does turn into a nap, it won't affect his sleep at night. Then follow these steps:

✔ Prepare your child by telling him he needs a little time alone in his room to rest. He may protest that he's not tired, but tell him in a firm and neutral tone that it's time for him to go to his room. Take him there and say, "Have a good rest — see you soon."

✔ This is quiet time but not necessarily sleepy-time, so tell him he doesn't need to be in his bed. Give him some toys and books or let him listen to a tape. Don't expect him to fall asleep, although later you may see him and Teddy zonked together on the floor.

✔ If he won't stay in his room, use a gate to create a safe and escape-resistant haven for him.

You can create a little ritual that signals quiet time is over. For example, give him a digital clock so he can announce when time is up, or better yet, play a musical tape or CD that runs as long as you want quiet time to last. When the music ends, he knows it's time for action again. But no cheating: Choosing a 3-hour Wagnerian opera isn't fair!

When your child has a lot of freedom in his room, you must be absolutely sure that the environment is 100-percent safe. Check outlets, lamp cords, sharp edges, and toys with small parts that can be swallowed (or put up his nose!).

Handling Common Bedtime Problems

Other than sleep problems, no toddler issue causes parents more concern than potty training. Having your neighbor assure you that no one ever walked down the aisle in diapers is hardly a consolation if your child's on her 20th pair of training pants or the preschool won't let Junior in until he keeps his pee and poop to himself.

Now add sleep and potty training together, and you have a formula for high anxiety.

The scoop on poop (and pee) at nighttime

The 2- to 3-year-old stage is prime time for learning to use the potty. This new development is a challenge for sleep routines because now you have to figure out how to keep her clean and dry when you're all asleep!

Parents have lots of questions about how to cope with the pee and poop and still get some sleep, and we cover the top two in this section, offering tips for keeping your sanity when you leave the diaper days (and nights) behind.

When should I expect my child to stay dry all night?

Surprisingly, staying dry at night isn't directly related to daytime potty use. And although some kids do it well before their parents start potty-training them, kids can't really be taught to stay dry at night.

In fact, kids tend to follow in Mommy's or Daddy's footsteps. So, to get an idea of when your child will be ready to stay dry all night, ask your parents when you reached this milestone. Although most children stay dry at night by their 5th birthday, those who wet the bed later than that often have a relative who did it too; it may not be as genetic as blue eyes, but there's a strong familial connection. In fact, when both parents were over 5 before reaching the dry-at-night stage, their toddler has an 80-percent chance of following suit.

Boys are more likely than girls to be late in developing this ability. But most pediatricians don't consider it bed-wetting until a child is past the age of 6. Up to that time, a child who wets the sheets is still within normal developmental limits.

As you work on toilet training, it's useful to recognize the difference between day and night. Nighttime dryness is primarily a physical issue; it happens when your child's body is ready. Daytime dryness, on the other hand, is as much a psychological process (a tug of war between babyhood and big personhood) as it is a physical one.

How do I know when my baby is ready to forgo nighttime diapers?

Potty training can be a stressful time, and many parents choose to keep their toddlers in diapers at night just to create an island of calm. At some point, however, the diapers need to go. You'll know your child's ready to make the switch if:

- ✔ She wakes up with a dry (or almost dry) diaper.

- ✔ She's wet in the morning but seems to have wet herself just before or after waking up.

- ✔ She's 3 or older, and she's asking to sleep in her panties.

- ✔ Your intuition tells you that she may take forever to wake and head for the bathroom because the comfy, convenient diaper is there for her.

Even if your child is still soaked in the morning, you may want to get rid of the diapers as she approaches her third birthday. Although you can buy large-size diapers, children this age often feel that diapers are baby stuff and would rather suffer through some wet sheets than keep wearing the white badge of babyhood.

How do I potty train if my baby is sleeping in the crib at night?

If your snookums potty-trains first, you obviously need a plan for the night because she can't get out of the crib by herself. Depending on your own sleep needs, you can follow one of these plans:

- ✔ Use diapers at night.
- ✔ Give her some help when the potty urge strikes.

Stories from the crib: Fancy pants

On Violeta's third birthday, she received three packages of beautiful new undies from her aunt. That night, Violeta insisted on wearing a pair of her new fancy pants to bed. Violeta had been using the potty during the day for many months, but she woke up each morning swimming. Her mom, Sofia, worried that soaking-wet new undies would affect Violeta's self-esteem the next morning.

However, because it was Violeta's birthday and she was so insistent, Sofia gave in. The next morning, she found Violeta wet to the gills but not the least bit upset. Violeta helped her mom strip the wet sheets from the bed, took a quick bath, put on dry panties, and was ready to face the day.

Sofia was glad Violeta took the experience so well, but she wasn't looking forward to washing wet sheets every morning. To make life easier for both of them, Sofia put three layers of absorbent towels over the bottom sheet each night. This way the sheet underneath stayed dry, and Violeta removed the wet towels each morning. Violeta still wet the bed, but wearing her fancy pants and taking charge of her own wet towels in the morning made her feel very grownup. Taking care of her own wet clothing allowed Violeta to be independent and eliminated the need for Sofia to intervene.

It turns out that Violeta's dad wet the bed until he was 6, and Violeta followed suit. But she remained responsible for her own body and stopped wetting the bed when she was physically able to — with no interference by Mom or Dad.

If your child frequently uses the "I have to go potty!" line but you think it's a ploy to get you in the bedroom in the middle of night, consider setting up a gate to convert the room to a crib and limit her movement out of the room.

If your child still calls for help with a midnight pee, you can leave on a night light and even put a small portable potty in the room so your tot doesn't need to leave her room.

What do I do when B.M. stands for blackmail?

A child who is potty trained or close to that goal quickly discovers that the words "I have to go to the bathroom" have an instant and almost magical effect on parents. What better way to get Mommy or Daddy back into the nursery at night than to say that powerful sentence? It's a rare parent who can say "No" to a request that seems so basic and necessary. However, make sure that you maintain your loving but firm stance and create an environment where your child can take care of her own needs.

If your child sleeps in a bed rather than a crib, you can expect her to use the bathroom on her own — even at night. Parents who still picture their toddlers as babies often worry that this expectation is too much for a little tyke. But in reality, toddlers find these steps quite simple, and they respond positively to the very grownup feeling of caring for their own bodies (although you can expect some resistance at first).

If you child resists handling potty chores on her own (and tries to get you involved) at night, she's craving your attention, not your help. Take this opportunity to tell her, "You're getting very grownup and you can do this." You're likely to find that she gains new confidence and becomes more willing to tackle other big girl tasks as well.

Getting the message across may take a few nights, but if you follow these steps you'll eventually succeed:

- Keep a night light turned on in your toddler's room so she can find her way to the door.

- If your child's bathroom is attached to her bedroom, keep a small light on there as well.

- If the bathroom is down the hall, put a portable potty chair in your toddler's room. Place it on an old bathroom rug to help absorb any messes.

- Put your toddler in pull-ups, training pants, or regular underwear so she doesn't need your help to pull her pants down. Also, buy pajamas with elastic waistbands so they're easy to slip down (or consider a nightgown if you're dressing a girl). Skip the one-piece flannel footies because they're just too hard for a toddler to manage.

- Put a couple of pairs of fresh undies and dry pajamas on the floor in case your child wets herself a little and needs to change.

- Have some dry towels handy so your child can put them on the bed if the sheets are wet.

Confronting the bogeyman

With each passing month, your child talks more *and* understands other people more. Oddly, this increased mental ability doesn't always translate into more rational thinking and behavior. On the contrary, at the age of 2 children begin developing out-of-proportion fears of all kinds.

Two- to 3-year-olds blur fantasy with reality because they simply don't have enough life experience to tell the difference. If you don't believe it, take a bunch of 3-year-olds to see a magician. The most amazing tricks won't impress them a bit — after all, from their point of view, things that appear and disappear are just a normal part of life! (See Chapter 7 for more on how your child's thinking impacts her behavior.)

Understanding the difficulty of distinguishing between real and unreal

Your child's fears about bogeymen in the closet and monsters under the bed stem from his incomplete understanding of the world around him. As a result, the Teletubbies are as real as his next-door neighbors, and Oscar the Grouch may live in your trash can. This overlap of the real person and the pretend character can be confusing and downright scary. So, if you're awakened by a crying toddler who insists, "There's a monster under my bed!" it's not just a ploy to get your attention. From his point of view, that monster is real.

An infant is secure that his needs will be met and his discomforts handled, but between 2 and 3 years of age, children become more aware of their own vulnerability and the fact that their parents aren't really all-powerful.

One interesting example of this change is that a toddler who falls down and hurts himself may yell at or even hit a parent who comes to comfort him. It's almost as if he's saying, "Why did you let me get hurt?" On some level, he still expects you to protect him against anything and everything, but when he figures out that you can't, he has to sort out some pretty big, complex feelings. As a result, you'll see some interesting behavior along the way — and some of it will involve sleep.

Debunking the demons

Your child's new fears and feelings can be magnified at night because of the darkness and his separation from you. If he calls for you, here are some ways you can make those things-that-go-bump-in-the-night a little less worrisome:

- ✔ **Avoid making fun of your child's worries.** Acknowledge them in your words and your actions.

- ✔ **Reassure your child verbally.** Tell him that you know he's worried about the monster but that monsters aren't real.

- ✔ **Show your child he's safe.** Take a broom or a flashlight and look in all the scary hiding places to prove it.

✔ **Leave a small flashlight in your child's bedroom.** This way, he can check the room out for himself when you're not there. (Be sure the flashlight is safe for toddlers — not too heavy, no sharp edges — and consider placing tape over the battery lid so little fingers can't get to the batteries.)

✔ **Place a nightlight in your toddler's room.** Try to find a spot where it doesn't cast scary shadows!

✔ **Keep your bedtime rituals quiet and calm.** Choose books that don't contain alarming images or words. Now is not the time for tales about snakes, spiders, or big scary dragons.

Of course, not all of your child's fears are about imaginary creatures. Some of them are about all-too-real monsters like robbers or murderers. If your little pumpkin worries about these real bad guys, assure him that it's your job to keep him safe and that you will.

Often, toddlers' fears stem from the television or movies, so be very careful about what your child picks up from the big or little screen. Even G-rated movies aren't always safe because your version of *tame* or even *cute* can be terrifying to a toddler. Do your best to pick toddler-friendly shows and movies, and try to look at them through a child's eyes so you can anticipate problems.

Just because your toddler wants to watch a show over and over, don't assume that it isn't scary. Often children are just trying to gain a sense of control over their fright. (Adults do this when they keep repeating a story about a scary experience.) Instead of allowing your child to keep watching an upsetting movie or show:

✔ **Talk to him about the scary scenes and help him understand that it's just make-believe.**

✔ **Let him know that you understand that the movie was too scary and that's why you're putting it away.** He may initially object, but inwardly he's relieved that you're protecting him from the frightening images.

Part III
Sleep Decisions that Involve the Whole Family

The 5th Wave   By Rich Tennant

"The bonding experience of co-sleeping has really evolved for us. Like right now, I'm bonding with my children, a monster truck, a doll house, 2 pets, Barbie, and a super hero."

In this part . . .

A famous Russian author once said, "All happy families are alike." But guess what — he was wrong! In reality, each family, just like each snowflake, is one-of-a-kind. This means that each sleep strategy needs to be unique as well and that family dynamics always play a role in how, where, and when your tot sleeps.

In this part we look at the ways that your baby's or toddler's sleep affects everyone in your family — from grownups to pint-sized siblings. In Chapter 9, we examine the new trend toward co-sleeping (sharing your bed with your baby) and discuss the advantages and disadvantages of this choice. Chapter 10 talks about managing the different sleep needs of two or more kids and offers advice for raising twins or welcoming an adopted child into your family. And in Chapter 11, we discuss the big role that day care and preschool play in your child's nighttime sleep and daytime napping.

Chapter 9

Keeping Baby Nearby? Co-Sleeping with Your Little One

. . . .

In This Chapter

▶ Picking a co-sleeping style

▶ Making the big choice: To co-sleep, or not to co-sleep?

▶ Settling into a routine

▶ Minding the do's and don'ts of co-sleeping safety

▶ Transitioning from co-sleeping to the big-kid room

. . . .

*L*ife's all about choices, and a big one for new parents is whether co-sleeping makes sense for you and your baby. *Co-sleeping* means your little one sleeps in the same bed with you or in a different bed in your room. It's a simple definition but a big decision — especially if your dream team includes a partner. So you're smart to weigh all the factors before you make your choice.

A reassuring note before you start: Any answer you pick will be the right one as long as it works for you and your partner. So let the experts squabble endlessly over who's right — the co-sleepers or the independent sleepers — and ignore them. As the ultimate expert on your baby and your family, make your own choice; both you and your baby will get a great night's sleep!

In this chapter, we outline the co-sleeping options and offer facts about its pros and cons, routines, and safety issues. We also provide important information about the next step: moving to a separate bedroom.

The Two Types of Co-Sleeping

Are you thinking that you'd rather snuggle up with your sweetie than have a crib in a nursery? Or maybe you lean toward the crib-in-the-room or *sidecar* option, where you put your baby in a bassinet or small bed next to yours. Both are excellent choices with lots of advantages.

When comparing the two co-sleeping methods, keep in mind that each approach has advantages and drawbacks, and the right decision is whatever works best for you. Many parents switch from one approach to another as Baby gets older. Other parents select one style and stick with it until Junior is old enough for a big kid bed. This section gives you the ups and downs of each plan.

The baby-in-your-big-bed plan

Putting your baby in bed with you is a co-sleeping strategy that has some weighty benefits. However, because of the potential dangers, it's a choice that requires serious thought and planning.

The hands-down benefits

Snuggling close to your baby is a wonderful feeling. In contrast, getting out of bed every hour or two to walk to another room can be a pain — even when you love your little dumpling dearly. So bringing your newborn into bed with you is cozy, comforting, and convenient.

Sleeping with Baby is an easy setup for these reasons:

- ✔ **You save money and hassle.** You don't need to buy a crib or transform your computer room into a nursery.

- ✔ **You don't have to get up as much at night.** If you're breast-feeding, you don't need to leave your warm, comfy bed when your angel says, "Feed me!" You just roll over and presto — it's snack time.

- ✔ **You're more in tune with your baby (and vice versa).** When parents and babies sleep together, they almost always lie on their sides facing each other. They also have more moments of sleep arousal (which translates into less time spent in deep sleep) and more moments of waking up. So Mom and Dad have lots of chances to take a quick peek and make sure all's well — and baby can do the same. Some researchers suggest that this closeness may help to lower the risk of sudden infant death syndrome (SIDS), an issue we discuss in depth in Chapter 4.

✔ **Co-sleeping in your bed helps set your baby's internal clock.** Babies can't tell day from night at first (more on this in Chapter 4), which is a big challenge for their sleep-starved parents. But babies who co-sleep quickly pick up on Mommy's or Daddy's waking and sleeping rhythms.

Contrary to what you may suspect, different bedtimes aren't a problem if you share a room. You can pop Baby into your bed in the evening and join him there later. Of course, this option is only available if you can situate your bed and baby in a way that ensures your baby truly can't fall. This approach puts some distance between parent and child but only until you go to sleep.

The most common concerns

So why is sharing a bed a hard choice? One word: safety. You need to work very hard to create a secure, baby-friendly environment, and this choice requires a very big commitment from any grownup that's in the bed with baby. (More on these issues in "If you're in the same bed" later in this chapter.)

The number-one worry about co-sleeping is whether it increases the risk of a baby suffocating. Even though this question is so important, the answer isn't a simple *yes* or *no*. These are the two main points of contention:

✔ **A deeply sleeping parent can roll over on her baby.**

True, a sleeping parent may roll over on a baby with tragic results. However, this is a *very* rare event, and the safety steps we outline in this chapter reduce this risk even further. And remember, sleeping in a separate bed (or room) isn't risk-free either.

✔ **Too much carbon dioxide (CO_2) can cause Baby to stop breathing.** CO_2 is the big clue for our bodies to take the next breath; too much CO_2 can lull the brain into saying, "I don't need to breathe right now," and that's very dangerous.

When Baby cuddles with Mom or Dad, they're nose-to-nose. As a result,

• Some of the CO_2 that a parent exhales enters Baby's airspace.

• Baby gets covered up more during co-sleeping than in a crib, and this can increase CO_2 levels.

- The risk of SIDS (which is greater for babies who sleep on their sides instead of their backs) is even more of a concern.

However, a tiny rise in CO_2 levels can actually stimulate breathing, which appears to happen with babies who co-sleep closely with their parent(s). The CO_2 level goes up enough to stimulate breathing but not enough to interfere with it. So co-sleeping *may* offer another way to reduce the risk of SIDS.

Studying a handful of families in the lab isn't enough to answer the co-sleeping safety question, so scientists are now looking at millions of families to see whether the behavior is risky in the real world. We can't dive into all the research in this book, but in short, co-sleeping is not the risk — the risk lies in the dangerous actions of parents while (or before) co-sleeping. When you eliminate those problems, co-sleeping looks like a safe option. (See the section "Tips for Safe and Sound Co-Sleeping" later in this chapter for specific advice.)

Sleeping together is more than a fad

Co-sleeping isn't just a fad. It always was — and still is — the choice for most of the world's parents. (The controversy about it isn't new, either – Saint Augustine took a stand against it back in the year 400!) Only one culture is out of step on this issue — Western-European-based societies. Here's a quick look at what other cultures do:

- In Bali, parents carry their babies all day, almost never putting them down, and co-sleep all night. Both parents and children sleep in bits and pieces throughout the day.

- In Japan, about ⅔ of families co-sleep, with Baby in a separate bed in the same room or (less often) in the grownup bed. About ¼ of these dads head off to the spare bedroom, leaving Mom and Baby together.

- In Brazil, nearly 100 percent of newborns and 80 percent of 2-year-olds co-sleep.

- Swiss parents hardly ever sleep with their newborns — but nearly ⅓ sleep with their toddlers.

- Babies in Germany and the Netherlands almost always snooze in their own rooms.

The separate-bed, same-room strategy

For some people, "Two's company, three's a crowd" takes on new meaning when Number Three has a cold or spits up all over your pillowcase. These parents want their own bed to offer a welcome bit of distance. The solution is a child's bed in your bedroom — together, but not *too* together. As a middle course, this choice joins same-bed co-sleeping as an increasingly popular arrangement. Depending on the age of your child, the bed can be a bassinette, a *sidecar* (a type of infant bed specially designed to be attachable to your bed), a crib, or, when the child is older, a bed.

The following are some advantages of this form of co-sleeping:

- ✔ **Your baby is right next to you but you still have some space.** If you're breastfeeding and using a sidecar, you can pick her up without getting out of bed. If you're using a bottle, you can pop her back in the sidecar when you're done and go right back to sleep. When she needs a pat and a reassuring word, you can offer both — and when you need a reassuring check, you just open your eyes!

- ✔ **The independent bed eliminates almost every risk of co-sleeping.** The bed is your territory and not baby's, so you don't need to worry about sleeping too deeply, draining your waterbed, or putting Great-Grandma's quilt in storage — as long as you put your honey bun right back in the sidecar after a feeding.

- ✔ **It's pee-proof.** If that no-leak diaper turns out to be less than perfect, the nearby bed gets soaked — but you don't.

- ✔ **It makes moving day simpler.** If you plan to move your baby into her own room when she's older, you can simply move the crib from your room to the nursery. The fact that your baby stays in the same bed makes this change easier for her.

So what's the downside? Really, only one: You may not like this way of sleeping together. Skin-to-skin contact is powerful, and having your baby nearby isn't quite the same as snuggling her up next to you.

Deciding Whether Co-Sleeping Is Right for You

The only people who really matter in the decision about co-sleeping are the people who sleep in your house — and, in particular, the people who sleep in your bed. But how do you decide what's right for them and for you? These questions can help:

✔ **Are you truly comfortable with the idea of co-sleeping?** Because co-sleeping isn't better or worse for your child, do what makes *you* happy. Some issues of personal comfort to consider include:

- **Comfort:** This sounds simple, but consider whether having your baby in your bed is physically comfortable or comforting for both parents. In your heart of hearts, does this setup feel right and make sense to both of you?

- **Intimacy:** This issue is clearly in the eye of the beholder. Only you and your partner can decide whether co-sleeping interferes with your time together.

- **Sleep disruptions:** As your child gets older, he can make sleep in a family bed or room bumpier by snoring, sleep-talking, and even sleepwalking. These issues seem to start after 18 months of age, but they're worth considering early to avoid painful interruptions of your sleep.

✔ **How does your partner feel about co-sleeping?** Co-sleeping is a big lifestyle change, and everyone needs to be happy with the decision. The great richness of two parents is their two perspectives, but this advantage becomes a challenge when they have to agree on major decisions like co-sleeping.

We recommend the following:

- Make the decision well before it has to be made, during a time free of pressure or crisis. Pick a quiet moment (rare as they are!) to have that chat.

- Listen carefully to the partner who really wants to co-sleep. But if one of you can't find a way to be comfortable with this, preserve the partnership and defer to the partner who wants to keep the bed as grownup turf.

- Remember that any adult in a co-sleeping bed must care deeply for your baby.

✔ **Have you contemplated the realities of co-sleeping?** Along with wonders of bonding and cuddling come the not-so-fun diaper smells and the lack of privacy. If you share your bed, you'll also make some changes in your bedtime routine and the bed itself. (For a quick look at these safety concerns, flip forward to "If you're in the same bed" later in this chapter.)

✔ **How do you feel about giving other kids (or Fido or Fluffy) the boot if you're co-sleeping in the same bed?** Co-sleeping is more complicated, less safe, and pretty darned uncomfortable if you have more than one kid in the bed (and an older child can never sleep next to a baby because it's dangerous). When your baby is little, the rule is: Only one kid in the bed at a time — and no pets. Be sure you and your family members are okay with this setup.

✔ **How long do you want to co-sleep?** Co-sleeping has no set time limit, but you need to have a limit in mind. Some parents co-sleep for three weeks, some for three years or more. The later section "Phasing Out the Family Bed" has more info on this decision.

If your answers to these questions give you the green light and you relish the idea of going cheek-to-cheek with your cuddle bug at night, then co-sleeping can be a great choice. On the other hand, if you cherish your privacy and dread giving up some of your adult pleasures (an evening glass of Chardonnay, your big goose-down comforter, or those spontaneous romantic moments — see "If you're in the same bed" later in this chapter), then a crib in the nursery can be an excellent way to go.

As long as your baby is safe in the setting you pick, he'll be happy, healthy, emotionally well-adjusted, and well-rested.

When Baby makes three: The issue of intimacy

One drawback to co-sleeping is that it makes romance tricky. Just plain cuddling isn't a problem. But what do you do when the sparks really fly?

If your baby is little and your bed is big, the answer is easy: Just scoot her safely to one side. Don't worry — she won't have the foggiest idea what you're up to, so you won't bother her a bit. Under the age of 9 months, infants don't know what's going on and aren't frightened by their parents being intimate. Many infants remain blissfully unaware for many months past this point.

When your child gets old enough to be aware, or if you're uncomfortable — some parents have a hard time getting in the mood with a little one in the room, even when she's tiny — then find another spot like a comfy futon or sofa where you and your

(continued)

(continued)

partner can be intimate. Just like babies, parents are resilient and flexible (which can be handy if that futon is small!). Every once in a while, if you can afford it, turn your sweetie over to a sitter and have a romantic night at a local hotel.

Of course, intimacy means more than just sex, so make time every day for grownup snuggling and conversation. That's especially important in those early months, because dads often feel a little left out when baby enters the picture.

And Dads: Remember that new moms need to know they're just as sexy and beautiful as ever. Even if co-sleeping makes intimacy a little trickier, make sure you keep the flame of romance alive.

Above all, share your feelings with each other. A new baby means change — in your sleep, your sex life, your days, your nights, and your relationship — and grownups react in a variety of ways to this big and exciting upheaval. Even if baby is sharing your bed, make time for some one-on-one with your partner so you can enjoy each other's company and explore your feelings about your new roles as parents.

Creating Your Co-Sleeping Routine

In the real world, parents tend to combine the different co-sleeping strategies. That's a good plan because a flexible sleeping style can keep everyone happy.

Considering a few options

Here's a handful of co-sleeping arrangements that seem to work well in the real world:

- ✔ **Your baby can start in your bed but end up in your room in a separate crib or bed.** If you choose this approach, have her spend time in the big bed with you before you fall asleep and let her enjoy another quick visit for each feeding. This way, you still get some cuddle time with your sweetie *and* you get your comfy bed all to yourself while you snooze.

- ✔ **Your baby can start out in her own crib or bed in the grownup room and end up in your bed.** This option allows for some flexibility. If your infant wakes up, it's okay to fall asleep together in your bed after feeding.

- ✔ **Your toddler can start in her bed in her own room and end up in your bed in your room.** This option is perhaps the most frustrating of them all — and usually it's the child's choice, not the parents'. But if you like this arrangement, it's certainly an option your child will enjoy. (See Chapter 8 for details on how to stop your tot from invading your territory if you don't want it to keep happening.)

Of course, if your baby sleeps with you in the same bed for even a little while, be sure to follow all the precautions for same-bed sleeping in the section "Tips for Safe and Sound Co-Sleeping," later in this chapter.

Assessing your situation

When you consider your own co-sleeping routine, the following questions can help guide your plans:

- ✔ **Do you have any habits that may make co-sleeping unsafe?** Examples include the two greatest dangers to co-sleeping: smoking and drinking. Another red flag is a parent who's often exhausted. Tired parents are at greater risk of rolling over onto an infant.

- ✔ **Do you have any sleep disorders?** If you do, avoid co-sleeping in the same bed with your baby. People with *sleep apnea* — a medical condition that causes them to stop breathing for longer-than-normal periods during sleep — can sleep so deeply they may not notice they they've rolled onto a baby. Sleep apnea is quite common and can be associated with conditions like allergies and obesity.

- ✔ **Are you willing and able to make your co-sleeping setup physically safe?** If you co-sleep in the same bed, you need to make sure you take all the necessary steps to be sure the bed, bedding, and placement of the bed are safe (see the next section for complete details on safety).

- ✔ **Does your routine feel right for you and your partner?** It's crucial to get an honest answer to this question: Do you *both* really like having your baby in bed with you? If so, great. If not, look at different options that can keep you close without making one partner uncomfortable. Feeling good about your sleep is very, very important, and needless suffering tends to have bad effects on everyone.

If your answers don't paint a clear picture, try charting the pros and cons of co-sleeping for each partner and see whether you can work out solutions and compromises that work for everyone. Table 9-1 shows how one family laid out their co-sleeping issues and came up with ways to handle each one.

Table 9-1	Sample Co-Sleeping Assessment Chart		
Co-Sleeping Issue	*Mom*	*Dad*	*Possible Solutions*
Sleep Schedules/ Restedness	No issues	Occasional exhaustion may be an issue	Baby can go in sidecar instead of big bed when Dad is very tired
Smoking/Alcohol	Mom allows Baby to be around relatives who smoke	Dad has an evening glass of wine	Giving up wine is okay with Dad; Mom will talk with Uncle Bob and Aunt Rita about smoking issues
Comfort	No issues	Dad's concerned about sleeping well on required flat bedding	Consider switching 100 percent to sidecar if Dad finds new bedding too uncomfortable
Intimacy	Mom's uncomfortable being intimate with Baby in same bed	No issues	Consider a bassinet in another room for Baby on romantic nights; bring him back to the family bed later
Timing	Mom wants to co-sleep for two years	Dad wants to co-sleep temporarily, maybe one year	Tentatively decide on one year; re-evaluate at ten-month mark

Our only caution with mixing and matching styles is that you pick a consistent routine and stick with it. For instance, if you put your baby to sleep in the big bed and move him later to a sidecar, do this each night. He'll get on a schedule more easily if he falls asleep and wakes up in a predictable spot each night.

REAL WORLD

Stories from the crib: A tale of two cities

When the sun sets over Tokyo, Yoshiro and Midori tuck 12-month-old Akio into their bed. Later, they snuggle up with him for the rest of the night. Akio wakes them up three or four times each week, and when he cries or fusses, it's always Mom's job to ease him back to sleep — an easy task with him close at hand.

In Tulsa, Kevin and Janet sometimes bring 10-month-old Kelly into bed with them for a brief stay before popping her into her crib. Most nights, however, they tuck her into her own bed, kiss her goodnight, and shut the door. If she cries during the night, they wait for her to go back to sleep on her own. When she doesn't, Kevin or Janet gives her a quick pat and then shuts the door.

Both Akio and Kelly sleep happily and well, and so do their parents. Yet the two families have very different sleep styles and different expectations. Yoshiro and Midori believe that sleeping with Mom and Dad gives Akio a sense of security during the night. When he cries, it means, "Mom needs to solve the problem." Kevin and Janet see Kelly's crying as a chance for her to learn independence. They also see the occasional middle-of-the-night visits as a job either parent can do.

Both families are making decisions based on what works for them and what's common practice in their cultures. In both cases, their solutions work just fine because babies can usually (and happily) adapt to an astounding range of sleep styles when parents keep schedules consistent and free from too much disruption.

Tips for Safe and Sound Co-Sleeping

The message from scientists, at least so far, is that co-sleeping is safe if you *make* it safe. So if you choose to snooze with your little sunflower, you need to follow a few basic do's and don'ts. Some of these rules apply only to same-bed co-sleeping, but if you're planning the crib-in-the room strategy or the sidecar option, you still need to keep general considerations in mind. In this section, we cover them all.

General tips no matter your method

Co-sleeping, if it's not done correctly, can cause physical harm or increase the risk of SIDS in so many ways that some experts (and at times even the American Academy of Pediatrics) simply advise: Don't do it.

But, after careful review of the medical literature, we have concluded that co-sleeping is much too common to simply say "Don't." More importantly, parents can make co-sleeping safe when they take a few critically important precautions.

This may be the most important section of the chapter. If you read only a few pages about co-sleeping, please choose these because they contain a crucial list of dangers.

✔ **Don't light up — even outdoors and even if you're away from your baby!** If you plan to co-sleep, this is the mother-of-all rules for Mom and Dad and anyone else who lives with you. (And if you're a smoker and getting a jump-start by reading this book while you're still pregnant, kick the habit now.)

Due to the unbelievably poisonous effects of tobacco smoke on the baby, the incidence of SIDS skyrockets when someone smokes in the same house, outside the house — whenever, wherever. The chemicals released by burning tobacco can impair your baby's ability to breathe, even if she breathes the residue off someone's clothing well after that person has smoked. In fact, one big study published at the turn of the millennium in the *British Medical Journal* concluded: "Co-sleeping has no impact on SIDS risk if the parents don't smoke." The no-smoking rule applies to every form of co-sleeping, even if baby isn't in your own bed.

✔ **Don't light up even during pregnancy.** This important advice is for the pregnant mother and everyone around her. Cigarette smoke actually shifts the developing baby's drive to breathe, reducing a baby's drive to get oxygen and increasing her tolerance for going without breathing.

The firsthand or secondhand cigarette smoke that the pregnant woman inhales actually causes a drop in blood flow to the baby's placenta. This very dangerous situation leaves the newborn more likely to stop breathing — a clear danger no matter where she sleeps but especially if she sleeps with an adult.

✔ **Keep the bedroom temperature comfortable.** A comfortable, not-too-hot temperature (ideally about 65 degrees F) reduces the risk of SIDS. If you sleep with your baby tucked next to you, your body heat makes it pretty toasty already — so keep your room comfortable but not too warm.

If you're in the same bed

In addition to the general safety issues, several concerns relate specifically to sleeping in the same bed.

Preliminary concerns

Before Baby hits the hay in your bed, keep these cautions in mind:

- ✔ **Consider holding off on same-bed co-sleeping until your muffin is 14 weeks old.** Newborns do have a higher risk for SIDS if they co-sleep in the same bed as their parents, but this additional risk vanishes when they reach 14 weeks of age.

  If you eliminate the major risks we describe throughout this list, you can sleep safely together even in the newest of the newborn days. Cheating on these safety rules, on the other hand, is even more dangerous in the first 14 weeks.

- ✔ **Avoid alcohol and medicines with sedatives.** Scientists report that the risk of rolling over on your baby during the night is almost nil *unless* you drink alcohol before turning in. If you or your partner indulges in the bubbly or tosses down a Scotch before turning in, your sweet pea is safer alone in his own crib or in a sidecar. Also, never co-sleep in the same bed if you or your partner takes medicines that cause drowsiness.

- ✔ **Stay well-rested (if you can!).** The risk of SIDS drops back to normal when parents get more than four hours of sleep the previous day. The moral: Sleep well, and you and your baby can co-sleep safely in the same bed. If you're burning both ends of the candle, pop your baby in the crib or a sidecar and go back to co-sleeping after you catch up on your own sleep.

- ✔ **Restrict co-sleeping with caregivers.** This safety issue is most urgent if your friend, relative, or hired help is watching the baby while you get precious time out. Be sure they do not sleep with the baby unless you feel they truly are very devoted, caring, and aware of your baby as your baby sleeps. The more connected co-sleepers are to Baby, the more alert they are to your little one's needs.

Concerns with the bed itself

If you're sharing a bed with your baby, then style and comfort take second place to safety concerns. Here's how to keep your little bambino secure:

- ✔ **Think firm, not soft.** Waterbeds and soft mattresses are out. Both types raise the risk of SIDS.

- ✔ **Go with flat, not fluffy bedding**.
  - Switch to light-weight blankets. Big, heavy blankets increase the risk of SIDS.

    Make sure blankets reach only to your chest, not up to your shoulders and definitely not up around your face.

- Thin pillows — not big, fluffy ones — are a must.

- Keep your bed's surface flat and uncluttered. Stuffed animals and down comforters need to go.

✔ **Keep your Baby away from walls.** Walls can be traps — if Baby sleeps next to a wall, he can get pinned between a parent and the wall — a dangerous situation. Hard rails or dividers are a no-no as well. (If you worry about your little sugar-pie falling out of bed, consider using a mattress on the floor, a crib, or a bassinet.)

✔ **Choose plain, not fancy.** Avoid headboards with cutouts or slats where Baby's head can get stuck.

✔ **Decide where your little sugar-bun goes.**

- **On the side? Stay low.** If your baby sleeps on one side of the bed, your safest setup is to keep your mattress on the floor. Don't forget to make sure the surrounding floor is covered with a carpet or rug.

- **In the middle? Be extra careful.** A little bundle of joy that sleeps between two adults is at higher risk for SIDS unless *both* of the adults follow every safety rule to the letter. So no fudging for either of you.

- **In it for the long run? Think ahead.** If you plan on co-sleeping into the toddler years, remember that toddlers almost never sleep in a straight line. They love to lie stretched out diagonally across the bed, with one arm poking you in the eye and one foot kicking your partner in the kidney. If you put your toddler on one side, he can only torment one of you at a time.

✔ **Make the couch an adults-only zone** — sleep with Baby only in your bed. Co-sleeping on a sofa increases the risk of SIDS nearly 50 times, a huge jump. (It's also dangerous for Baby to nap alone on a couch.)

Phasing Out the Family Bed

At some point, your little lady will get out in the world — but for now, she just needs to get into her own room! The age that she makes this transition depends on your situation and your comfortable level, and it varies from family to family. In this section, we offer guidance for making the big switch to independence.

Baby, meet nursery!

If you decide to switch from co-sleeping to a crib in the nursery any time before the 1-year mark, just pick a night and make the move. Be sure to follow your usual bedtime routine before tucking your sweetie into his new crib. If your child doesn't feel like making the switch but you're ready for him to move on, count on some hurt feelings *and* be prepared to manage them.

Your child needs the chance to adapt to this new place that you call *his* bedroom. Let him fuss for a while the first night or two, but if he howls at the moon for more than 15 minutes, head to Chapters 5 and 6, where we go into more detail on managing this kind of reaction.

Toddler, meet big-kid bedroom!

If you're considering making the switch from co-sleeping to independence with a child who's at least 1 year old, look for cues from your toddler to see whether she's ready. Sometimes, children — not parents — are the first to decide they're ready for a big-kid room. Some signs to look for include:

- ✔ Resistance to going to your bed
- ✔ Wandering out of your room to lie down and sleep elsewhere
- ✔ For older children who are able to talk, when they say so!

When you do decide it's time to make a change, do so in a way that continues the closeness you have with your youngster so she doesn't feel as if she's been thrust into a whole new situation. If your toddler is aching to have her space, you're in luck — just introduce her to her new room, help her feel comfortable in her new space, and settle in for a good night's sleep. If your toddler is less than eager to leave Mommy and Daddy's room, though, you're in for a bit of a struggle — nothing you can't handle, of course.

Smoothing the move for a resistant tyke

If the transition is your idea and not your toddler's, follow these steps to make the transition easier:

1. **Explain to your toddler that she's getting very grown up and is ready to have a big-girl room all for herself.** Above all, let your little moppet know that you're excited about

her new grownup room and proud of her for taking this big step toward independence. (It's natural to feel a little weepy about the change yourself, but try not to let it show.)

2. **Give her some ownership in the big move and the new place.** Let her put her favorite toys (and maybe some new ones) where she wants them and let her help pick out her sheets and blankets.

3. **Move your bedtime ritual to your little sugarplum's new room.** If you had a rocker in your room, move it so you can enjoy story time and quiet play time together in the new room.

4. **If your toddler has a bed and not a crib in her new room, lie down with her for the first night or two just until she falls asleep.** That way, she doesn't have to say "Goodbye" to her old bed and her beloved sleeping buddy all at once.

Remaining firm

As we mention in the beginning of this section, expect to have a few rocky days when you make this big leap to independence. Stay firm and don't backslide or else you'll go through the same struggle again later.

What does *firm* mean? It means you stay out of her new room long enough to accomplish two goals:

- ✔ **Convince your child that the change has indeed happened:** Going in to check on her only confuses her. She doesn't understand that you're just checking, so she concludes that you're coming in to spend the night.

- ✔ **Let your child have the time and space to make the change work:** Each time you appear, you open up the option that you're managing this problem for her.

As rough as this transition may be, it is also brief. In our experience, such transitions usually take one to two nights, rarely more than a week if parents handle it as we advise (see Chapter 5). This length of time is typical for all young children — infants through 10-year olds.

If your toddler wants to wander, see the tips in Chapter 8 for keeping her safely in her room.

Chapter 10

Move Over, Darlin'!
When a Sibling
Enters the Picture

*Y*our first time as a parent was a leap into the great unknown, but now you're a pro at everything from changing diapers to bandaging boo-boos. You're at the top of your game, and it shows.

Your new baby feels this confidence, and as a result, there's a good chance he sleeps more soundly than your firstborn. It doesn't *always* work this way because each baby is a unique little person. But even if your new cherub is a holy terror at night, the tricks you mastered the first time around can help you stay on top of the situation this time around.

However — you knew there was a catch, didn't you? — it's not just Baby #2 you need to worry about. In fact, even if your firstborn has this sleeping thing down pat, she's likely to be the one who's up at all hours, demanding attention while your new little angel sleeps peacefully.

In this chapter, we explain why a sibling's arrival can throw even the perfect sleeper's patterns into chaos and what you can do to head this problem off at the pass. We also talk about balancing bedtimes for your brood — a tricky issue when Baby needs quiet and your wide-awake older child wants to sing the *Hokey Pokey* or bang on her new birthday drum. In addition, we look at the special sleep issues that adoption raises and the double joy (and double trouble at bedtime) if your bundle of joy turns out to be twins.

Understanding How Baby #2 Affects Baby #1's Bedtime Behavior

Parents know that a sibling's arrival is a big deal for an older child, and they watch carefully for signs that #1 is having trouble coping. Alarm bells go off in their heads when their toddler gives the newbie a pinch or gets too rough when *helping* the baby.

But children often show their emotions in more subtle ways, and one of them is by having trouble sleeping. When young children deal with big conflicting feelings — and a new brother or sister really stirs up those feelings! — this turmoil can creep into their consciousness as they cycle through deep and light sleep at night. (Check back to Chapter 2 for more on these cycles.)

This turmoil explains why the sweetie who says, "I love my little brother" can be up at 2 a.m. saying, "I lost my Teddy," or "I had a bad dream." The inner conflict also explains why the little angel who keeps her feelings under wraps — who doesn't sneak a pinch or a poke — often has the biggest nighty-night issues when baby moves in. One way or another, those powerful feelings need to come out.

Luckily, some simple strategies can help you get your older child back on the track to Sleepyland. In the next sections, we look at techniques you can use before a sibling arrives and ways to help a toddler who's already dealing with a new brother or sister.

Making Room for Baby

Remember those old black-and-white movies where babies slept soundly in a dresser drawer? It's a different story these days, with more paraphernalia for Baby than ever before. Depending on the age of your firstborn, you may have a huge array of decisions about where Baby #2 will lay his little head.

Figuring out where Baby will live

Some parents feel strongly that each child should have his or her own room. If you have the space, this setup has lots of pluses:

- ✔ A newborn's crying is less likely to wake the older child.

- ✔ When Mom or Dad feeds or changes the newborn in a shared room in the middle of the night, it may disturb the older child.

- ✔ A toddler who's struggling with sleep and getting in and out of bed may disturb a newborn who's just getting used to finding his own way to sleep.

- ✔ A room of her own can help a toddler feel less displaced, which can soothe some of that sibling rivalry that disturbs sleep.

Handling the shared-room situation

The one-room-per-kid plan is great, but children end up sharing a room for plenty of reasons — and the good news is that doubling up (or even tripling up, in some cases) can and does work for millions of families. Check out the following questions to size up your shared living quarters:

- ✔ **Do I have to worry when my toddler and baby aren't the same sex?** Not really, at least for the first three years. (Later on, you can get a screen to divide the room and provide some privacy.)

  Also, a child who's starting potty training may begin to develop a keen sense of modesty. Do what you can to accommodate her while she's figuring out how to be in charge of her own body.

- ✔ **Is it all right to put the baby in with my oldest child instead of with the child who's closer in age?** Yes. This arrangement often works quite well. In part, it depends on the sexes of the children — especially if this is a long-term arrangement.

- ✔ **I'd like to keep the baby in my room for the first few months. Is this okay for the baby and will my older child feel resentful?** Yes — and yes! Keeping Baby close is a great idea, but your toddler may raise a fuss about it. If so, calmly and matter-of-factly explain that keeping Baby with you allows everybody to sleep well. You can also talk about when Baby will move into another room. (See Chapter 9 for more details on sharing a room with your baby.)

Setting up the room

You may not love the lack of symmetry of a crib and a bed in the same room, but your kids will be fine with it as long as you prepare the older one for the change and make her feel at home. Here are some ways to do just that:

- ✔ Include #1 in preparing the room for two. She can help you rearrange the furniture and pick out items for the new room.

- ✔ Try not to clutter the room with baby stuff. Keep some of Baby's items in your room or elsewhere in the house.

- ✔ Invest in some inexpensive shelves for your older child's possessions so she has a place to call her own. You can even label the shelves (for instance, make a colorful sign that says *Sara's stuff*).

- ✔ Even if privacy isn't an issue, think about purchasing a light-weight screen to divide the room. This gives the older child a sense that she still has her own space.

Preparing Numero Uno for the Big Event

If your new baby is still resting cozily inside Mommy, you have a golden opportunity to nip your toddler's sleep problems in the bud. An ounce of prevention really is worth a pound of cure at this point; taking a few steps now can spare you nights of sleeplessness later.

The following sections offer great tricks so your toddler can rest at night rather than toss and turn about that sibling on the way.

Giving your toddler a heads-up

Children don't like big surprises, especially if they involve major life changes. You don't need to break the news the instant the pregnancy test reads *positive,* but don't wait too long. You may hear some people say, "Wait until right before your due date." We disagree. Your toddler can't miss the fact that Mom's getting a great-big tummy, and she overhears those grocery-store questions like "So when's the baby coming?" "Are you excited?" "Wow, are you ready for the big day?" Your toddler's smart, and she'll be on these clues like Sherlock Holmes on a footprint. So make your toddler part of the inner circle for the blessed event.

When you begin to freely discuss the event with others, it's time to let your older one in on the secret. Toddlers don't have a good grasp of time, so keep the news simple and straightforward and offer helpful clues. For instance, you can say, "We'll have a new baby at our house at Thanksgiving time."

A young child can't fully understand what being a big brother or sister means (it's hard enough for *you* to imagine having a new arrival!), but here are some ideas to try out during the waiting period:

✓ **Point out other newborns when you're out.** Tell your child, "Our baby will be very small like that," or "Look, this baby can't walk or talk yet. See how little her hands are?" These casual comments help your toddler know what to expect a few months down the road.

✓ **Talk to your child about all the big-boy things she can do already (talk, drink from a cup, and so forth).** Let her know that the new baby won't be able to do those at first.

✓ **Avoid telling your older one how much she'll love the new baby.** Even before the arrival, #1 is likely to have some ambivalence about this big change. If she feels like she *has to* love the baby (but she's not sure she will), worried thoughts and sleepless nights may ensue.

Creating a special book

Children love a good book — especially when it's all about them! A book just for your toddler, with pictures and words about her role in the new baby's arrival, is more enchanting to her than the glossiest book from the library.

To create this singular sensation, buy an inexpensive photo album and use magazine photos, drawings, and index cards to make a special nonfiction story about your toddler and the new baby. See Figure 10-1 for a good example of how to set one up.

Make sure your toddler takes center stage in each caption to help her feel like an important part of this new family adventure.

Include the need-to-know info in your book — for instance, who's going to stay with your older child when you go to the hospital — but don't forget to add the feelings part, too, because those pesky sensitivities really get in the way of sleep. State in plain words that your child will be excited to be a big sister but sometimes she may feel mad because the baby takes so much of Mommy and Daddy's time.

While Mommy is in
the hospital, Samantha
will be with Grandma.

At night, Samantha
and Daddy will stay
and sleep at home.

Figure 10-1: A personal book helps prepare your child for future events.

Playing musical beds early on

Planning to keep your older child in the crib for awhile? If so, borrow or buy another crib for your new arrival, or let the new little bundle sleep in a bassinet for the first few months. Assuming there's no risk of jumping out of the crib, let your toddler keep her own nest rather than moving her into a new crib, even if it's newer or prettier. From her point of view, there's no place like home — and that crib is her little home at night.

If you're not sure whether your toddler will be ready for a big bed when baby arrives, err on the side of caution. Rushing a young toddler (under 2 years) into a big bed right before the stork comes can be too much change to handle.

Some babies make an early entrance, so don't get caught with your crib rails down! Give your first child time to adjust so she doesn't feel like you're evicting her to make room for that new kid. (See Chapter 7 for tips on moving your toddler to a big bed.) In addition, make the transition feel like a move up instead of a move out. Try the following tried-and-true tricks:

✔ Let your sweetie shop with you for special sheets, pillows, and room decorations.

✔ If you're switching your older child to a new room but she's still in a crib or toddler bed, keep the old bed for a while instead of switching two routines at once.

> ✔ If #1 is getting a new room, add something special like a child's tape player and some new sleepy-time CDs to make nighty-night time something to look forward to.

Handling the Emotional Tug of War When Baby Arrives

When your new little sweetums arrives, you may find you're dealing with three nightly feedings *plus* a toddler at 2 a.m. saying, "I wanna rock with you, too!" If so, you need to get your firstborn back on the nightly path to Dreamland.

The first step is to look at the situation from your toddler's viewpoint. In Chapter 8, we talk about the toddler's emotional tug of war: On one side is the baby who doesn't want to grow up, and on the other side is the big child. This conflict heats up when your toddler is no longer the baby but the big sister. Suddenly the baby side of the rope starts looking even better — especially when #1 sees the newcomer getting away with fussing and pooping his pants while she's expected to act like a big girl.

At the same time, your toddler has another tug of war going on in her mind: "Should I be loving or unkind?" "I'm proud because Mommy says I'm a big help with the baby." "I'm mad because Daddy's playing with the baby and he's not paying any attention to me."

This inner debate continues all day and even laps over into dreamtime. To quiet your toddler's inner volcano so she can sleep through the night, give your little bundle-of-feelings a chance to sort out her emotions in the sunny hours. Just like a grownup, she can get a better grip on her feelings if she talks it over with a good friend — and that's you. In this section we show you how you can help.

Be sensitive but firm

Your daughter may love her brother — some of the time — but not always. This fluctuation is perfectly normal, and she needs to hear from you that it's okay to love the baby sometimes and be pretty mad at him (and you) at other times. When you do, you acknowledge the ideas she already has and give her a wonderful gift of letting her know that you understand how she feels. Parents who don't allow tots to express their negative feelings will feel the repercussions. A toddler's reactions can take many forms, but sleep troubles are one of the most common — so acknowledge your sweetie's feelings in the day, or you'll get the message a different way at night!

Stories from the crib: A trashy tale

Jon and Jenn knew they were in for some sleepless nights when they brought their second son home from the hospital, but they didn't expect 2-year-old Luke to be the one up at night! After consulting with his pediatrician, they understood that even though Luke seemed to love his new sibling, some big feelings about having to share Mom and Dad were interfering with his sleep.

Jon and Jenn helped Luke express his ambivalent feelings about the baby and gave him permission to be angry when the baby cried and demanded attention from Mom and Dad. His response almost knocked them over: After listening to their supportive words, he screwed up his face and yelled, "Yes, I am so angry I could throw you all in the garbage!"

Jon and Jenn were able to see the strength of their child's feelings *and* the power that their words had in helping Luke sort those feelings out. Soon, this little guy was back to sleeping through the night.

Being firm with your confused little tyke is as important as being understanding. If you spot your love-bug's gentle pat on Baby's arm turning into a hard squeeze, you need to set limits. When you step in, acknowledge her feelings and offer a safe release valve for them.

For instance, you can say, "When I see you hurt your brother, I know you're angry with him. You can be as angry as you want, but I will not let you hurt him. When you get those angry feelings, you can punch your pillow really, really hard." Or let her stomp her feet or say, "I'm angry!" as loud as she wants. Here's another idea: If your child wants to draw an *angry* picture or tell a story about her feelings, you can help her turn her words or picture into a special-feelings book that she can refer to when she's upset about the new baby.

Plan ahead

At times when baby gets your undivided attention — feeding time, for instance — you can count on your toddler to throw a monkey wrench into the works. As soon as you settle down in a comfy chair with your newborn, you're likely to hear, "I need a drink!" or "I'm hungry!" or "I want that toy on the bookcase."

Anticipate this attack of toddler jealousy and ward it off by making a special bag for your older child. (A sturdy canvas bag is a good choice because it lasts a long time and it's easy to throw in the washer.) Be sure it contains a fun selection of snacks and toys, and try to rotate the contents once a week.

At Baby's feeding time, get the bag and tell your toddler, "I need to feed the baby right now, but here's your special bag — let's see what's inside today!" Your big girl may still whine, but at least you both know that she's getting attention, too.

The Juggling Act: Managing Multiple Bedtimes

Think it's a challenge to get one child to sleep? Add a brother or sister to the mix, and the fun really starts. But they'll all have sweet dreams — and so will you — if your bedtime strategies take family dynamics into account.

In the following sections, we explain how to satisfy each sib's needs for naps and nighttime. In addition, we offer tips for those times when your newborn squalls nonstop and your toddler says, "I can't sleep with all that crying!"

The bedtime balancing act

Did you ever watch a juggler spin several plates on sticks all at once? Well, that's nothing compared to getting a couple (or more) kids to sleep at once! When children are very young, it's helpful to take a Zen attitude and just remember the old adage: "This too will pass." But then again, even the hardest jobs can become more manageable.

Putting your kids to bed

Getting one child to sleep is easy when you get the knack of it. Trying to get two kids tucked into bed, however, is a little like herding cats. Your little one is busy crying or pooping or spitting up. Your toddler is jumping on the sofa or begging for a story or saying, "Can I watch my favorite movie again?" And nobody's tired except you.

You have several options for making the bedtime ritual go more smoothly:

✔ **Divide and conquer.** If you have a partner, developing a plan to share the responsibilities is the best. For instance, you can decide that you'll give Keisha her bath, feed her, and change her. Your partner can help Samuel with his jammies, read his bedtime story, and tuck him in. It's surprising how much easier bedtime is when everyone knows the drill.

✔ **Find a helper — real or cartoon!** If you're single-parenting or just have a spouse who's conveniently absent at bedtime, you may need to do a little compromising:

- An appropriate video may be a lifesaver if it keeps your toddler occupied while you're with the baby. By appropriate, we mean something very calm and soothing — nothing with loud music, scary images, or complex plots that keep your little one awake.

- Hiring a young neighbor to come over for an hour can be just the ticket for some nighttime relief. Even a 12-year-old can play with your toddler as you get Baby down to sleep, and kids usually work cheap. You're home, so the sitter's maturity isn't a big issue.

✔ **Break out your toddler's special bag while you're getting Baby ready for bed.** For nighttime use, fill the bag with quiet, sleepy-time toys and books like an Etch-a-Sketch or a doll that your love-bug can undress and get ready for bed For the low-down on your toddler's special bag, see the section "Plan ahead," earlier in this chapter.

✔ **If you have older kids in your home, enlist their help in getting your toddler ready for bed.** Teens can be very handy (especially if you offer to bump up their allowance or cell phone minutes in exchange for extra responsibilities), and even a 4-year-old can feel mighty proud if she gets to help out in a grownup way. Another plus: Toddlers often comply more willingly when a big brother or sister is running the show.

Never allow a child under the age of 12 to supervise a bath or any other activity that requires adult guidance. Instead, assign safe jobs like reading a book or helping with jammies. Also, if you have teenagers and want them to babysit when you go out for dinner or a movie, make sure they attend a Red Cross babysitting class or similar training program. The more they know, the safer your little ones are.

✔ **When your baby is still at the newborn stage, start your toddler's bedtime ritual right after Baby is fed and down for the count.** This way you'll feel more relaxed as you bathe your older child or read to her. Everyone picks up on the tension if you feel rushed because you're listening for Baby to wake.

✔ **If your newborn hits his alert stage right when it's big sister's bedtime, trying putting him in a carrier and having him with you as you go through the older one's bedtime routine.** Even though you really want to attend to your older one's needs, the baby will get a lot out of your interactions by hearing the splashing water in the tub and listening to the bedtime story.

Dealing with a finicky toddler

Don't be surprised if your toddler goes through a stage where she acts like she prefers one parent over the other. It's heartbreaking when your beloved child runs away from you hollering, "No, Mommy do it!" or "I don't want you, I want Daddy!" But the reassuring fact is that this isn't about you. It's just a phase, as they say, and she's likely to switch favorites a month or two later. Nothing is as fickle as a toddler, especially when she realizes what a stranglehold she has on your emotions.

Problems can arise during this phase when you try to get two kids to bed. For instance, if your toddler insists on Mommy, Daddy can't really take over the breastfeeding chore! When your toddler snubs one parent and it wreaks havoc on your bedtime plans, here's a strategy that can calm the waters (usually within a few days):

1. **Don't give in to your child's demands.** "No" is a perfectly reasonable answer. If you do stand your ground, make sure you never sink to your child's level with your response. (We don't mean that you can't get on your knees and look her straight in the eyes — that's a good thing!) We mean don't respond in a childish way. (We know one Dad who was so hurt by his child's words that he replied, "Well, I don't want to be with you either!")

2. **Reflect your toddler's words back to her.** For example, say, "I hear that you'd rather have Mommy give you your bath. She is busy now, so I will help you wash up. When you're through, Mommy will come in and read you a book and kiss you goodnight." This matter-of-fact talk helps your child see that you understand her wishes but can't give them to her right now. She may throw a fit, but don't worry — she won't hold a grudge.

3. **If your child still carries on, restate your understanding, continue to hold your ground, and make your child take a breather.** For example, simply say in a neutral voice, "I see you are still mad. I will wait until you are calm, and then you can have your bath." Yelling and punishing may solve the immediate problem, but they do nothing to stop it from happening again. Your cool and calm demeanor (even if you're bubbling over inside) will help your child relax.

4. **If you child rants so long that it's too late for a bath or a bedtime story, conclude the bedtime routine and head straight for the bed.** For example, say, "Tomorrow, I think you'll be able to listen and have your bath and all your bedtime stories."

This is one time, however, when your gut feeling needs to come into play. If you sense that your older child really is coming up short in the parental-attention department, you can say, "I see you need to be with me right now. I'll put the baby in his crib, and we can spend some time together." Firmness and consistency are good, but sometimes bending the rules is a wiser strategy.

The crying game: Keeping one kid from waking the other

Your home can get pretty noisy when you're walking the floor with a squalling newborn or letting an older baby cry himself to sleep. All of this commotion can roust your toddler out of bed, and you may find yourself bouncing one weepy child on your hip while the other one clutches your leg sniffling, "I can't slee-ee-eep."

There's no surefire solution for this problem, but luckily it's usually temporary. If the situation leads to frazzled nerves, here are some techniques you can try:

✔ Put your baby to bed first, before your toddler's bedtime. You can even enlist your toddler's help in listening for the baby crying.

✔ If your baby is 4 months or younger and he's not in your room, move his crib farther away from your toddler's room. (Or put your newborn in a much-more-transportable bassinet and leave the crib where it is.) This arrangement only works until you're ready to teach your new baby to get to sleep on his own; at that point, he needs to have an established room (see "Making Room for Baby" earlier in this chapter).

✔ Let your older child sleep in another part of the house. A sleeping bag and makeshift tent in the den can be a real treat for a child who's nearing the 4-year-old mark. Of course, you need to make sure your toddler's new environment is every bit as safe as her own room.

✔ Get your older child out of the house at nighttime, at least for a few nights. If your toddler enjoys sleepovers with close and trusted friends or family, now's the time to have another! But bring her home in the daytime so she can enjoy her regular activities.

The daytime dilemma

Your toddler loved her daytime schedule back when she was the center of the universe. But what happens now, when Baby needs a two-hour nap in the afternoon and your toddler wants her library story-time?

This question has no right answer; in fact, in the same family, the answer may change from day to day. However, here are some guidelines that can help you cope with conflicting demands:

- ✔ **Try to coordinate naps as much as possible.** If your toddler already gave up her morning nap, you may still manage to get both children down at the same time in the afternoon. Try putting Baby down first so you can have a few alone moments with your toddler. Even a young toddler can be patient when she knows her turn is coming next.

- ✔ **If your new baby is a fuss-budget who loses it at the end of the day when he misses his nap, think of alternative ways to get your older one to playgroup or story hour.** One idea is to co-op baby-sit with a friend or neighbor: You take the big kids to nature class on Friday while the other adult watches your baby. On Tuesday, you trade places, and your buddy drives the older kids while you watch the littler ones.

- ✔ **If your older child is in preschool and Baby heads for dreamland just as you need to walk out the door, try to nudge Baby's schedule in a more convenient direction.** For instance, if Baby still wakes up at night to eat, try to postpone the last pre-morning feeding so that (with luck) he sleeps a little later and then naps a little later as well.

- ✔ **Consider getting a front baby-carrier.** Babies can sleep quite happily in these carriers, and they enjoy the movement as well as the feel and smell of Mom or Dad. With this set-up, you have your hands free for your toddler.

Here's the hardest piece of advice to follow: Relax! No matter how hard you try to juggle naps and toddler time, you can't always succeed. The good news is that babies are resilient, and your little love-bug will thrive even when your schedule doesn't fall neatly into place.

Welcoming an Adopted Baby into Your Nest

Some newborns arrive by very special delivery: an adoption. If this is the case in your family, be sure to make your toddler a big part of this happy event.

Families often face many unknowns when they adopt: When will the baby arrive? Will we need to travel to another country? How old will the baby be? Will the baby be healthy?

When grownups are up to their ears in all the logistics of an adoption, they can overlook the fact that their older children have their own hopes, fears, and questions about this enormous life change. And those feelings — like any strong emotions — can affect a toddler's sleep, both before and after the new baby arrives.

Soothing your toddler's pre-arrival jitters

When you adopt a baby, lots of powerful emotions come into play. Your toddler soaks up these emotions like a sponge and often reflects them by resisting bedtime, tossing and turning, having nightmares, or waking up in the night.

To set her mind at ease, keep her in the loop. She's going to overhear conversations and know that something's up. When she can't find out the truth, she fills in the blanks — and a toddler's imagination can conjure up some scary ideas.

So give her the scoop in words she can understand. Create a picture book (see that section in this chapter) about the new baby. Tell your toddler in simple terms what to expect. Let her help set up the crib and go with you when you buy bottles and blankets. To make being the big kid more palatable, get her something that only an older child can use — for instance, some washable markers or modeling clay. But don't go overboard; material possessions are not the key to soothing sibling feelings. And be ready with answers to these questions:

- ✔ **When is the baby coming?** To help in answering this question, make a *backwards* calendar — an open-ended chart to which you can add days until you get a better idea of baby's arrival date. Think of this calendar like the countdown to a shuttle takeoff. If you think it'll be two weeks, make 14 squares, the last square holding a picture (if you have one) of your baby or a picture of some baby item like a crib. Each day, your older child can put a sticker or make an *X* in the spot as you get closer and closer to baby day. If the wait is longer than you anticipated, add some extra squares.

- ✔ **How old is the baby?** If you know your new baby's age, tell your toddler — and point out children about the same age so she knows how big a baby to expect.

- ✔ **Where does the baby live now?** If your new cherub hails from a different country, explain this to your toddler. You can even get a globe or a world map to point out where the baby lives now. Perhaps you can try to learn some words in the baby's native language or taste some foods from Baby's culture.

✔ **Why is someone else's baby going to be part of our family?** As toddlers approach 2½ years, their newly sophisticated thinking can lead to some wild conclusions. Adoption undermines one of a child's most fundamental beliefs — that a family is safe and unchangeable — because a baby from somebody else's family is now part of hers. When you talk to your child about adopting, repeat again and again that she is part of *your* family forever.

Ensuring a happy and peaceful homecoming

Any new arrival is a big transition. When Mom's pregnant, the older child has plenty of opportunity to get ready; she notices Mom's changing body, sees the preparation for the room, and hears the world talking about this new baby. But in an adoption, you may have only nine hours, not nine months, to get ready. No matter how much you try to prepare your toddler, the process will most likely move rapidly. So be sure to retain as much consistency in your toddler's life as possible; it's one of the keys to a good night's sleep.

If you need to travel without your child to get the new baby, the best option is to have one parent stay behind. If this isn't possible, prepare your child thoroughly for your departure:

✔ Let her stay in your house with a sitter or relative if you can.

✔ If she needs to stay away from home, send her with lots of comfort items like favorite toys and blankets (and maybe one of your old sweaters or jackets).

✔ Leave a photo album and tapes of yourself reading a favorite story.

✔ Call her as often as you can.

Expect your toddler's bedtime rituals to take longer — or even disintegrate — when your new baby arrives. When this happens, be patient and rebuild your routine from the ground up. (See Chapters 5 and 6 for ideas on encouraging a bedtime routine.)

Don't be surprised if your toddler refuses to sleep in her own room. She's reacting both to the new baby and to her fears of separation. One valid philosophy at this time is this: Rules are made to be broken. So, if you don't mind having a party of three in your bed, let your toddler sleep with you for a little while — or put a mattress or sleeping bag on your floor for her.

On the other hand, an established bedtime routine still works best for many families. (And it helps to have at least one kid who has the bedtime drill down pat!)

Getting your adopted baby to sleep

Is your adopted child a newborn? If so, the advice in Chapter 4 works just fine. If he's older than 4 months when you bring him home, however, you may need to backpedal a bit before you move forward.

Older adopted infants and toddlers arrive with their own sleep habits and rituals, and changing them takes time and patience. If possible, get a detailed description of how your baby's former caregivers put him to sleep at night and for naps. Your dark, quiet bedroom may be just the opposite of the well-lit, noisy room your little buttercup is used to! Expect some trial and error as you figure out how to ease your sweetie into a nightlife that's probably very different from his old routine.

Daytime stress invades the sleeping hours. As a result, the night hours can be rocky until your beloved stranger comes to know and trust you and feels comfortable with the sights, sounds, and smells of his new home. Your new baby's age, temperament, and former environment all influence how quickly he adjusts.

Consult with experts about the issues that adopted babies and children face. If your new child is a toddler or older, these issues can include life disruption, grief at losing their former world and caretakers, and attachment problems. You can find lots of ideas for dealing with these problems in *Adopting For Dummies* by Tracy Barr and Katrina Carlisle (Wiley).

Doubling Your Pleasure

When twins enter your life, here's our best advice: Open your mouth and yell, "HELP!"

Our second piece of advice? Get that help! The first few months with twins are an endless cycle of feeding, pooping, and crying, and the best way to keep your sanity is to share the load. If you can't rustle up grandparents or other free helpers, an adult helper is the best investment you can make. If money's tight, try to find a reliable teen that can come in after school.

You need all the help you can get, especially at sleepytime. Twins often have special sleep issues (for instance, many are premature or smaller-than-average and need extra feedings). They also have different personalities — even when they're identical twins — and that means double trouble when you try to get them on a schedule.

The following sections offer tips on dealing with two sleep-resistant tots without losing your marbles. In addition, we cover sleep arrangements as your twins grow and how to cope with twins who develop at different speeds.

Deciding where your twins will sleep

One friend with twins says, "My babies didn't sleep well until I reunited them in the crib. They fell asleep more quickly and slept longer. I'd find them curled up like little spoons, touching each other's hair."

Some parents find that twins sleep better in the early months when they share a crib. That's no surprise — after all, they shared a much smaller space for nine months! Other parents say their twins are just as happy in separate beds or even separate rooms.

If your twins do share a crib, make it a temporary arrangement. By the time your cuties are about 3 months old, they need separate spaces for safety's sake. In the meantime, if one is a sleepyhead and the other is wide awake:

- ✔ **Tend to the calm baby first.** After she's asleep, you can focus your attention on your other little rascal.
- ✔ **Look for clues.** Why isn't your wide-awake twin longing for bed? Ask yourself these questions:
  - Did this baby feed as well as her twin today?
  - Did this baby take a longer nap?
  - Was this baby more stimulated, making her all wound up? Or was she under-stimulated, leaving her ready for action?

- Is this little darling coming down with a bug?

- Is this twin always the tyrant at bedtime? (If so, it's a temperament issue.)

✔ **Make a plan.** Depending on the issues you identify, a calming bath, a feeding, or a long rock with Mommy or Daddy may be just the ticket.

✔ **Have a backup crib.** If your little fussy-face simply refuses to calm down, pop her into a portable crib so she doesn't wake up her sleeping sib.

Balancing the eat-and-sleep scheduling teeter-totter

Tiffany's down! Tamara's up! Parents of multiples can feel like puppets, with their babies pulling the strings. Everybody agrees that getting twins on the same schedule is the first step, but that's easier said than done.

However, give the schedule a try. Your dynamic duo may surprise you by going along with the idea. The following two steps make a good game plan, based on the fact that feeding and sleeping have a strong connection:

✔ **When your first baby wakes to feed, rouse the other sweetie as well.** It isn't always easy because a newborn in deep sleep is totally zonked.

   Hint: Take off your snoozer's swaddling, and put a little bit of slightly cool water on the bottoms of his feet.

✔ **If you bottle-feed, have another adult feed one twin so you don't need to prop a bottle. If you breastfeed, buy a pillow that allows you to comfortably feed two hungry mouths at once.** (Or your helper can wake up Baby #2 while you're feeding Baby #1.)

Some parents don't like the idea of manipulating their babies' internal hunger alarms. That idea may be okay in the ideal world, but in the real world of twins, ideal doesn't always work! Getting your two babies on a single track doesn't hurt them at all. In the long run, the schedule makes you happier, more rested, and peppier. And that's a big advantage for everybody.

If your babies absolutely refuse to synchronize their internal watches, you may need to take turns with a partner. You can trade off nights or do split shifts so each partner gets half a night of sleep. But if you're parenting twins on your own, it's worth a few difficult nights to switch one of the babies to the other one's schedule. Here are some tips for accomplishing that mission:

- ✔ Even as newborns your babies have different temperaments, so try getting the easier-going one to make the switch.
- ✔ Start by waking the baby you want to switch 15 minutes earlier (or letting him fuss 15 minutes longer) at each feeding until you get your little pair synchronized.

Creating a bedtime ritual and adapting it for each child

Just like other siblings, twins tend to develop at different rates — and that's true for their sleep patterns as well. As a result, you may need to adjust your bedtime routines (and expectations) to meet the needs of each twin. If you have a partner, try divvying up the bedtime ritual so each twin gets individual treatment. Here are two more tips:

- ✔ Nighttime baths are often part of a bedtime ritual, but if your scallywags end up working each other up into a frenzy of splashing excitement, consider separate baths or just bathing them every other night.
- ✔ You may find that each twin has a special bedtime book. Consider reading each twin's particular book to her alone, before the tuck-in. (Accept the fact that the other twin will likely be hanging over your shoulder as you read). Then, choose a book that both will enjoy as the last piece of your routine.

Using separate rooms for older twins

Twins are an endless source of laughter and frustration as they grow, especially when they start talking. At bedtime they make you giggle when they chatter like magpies, discussing the day's events in baby-talk. Later, they drive you nuts when they're so full of beans that they keep each other up.

If your duo gets so rambunctious that sleep is your impossible dream, you may need to put them in separate rooms for a while. Don't be surprised if they object because most twins want to stay together, at least in the early years.

If your kids are old enough to really object to being separated, then they're old enough for you to set limits — and stick to them. For instance, tell them that if they're not quiet after 15 minutes (set a timer), then one twin will have to move. If neither one volunteers to leave home base, you can literally draw straws. You may hear some loud objections, but if you stand firm, the separation will probably last only a few days. Most twins figure out what they want (to be together or to be apart at night) and tailor their behavior to achieve their goal — and yours!

Chapter 11

Your Dream Team Grows: Preschool, Day Care, and Sitters

· ·

In This Chapter

▶ Linking daytime care and nighttime sleep

▶ Considering the choices: Away from home or in the home

▶ Keeping your focus on sleep and safety issues

▶ Creating and maintaining a positive atmosphere for your toddler

· ·

*P*olly hangs out with Grandma on weekdays while Mommy works. Damon's parents hire a sitter twice a month so they can enjoy a romantic evening. And Juan and Manuel started in childcare when they were 2 months old; their parents say, "We need to work two jobs if we're going to send twins to Harvard!"

What do these families have in common? Each one calls on other people to help care for Baby — preschool teachers, child-care providers, relatives, or sitters. And each family's extra dream-team members play a big role in how well their little ones sleep at night.

In this chapter, we look at how daytime stints at school, Nana's home, or a sitter's house can mesh with your sleep routines. We also explain how to reduce separation-related sleep upsets by choosing your child's day-care providers wisely, by communicating your baby's sleep issues to them, and by enlisting their help for your wee one's transition.

Understanding How Caregivers Affect the Sleep Routine

Getting your honey bun to sleep is tough enough when all the stars are perfectly aligned and you're the only one calling the shots. Add another person or two to the mix, and you can see why even a good sleeper can throw you a curve at beddy-bye time.

Choosing the best child-care situation for your family takes some thought and homework — and you're not finished when you've made that decision. You still need to be in constant communication with your caregiver to make sure everyone's giving your child the same messages about napping and sleeping through the night. This section provides some insights into the benefits of each type of care and the sleep issues that may arise.

Preschool and day-care centers

Preschools and child-care centers are popular choices for lots of good reasons. In good programs, children get a happy learning experience and a chance to socialize. Good preschools and day-care centers are licensed and supervised by the state; many seek out state or national accreditation. And you don't need to worry about that morning call from Nana or the nanny saying, "I can't come today — I'm sick!"

However, if you pick a preschool or day care, be ready for some fussy days and sleep-deprived nights. To understand why, think back to your first day in kindergarten — or even your first day at a new job. You worried, "Who's going to be in charge of me?" "When's lunch?" "Where do I go to the bathroom?" No matter how young or old you are, learning the ropes at a new place is a challenge.

This challenge is even more stressful for a tot in preschool or day care because he adds an elephant-sized worry: Is Mommy or Daddy *really* coming back for me? If your tyke is 12 months to 2 years old — when the fear of parting really sinks its claws in — he probably worries that your bye-bye wave is the last he'll ever see of you.

All of these worries can play havoc with your child's sleep. Here are some possible problems to anticipate:

- ✔ **Napping at school:** When your child is happily playing in the sandbox or painting a masterpiece, he can be the model student. But when the teacher turns down the lights and says, "Naptime," you can bet that your tot's thoughts go directly to you and when (or whether!) you're coming back. Naps at school can be a tough time — especially if he worries that he'll miss your return. He may respond by fighting sleep.

✔ **Napping at home:** Even good nappers may have difficulty at home after they start school. Schedules are different, and they get used to sleeping in a group. They may even fight that afternoon nap on the weekend because it takes them away from Mommy or Daddy. (See our "Weekend Waker" story later in this chapter.)

✔ **Nighttime sleep:** Leaving home is a big step and a big separation, but a child who seems fine with daytime separations may fight sleep at night simply because it's *another* separation. Until your child begins to feel really comfortable at school, you may find yourself dealing with some nighttime awakenings.

Because separation anxiety can be in full gear at this age, we recommend waiting till your tot is 2 years or older if preschool is only a socializing experience. Toddlers younger than 2 years don't need to be in a preschool program for socialization — a play group, play dates with the neighborhood kids, or a toddler gym or music class can give these toddlers all the social skills they need.

Stories from the crib:
The weekend waker

Raphael and Luisa found a great preschool for Julia, their 2-year-old. Julia played hard and happily all morning, and the staff reported, "She's always one of the first to fall asleep at naptime."

Weekends, however, were another story. Julia napped just fine in the mornings, but in the afternoon she popped up like a Jack-in-the-Box. This perplexed her parents. What turned their weekday napper into a perpetual motion machine on Saturday and Sunday?

Julia's preschool director explained that this pattern is quite common in preschoolers. Weekends at home with Mommy and Daddy are just too exciting to waste on naps, even for the most frazzled toddlers. At school, on the other hand, a long snooze helps to pass the time until Mom or Dad shows up.

When Raphael and Luisa understood why Julia shunned weekend naps, they decided on a compromise. Rather than insisting on an afternoon nap on weekends, they scheduled some quiet downtime. Often, as she listened to the soft music, assembled puzzles with Mommy and Daddy, and listened to her favorite stories, Julia would doze off for 30 minutes or so — just long enough to recharge her batteries so she could enjoy her evening with her parents.

However, working parents may not have the luxury of waiting for the perfect moment. If that's your situation, don't worry. Your little one may have a few rocky days and nights, but there are ways to minimize those slumber setbacks (we cover them later in this chapter as well as in the age-related chapters in Part II). These tricks also work great with older tots who still find it tough to say "Goodbye" to Mom or Dad.

In-home caregivers

Home care is a great alternative for babies and toddlers who may be intimidated by the hustle and bustle of a large center. Younger ones also benefit from the consistency that a single caregiver provides, and this can mean better sleep for both of you. You have a few options: a family member, a nanny, or an au pair. We cover all three in this section.

The family affair

It's a match made in heaven when Grandma and Grandpa — or any other relative you love and trust — watches your little munchkin for you. The love connection between your sweetie and her family members is powerful insurance that she'll be happy and safe.

However, no one's perfect — not even your mom or dad. If you want your little sunflower to be safe and well-rested in the day so she can sleep stress-free at night, know what you're getting into when you ask your parents to pinch-hit for you.

Problems can crop up when you make babysitting a family affair — and these problems can create cracks in your carefully-crafted sleep routine. Here are three all-too-common hitches in the get-along:

- ✔ *Free* **can come with strings attached.** Often, family members baby-sit free of charge. That sweet deal saves you a bundle of cash, but a volunteer who doesn't follow your game plan is hard to criticize.

- ✔ **Different styles can cause friction.** Grandma's or Grandpa's deep emotional attachment can sometimes lead to a strong reaction to your parenting style — especially when your folks don't agree with your sleep strategies.

- ✔ **History repeats itself.** Remember the mistakes Mom or Dad made with you? Most likely, they'll make the same mistakes with your toddler. If they do, you'll need to decide whether to lay down the law or grin and bear it.

A few examples: What will you do if your mom still insists on washing your tot's mouth out with soap when she says a bad word? What if your dad vetoes healthful, whole-grain peanut-butter-and-banana sandwiches in favor of marshmallow fluff?

Before asking your mom or dad (or another relative) to sit for you, think through your decision and be sure your relationship is strong enough to handle the sticky issues. If it is, go for it. If not, paying extra money for a sitter may be a wiser choice.

A nanny or au pair

When you're choosing a person to care for your angel in your home, weigh the differences between nannies and au pairs.

A nanny comes with many built-in advantages and a few drawbacks:

- ✔ If you use a good agency, the greatest advantage is that your nanny is already well-versed in bedtime safety rules.

- ✔ A major drawback is that a trained nanny may also feel she has the know-how, so she may try to override your rules. Although kids are pretty smart and quickly pick up on different standards, big differences in sleep expectations can take a toll on their sleep.

   For instance, if you and your nanny differ about how long (if at all) a baby should cry before falling asleep, you can bet your diaper bag that your child's sleep routine will suffer.

Au pair is French for *on par* or *equal to*. In plain English, an au pair is usually a woman from another country who stays with a host family for free (and gets a little money, too) in exchange for child-care and sometimes light housekeeping. When comparing au pairs with nannies, these are some differences:

- ✔ A typical au pair is young, inexperienced, and has little or no training in child development. Think of au pairs more as working tourists than childcare experts.

- ✔ These young adults have their own needs that may cause some bumps. For example, they may become homesick or find the nightlife in your hometown a little too appealing.

- ✔ Because au pairs come from different cultures, their ideas of child-raising may not mesh with yours.

- ✔ Au pairs are cheaper — a big plus if money is tight.

✔ Like nannies, they can give your little cherub one-on-one attention and cater to your nap and bedtime schedules.

✔ Unlike a nanny, an au pair generally doesn't have a predetermined idea of how to get your little one to sleep.

Her adaptability can be good news and bad news. You can explain your bedtime rules to her and she'll agree to them. But she may have trouble following through because of her inexperience.

Au pairs are great if you use them as intended — family helpers who fill in when Mom and Dad aren't available. We don't recommend the use of an au pair for full-time care when a child is under 3 years of age. If the child is truly attached to the au pair (which you want!), the sense of loss when she leaves can feel like a death — the complete disappearance of a loved one.

Hiring Help that Supports Your Sleep Strategies

Angie sleeps like an angel after a day at her new day-care center, but Kyle's bedtime ritual is falling apart. Roberto doesn't nap for his new sitter and he's a real bear at bedtime. Dustin willingly grabs his blankie when the nanny says, "It's naptime," and then goes off to bed happily for Mommy at night.

Why do some kids make the transition to day care without a glitch in their naps or nighttime dozing while other kids go off the rails? One reason is that kids sleep well only when they like, understand, and feel safe with the people in charge of them — which is why successful sleep can hinge on finding just the right setting or person to provide day care for your tot.

Looking for the right day care

To make your child's days easier and keep your nights quieter, seek out a program that's sensitive to his needs. Finding the perfect place takes time, but it's well worth the effort.

What should you look for at each school? First, make sure the director appears knowledgeable and available; look for someone who can support you with reliable information when your sweetie pie has an issue. Next, focus on the issues that are deal breakers for you. *Choosing Childcare For Dummies* by Ann Douglas (Wiley) covers this topic in great detail, but here are few pointers that pertain to sleep:

- ✔ **Say "No" to any program with a *drop-and-run* policy.** This policy means that the staff discourages you from staying while your child gets acquainted. Instead, they want you to simply walk away — even when your toddler struggles and cries. This scenario is likely to cause a strong negative reaction (can you blame him?). And it can lead to bedtime clinginess, disruptive behavior, and nighttime awakenings.

- ✔ **Ask specific questions about naptime requirements.** If your child is still an infant, make sure there's enough staff so your baby can conk out on his own schedule. If your toddler still takes two naps a day, what sort of accommodation (if any) is the staff willing to make when the rest of the class takes just one nap? *Note:* An alternative may be to have the toddler join the infant class for the morning snooze.

- ✔ **Ask what happens when Junior is no longer napping.** Even children younger than 2 are sometimes ready to forgo all naps. Find out what sort of accommodations the school is willing to make for a non-napper of any age.

If possible, leave your little darling home when you take your tours (unless you still have an infant trussed to your chest). A mobile baby or toddler can distract you from your mission, and an older child can get confused about which school will be his.

Considering a sitter

When family members can't pitch in, you may need to look outside your home for someone who can give you a break from the rigors of raising a child. Sitters aren't just a luxury; they're an important part of the picture for families with young children. Using a sitter allows you to get out in the world of fun, away from your work at home or the office. And this break provides an important opportunity for you and your partner to reconnect over something other than rice cereal and strained plums.

Picking the right candidate

Although it's a favorite plot for offbeat television movies, few babysitters actually turn out to be crazed axe murderers! However, picking a sitter you can trust to keep your child safe, happy, and sweetly asleep at night can be a real challenge.

The best choice, obviously, is a highly trusted friend or family member. But if your pals and kin are off at the movies or out snow-boarding on the weekends, where else can you turn?

The simplest answer is to hire a neighborhood teen who's looking for some extra spending money. But before you think about trusting your angel to the kid down the street, ask yourself these questions:

- ✔ **How old is old enough?** Leaving your baby or toddler with a child under 12 years old is unsafe (and illegal in some parts of the country). But 12 isn't necessarily a magic number because lots of brand-new teens are totally unprepared for the responsibility of caring for a little tyke. On the other hand, some 20-year-olds can't be trusted with a Pekingese! So go by maturity, not just by age.

- ✔ **Does your child have special needs?** If your child takes special medications, uses a breathing machine, or has feeding issues or serious behavior problems, don't expect a teen to cope.

Asking lots of questions to make sure Sweetie will be safe

A good boss asks plenty of good questions at a job interview. In this case, you're the boss — and there's no more important job than watching your wee one and staying on top of her schedule and nighttime safety. So be sure to give your wanna-be sitter a good (although friendly) grilling. Some key questions to ask:

- ✔ **How much experience do you have?** Look for a candidate who's already trained on someone else's kids. If possible, check with those families to see whether the sitter did a good job. For instance, did the sitter follow the family's sleeping routine, or did the parents come home to find their child sleeping on the floor clutching a video game?

- ✔ **Did you ever take a babysitting class?** If the answer is "No" but you like the sitter, consider offering to pay for a course (as well as paying her for the hours in class). It's a small investment to make for a safe sitter, and it demonstrates your own seriousness about his work. Community centers, YMCAs, and the Girl Scouts of America routinely offer these classes.

- ✔ **Do you have younger brothers or sisters?** This qualification isn't a must — but older sibs often are pros with diapers, bottles, and bedtime stories.

- ✔ **Can you handle a houseful?** Give your potential candidate a couple of *what-ifs*. For instance, what if the baby is screaming for a nighttime bottle at the same time the 3-year-old needs to use the potty? Your candidate's responses show you how quickly your candidate can think on his feet and how well he can cope with your mischievous herd.

If your candidate passes your interview with flying colors, make your next step a test run. Pay your sitter to watch your child for a few hours while you're at home. After the initial getting-to-know-you period and a thorough review of the house rules, give the sitter a little breathing room; let her handle everything — diapers, feedings, and a nap or bedtime.

By keeping your distance, you give your sitter and your tot a chance to size each other up while you check out the sitter's skills. Listen to the conversations and observe the interactions. If your child appears comfortable, resist the urge to hover (it sends the message that you think something's amiss). Obviously, you want to quickly intervene if necessary, so find something to do like cooking up a pot of stew in the kitchen while they play in the nearby den.

After you've handed over the greenbacks and waved goodbye, do a gut check:

✔ Did it go well?

✔ Did your tot warm up to the sitter?

✔ Is a little voice inside you saying something's not quite right?

Go with your instincts — you'll never have fun out on the town if you're anxious about your sitter.

Laying out the Sleep Routine

Families get used to nap routines — you naturally stick with what works. But if your angel's at day care or home with a sitter, you'll need to make some adjustments. This section explains how to get everyone in synch.

In day care

If you hate to see your toddler's morning nap go but the staff at his program thinks he's ready for this switch, sit down with them and talk it over. Together, you can work out a plan for making this change as painless as possible. Base your plan on the staff's feedback as well as your own observations. Here are some tips:

- ✔ **Find out why the staff thinks it's time.** Maybe it takes the staff 30 minutes to get Junior down for a nap that lasts just 15 minutes — or perhaps they find that his little catnap at 10 a.m. keeps him from getting good sleep at 1 p.m.

- ✔ **Look to the bedtime hour.** If your baby's bedtime at home has shifted (maybe he's now happy and playful until 8 p.m. instead of zonking out at 7), it may be a clue that his nap needs are changing.

- ✔ **Give it a try.** After a few days, the staff may tell you that your sweetie is now sleeping a full two hours at one stretch instead of 15 minutes in the morning and 45 minutes in the afternoon. This change is a pretty strong sign that you made the right decision. And a longer nap in the afternoon may have added benefits: You get to pick up a well-rested, less cranky child.

A different problem arises if you want your toddler to skip a nap that's part of the program's schedule. We generally think parental instincts are worth gold, but in this case, the teachers' or caregivers' instincts may be more on the mark. This is the time for a little introspection on your part.

If your goal is to get your exhausted toddler down right after dinner so you can have a whole evening alone after a long day at work, you may be doing your child a real disservice. Your child needs to sleep at school and go to bed a bit later at night for several reasons:

- ✔ A good program is busy, exciting — and tiring! Often, your little one needs an afternoon siesta just to keep up. If he doesn't get it, he may be cranky or weepy and have trouble coping later on in the day.

- ✔ An overtired toddler spells trouble at twilight. Little rug rats who don't get forty winks in the afternoon can be too stimulated to unwind (putting a real wrinkle in your evening plans!).

- ✔ After a good nap at school, your little one is rested enough to enjoy a bedtime routine that allows for a lovely reconnection with you at the end of the day.

If your day-care program expects your toddler to snooze for two or three hours, it's fair to ask for a shorter naptime. Some toddlers like to sack out for hours at a stretch, but many others fancy a shorter rest. If you do your homework and pick an understanding and flexible program, you can probably work out a compromise with the staff.

Of course, some children really don't require naps. If your child falls into that category, find a program that provides a non-napping room with a staff member who offers quiet toys and activities until the other children are up.

At home

With an in-home sitter, aim for consistency in your tot's sleep routine, but don't fret if you're not always on the same page (or even the same paragraph) with your caregiver. Adapting to different routines isn't traumatic for your sweetie as long as the schedule doesn't spin out of control. Here's how to combine consistency with flexibility:

✔ **Nap times:** You can't cast naptime in stone, but do expect any caregiver to stick closely to your schedule. A half-hour variation or a once-a-week change of schedule doesn't hurt, but a different nap time every day throws a baby's life out of kilter. *Note:* Be sure to spell out your child's usual naptimes in writing so your sitter has a benchmark.

✔ **Sleepy-time rules:** Do you let your little pumpkin cry himself to sleep or do you pick him up at the first whimper? Do you put your toddler down precisely at 8 each night, or do you allow some flexibility? No matter which strategy you choose, encourage the caregiver to march to the same drummer.

Keeping your Baby Safe and Happy

No matter who sits for your children at your home — big brother, the cheerleader down the street, Grandma, or your best friend — you need to give them tools for safe sitting and the info they need to keep your sweetie cozy. For safety's sake:

✔ Make two charts, a *contacts/emergency information* chart and a *routine and scheduling* chart, and show them to your sitter. Be sure to include your first and last name — you'd be surprised how many sitters don't know these basics! (See the Cheat Sheet at the front of this book for a good go-by.)

✔ Don't take safety rules for granted. Your sitter may say, "I raised six children — I think I know how to keep a baby safe!" But he may not, especially regarding sleep. Be ready to take a stand, lovingly but firmly, on sleep safety issues — and spell them out in your instructions (see the Cheat Sheet at the front of this book).

For you baby's comfort, cover these bases before you leave:

- ✔ Set out in plain sight everything your sitter will need including pajamas, diapers, snacks, and toys.

- ✔ If your sitter is new to your house, offer a quick tour of every room that's not off limits.

- ✔ Make sure your sitter knows how to: use the television, turn alarms on or off, use the microwave, and handle baby monitors or other equipment. The more comfortable your sitter is with the ins and outs of your home, the more relaxed your baby will be.

Managing Toddler Anxiety

As babies and toddlers start to figure out their world, they can become little worrywarts — and these worries can deeply affect their behaviors, especially sleep. So take the time to help your child transition to new places and new people; it'll give you a blue-chip payoff in the end.

Earlier in this chapter, we detail how to acclimate your child to a sitter in your home. But adjusting to a whole new physical environment — a day-care center, preschool, or sitter's home — takes a bit more time and a little ingenuity. This section gives you some tips for the transition.

Easing her into day care

Be ready for a few sleepless nights before and after your toddler starts preschool or day care. To ease your toddler's anxieties, do a little prep work and be on hand when she takes this big step:

- ✔ **Be a shutterbug.** Stop by your child's new program before starting day and bring a camera. Take pictures of the play tables, the swings, the bathroom, the staff members, the lunchroom, the cots — anything that gives your little snookums a sneak preview of her new home-away-from-home. This way, she knows what to expect. (You can even make a book about the new program — see Chapter 10 for a variation on this theme.)

- ✔ **Create a memory.** Make a little photo album of family pictures that your child can take with her each day. (Include Spot and Fluffy, too.) Use photos you can replace in case they get lost.

- ✔ **When you arrive, plan to stick around to help your little angel get acquainted with her new friends.** In fact, see whether you can slowly increase your pumpkin's time at the center (check the steps below for a smooth transition).

A good program will be happy to go along with your step-by-step approach to ease your tot into a full day. If a program doesn't let you do it, find another place for your pumpkin.

✔ ***Never ever* sneak out without saying "Goodbye" to your child** no matter how tempting it is. Even if your goodbye is mingled with tears, your child needs to know that you're coming back; you aren't just disappearing.

If your little cherub is starting a full-time program:

1. **Bring her (and plan to stay at the program yourself) for a couple of hours the first day.**

2. **Have her stay progressively longer each day (and stay at the program yourself).** As she gets more comfortable with her new world, leave the room for increasing amounts of time.

Stories from the crib: Schooldays, night daze

Andy's mom, Heather, expected preschool to be a piece of cake. "He never fussed when sitters came," she says, "and I had him in childcare for months with no problems." But while other children cheerfully said "Bye-bye!" and marched into the classroom each morning, Andy grabbed at Heather's legs and said, "No! I want to go home!" At night, he couldn't fall asleep, and he didn't want Heather to leave the room.

The director of Andy's preschool explained that even children who do fine with sitters or child-care providers can be overwhelmed by preschool — especially when they're in the grips of separation anxiety. To help Andy cope, Heather rearranged her work schedule so she could spend a week in the classroom with Andy, and his teachers went out of their way to welcome him. Soon Andy was one of the gang — and he started sleeping soundly again.

Latoya had the opposite experience. Her daughter, Lydia, appeared to love school. At home, however, bedtimes became a big struggle. Lydia also started getting up in the middle of the night and asking for water or a hug.

Latoya told her pediatrician about the problem, and he clued her in: Lydia loved school — but she also hated being away from Mommy. That conflict, he said, intruded on Lydia's sleep. When Latoya understood the connection, she talked with Lydia about her big conflicting emotions. She said, "I know you have fun at school, but I also know that you miss Mommy." Just having Mom put her feelings into words made Lydia feel better and helped her fall asleep more easily.

3. **Stay for nap-time the first day.** When you help the caregiver get your little one down, you reassure your tot that sleeping at school is okay.

4. **Let the caregiver put your baby down the next day, but stay close by.** Again, this gives the strong message that she's safe sleeping there.

5. **Do the vanishing act when your child has a comfy feeling at school.** At this point, you can say "Goodbye" with a quick kiss and a cuddle.

This process can take a week or longer, so keep your schedule open!

Playing musical houses successfully

In a perfect world, Mary Poppins shows up every morning on your doorstep. In the real world, getting *anyone* to show up can be hard. You may need to cobble together a week's worth of childcare by using sitters some days and day care or preschool on others.

Babies are resilient, and they can handle this game of musical houses. But to make it easier, try these approaches:

✔ **Keep your baby in one place for as many days in a row as you can.** For instance, see whether Grandma can take the Monday-Tuesday-Wednesday shift and Aunt Rita the Thursday-Friday shift.

✔ **For naps, play it by ear.** Your tot may nap at different times in different settings and do just fine. But if the nap schedule dissolves into complete chaos, try to get it back on track. One idea: Can at least one sitter come to your house to cut down on disruptive moves?

✔ **When your baby reaches the 15-month mark, introduce a calendar to help her know where she's going.** Make a simple strip with 2-inch blocks to represent each day. In each block, stick a photo of that day's sitter. Make photocopies of the strips, placing one on your fridge and one at each sitter's house. If a change occurs, simply make a new strip.

Part IV
Dealing with Special Circumstances

The 5th Wave   By Rich Tennant

"The victory rolls settled him down, but I think the power dives are what'll put him to sleep."

In this part . . .

*L*ife takes lots of interesting (and sometimes surprising) twists and turns. Often, we celebrate happy changes — a new job, an exciting move, a wedding in the family. Other times, unpleasant surprises like illness or divorce give us a jolt. Many changes — birthdays, the first day of kindergarten — are predictable. Others, like the arrival of a baby weeks ahead of schedule, can take us completely by surprise.

In this section, we look at three special and challenging situations and how all three affect your tot's sleep (and yours). In Chapter 12, we talk about how to cope if your love-bug arrives before her due date, and we explain why your early bird keeps you awake round-the-clock (and why *you* won't be getting to sleep for a while). In Chapter 13, we offer advice about your baby's or toddler's sniffles and rashes as well as chronic medical issues that can disrupt your tyke's sleep. And in Chapter 14, we talk about keeping your little one sleeping like an angel even if big or little life changes have your household in a tizzy.

Chapter 12

Sleep Tips for Families with Premature Babies

*W*hat's the first rule about kids? They're unpredictable! Some little rascals prove this point right off the bat by showing up a little (or a lot) before their due date.

If your baby made an early appearance, you have some extra challenges with parenting — and one of those challenges is to help your sweetie sleep. Early birds have many of the same feeding and sleeping issues as full-term newborns, but they also have the extra job of playing catch up. So a preterm baby sleeps, eats, and acts like a newborn for an extra-long time. In addition, some preterm babies have health issues, ranging from mild to very serious, that can greatly affect a family's sleep. The good news is that premature babies, if healthy enough, finally outgrow that first stage of non-stop wake-up calls.

In this chapter, we outline the three reasons early birds keep their parents awake and tell you how long it may take to get your nightlife back to normal. We also give you our insight on adjusting your life to meet your little one's needs while keeping your sanity! Finally, we give you a full rundown on how to keep your premature baby safe — a vital part of parenting these wee ones — and share a sleep-promoting trick that comforts your baby as you get her to sleep.

Noting Age-Specific Problems in Premature Births

The term *premature* covers lots of territory. Babies typically stay in the womb for 37 to 42 weeks, and anything before that is *preterm* or *premature.* (Anything after 42 weeks is *postmature*, but modern delivery methods have sharply reduced the chance of that situation.)

In the womb: Stages of development

About one in ten babies arrives early, but the issues you encounter as a parent depend largely on *how* early. A quick look at a baby's development shows why.

Prenatal (before birth) growth takes place in neat thirds, with dramatic changes occurring in each trimester:

- ✔ **In the first trimester (the beginning to 12 weeks of pregnancy):** The fertilized egg transforms into a body with all of its organs.

- ✔ **In the second trimester (13 to 26 weeks):** The newly-formed organs start to do their jobs. For instance, the lungs that developed at the end of the first trimester don't start to breathe until the end of the second trimester.

- ✔ **In the third trimester (27 to 40 weeks):** A baby's body stockpiles nutrients, fat, and water in preparation for life in the outside world. His body also adds the finishing touches so that every part — lungs, heart, even skin — can function from the get-go. By his arrival day, he can maintain his temperature, eat on his own, and breathe without any reminders.

When a baby arrives before the end of the third trimester, his body still undergoes the third-trimester changes, but some or all of them happen outside the womb. That adjustment is a challenge, especially for a very premature baby. *Note:* The word *premature* carries many meanings, so it's more helpful to look at the *degrees* of prematurity, which depend on the length of the pregnancy:

- ✔ **Birth at 24 to 26 weeks (severe prematurity):** A baby born at the start of the third trimester can have serious medical problems (particularly if his lungs don't work well). These problems can include:

  - • Very serious breathing troubles that require ventilator support and high concentrations of oxygen

- Frequent and potentially serious infections

- Bleeding in parts of the brain; the more premature the birth, the more likely this complication is

With or without these serious medical challenges, the severely premature baby still grows. In fact, growth is the most powerful tool he has to help him develop into a healthy infant.

✔ **Birth from 27 to 29 weeks (moderately severe prematurity):** A baby who arrives this early still has big issues, but the chance of serious problems drops significantly. These problems can include:

- Very serious trouble breathing

- Potentially serious infections

- Bleeding in the brain

✔ **Birth from 30 to 34 weeks (moderate to mild prematurity):** By 30 weeks of pregnancy, the chances that a baby can breathe well and avoid serious illness improve greatly, and these chances improve further with every week of pregnancy. Better lung power means better health in several ways:

- Normal, calm, and effective breathing can define the overall medical course of a premature infant.

- When lungs function normally, the risk of severe infections or bleeding in the brain drops dramatically.

- Good lung function allows the premature baby to devote valuable energy to the key goal of growing.

✔ **Birth from 35 to 36 weeks (near-term):** Although a baby is technically premature at this point, his lungs are so mature that serious issues are unlikely. However, three key challenges still remain (see the next section for more details on these issues):

- Maintaining his own temperature at 98.6 degrees

- Eating without extra help

- Breathing in a regular, uninterrupted rhythm

Each baby is an individual, of course, and a small number of 25-weekers have no serious medical issues or long-term special needs. And needless to say, illness is a risk even for full-term infants. But to a large degree, the length of your baby's stay in the womb affects his health — and sleep — issues.

Out of the womb: The catch-up game

If you're tall, short, left-handed, or freckled, those traits last forever — but being premature is a temporary condition! Like other babies, preterm babies can experience long-term health issues, especially if they're very premature. But prematurity ends as soon as Baby catches up on the developmental steps she skipped in the womb. One year past their due dates, a healthy premature infant is no different from a healthy full-term infant in many ways.

Unfortunately, illness is a big threat to a premature baby, and the smaller your baby, the more medical challenges you're likely to face. But small size, in the absence of health complications, may not cause long-term problems.

If your tot has serious medical issues (for instance lung, brain, or immune system problems), she'll probably spend time — maybe weeks or months — in the Neonatal Intensive Care Unit (NICU). Even preterm babies without serious medical problems often need to stay in the hospital till they get big enough for the outside world.

After your baby is medically stable, your journey toward taking her home takes a big step forward. She's likely to be ready for the big day when she reaches the three key goals (we note these in the previous section about birth after 35 to 36 weeks of pregnancy):

- ✔ **She can eat like a pro.** At first, your little cherub may need a feeding tube because she has trouble swallowing. To be safe at home, she first needs to master the skill of feeding from breast or bottle.

- ✔ **She's not chilling out.** Keeping warm is harder than it sounds because the body needs to do two jobs: generate heat (the brains' job) and keep it inside (the skin's job). Both of them are big challenges when prematurity enters the picture.

  The smaller your baby, the more surface area she has in relation to her size — and the easier it is for heat to escape from her body. When she weighs 4 pounds, her skin is probably sufficiently thick and well-developed to keep heat in or let it radiate away from her body. At the same time, her brain figures out when she needs more or less heat *and* then adjusts her skin to keep her at a cozy 98.6 degrees in a warm room.

- ✔ **She gets the art of breathing down pat.** Your baby's lungs don't start working until the third trimester, and her brain doesn't master the art of breathing reliably until about the 35th week of development. This late development makes sense because Mom provides for Baby's every need in the womb — breathing isn't necessary.

The late development also explains why babies born before 35 weeks run the risk of forgetting to breathe. When that happens, they need a little stimulation — a back rub, a tap on the foot, or even a little extra oxygen — to get back on track. Your baby stays in the hospital until her brain and lungs figure out the ins and outs of breathing, and when you welcome her home she may still be on medications and a breathing monitor. These precautions ensure that she takes every breath just when she needs to.

When you bring your baby home, she continues playing catch up. In the next few sections, we cover her needs from that first day at home until the day her body successfully completes the steps it skipped before birth. For more detailed information on sleep after that milestone, check out the chapters in Part II.

Understanding the Special Needs of Premature Babies

The primary reason your little honey bun keeps you bouncing out of bed so often is that he has to get used to the world after being in your womb.

Life in the womb is like a stay in a 4-star hotel because Mom meets so many of her developing baby's needs. Check out the womb's unique features:

- ✔ It keeps the temperature at 98.6 with no effort on Baby's part.

- ✔ It offers the oxygen Baby needs without using his lungs.

- ✔ It serves up his meals without any need to eat them.

- ✔ It manages crucial chemical reactions via the placenta, which also takes out the trash by removing waste products.

- ✔ It lets your sweetie sleep and develop with little stress or noise.

Birth propels your baby into a journey of increasing independence — a tough road at first for a premature baby. Your cherub suddenly has to maintain his own temperature, breathe, eat, pee, poop, and manage all his own chemistry. That's a big leap for a newborn — especially for one who shows up early. He also faces these three big challenges when it comes to sleep:

✔ **He needs to play catch up.** Sleep develops over time — just like organs, hair, and those cute little fingernails. Even a full-term baby has immature sleep patterns, so preterm babies need extra weeks to catch up for missed time in the womb. (See the previous section for more on this catch-up period.)

✔ **He has a giant appetite.** For the first few weeks or months, your little rosebud needs to eat like a sumo wrestler — and that means more wake-up calls.

✔ **Medical issues, a serious risk for preterm babies, can also disrupt his sleep.** Resolving these problems adds to sleep challenges when the big homecoming day arrives.

In the following sections, we look more closely at how these three issues can make preterm babies a handful for Mom and Dad. But don't despair; later in this chapter we offer tips for getting through those first few months.

Growing into a sleep pattern

Just like a full-termer, your preterm baby starts out with an immature sleep pattern. She eventually develops a more mature one, but she does it just a little _more_ slowly than a full-term baby.

The development of sleep patterns

All newborns have sleep cycles that consist of the following forms:

✔ **Active sleep:** Later in infancy, your baby will develop _Rapid Eye Movement sleep (REM)_, a special phase of sleep where many dreams occur. But before the mature REM phase develops, this phase is called _active sleep_. It's a large part of sleep for newborns and especially for premature infants.

✔ **Quiet sleep:** Another immature state, _quiet sleep,_ later matures into the stages of sleep (see Chapter 2 for info on these 4 stages). In newborns — and especially premature babies — these stages aren't yet distinct.

✔ **Indeterminate sleep:** This third type of immature sleep is partway between active and quiet, deep sleep.

Your preterm baby's sleep and a full-termer's are very different because your little love-bug starts out sleeping like a baby who's still in the womb. Here's how her sleep develops before and after birth (we give you a quick overview here, but see Chapter 2 for more info):

✔ Near the start of her third trimester, your baby's brain starts cycling between wakefulness and sleep, although much of her sleep is the active form. At this point, the lines between sleep stages (see the previous bullets) are blurry. Your sweetie really isn't awake, so we don't know why she starts to snooze!

If your sweetums arrived very early (prior to 30 weeks of pregnancy), she spends about ⅔ of her first days after birth in active sleep.

✔ In the third trimester and for some time after birth, a baby briefly experiences indeterminate sleep, cycling from active to quiet and back to active sleep. She is also fully awake at times, and sleep probably plays a bigger role in her well-being.

✔ By the time she reaches her expected due date — that is, the date Mom's pregnancy would have reached 40 weeks — a baby spends only half her time in active sleep (an early version of REM — see Chapter 2 for details). As active sleep diminishes, the sleep stages begin to develop, and alert wakefulness continues to advance.

✔ When a baby passes her expected due date, she develops more mature sleep patterns — just like a full-term newborn. In just a few months, her four stages of sleep (see Chapter 2 for more info) become better defined, and she develops a sleep/wake pattern that's very much like an adult's. As these changes take place, sleep plays a more mature role in forming memories and promoting healthy brain function.

Reaching sleep maturity

After your sweetie reaches her full-term due date — if she doesn't have significant medical problems — her sleep patterns start to follow the same path as a full-term baby's. So, if she arrived four weeks early, you can figure on an extra month of newborn-style sleep. If he arrived ten weeks early, you're in for a longer haul.

Of course, premature babies (just like full-term babies) are unique little individuals, so some develop regular sleep habits faster than others. Follow the advice in Chapters 4 through 8 for advice on a baby's age-specific sleep issue, simply adjusting for your baby's weeks of prematurity.

To know what age range to go by:

✔ Subtract the number of weeks your baby was premature from her actual age; use that adjusted age to anticipate what to expect sleep-wise. (For example, if your little tootsie came a month early, she's ready for the steps we outline for 6-month-olds when she's about 7 months old.)

✔ If your baby was severely premature, consider using the date of her discharge from the hospital as the starting point for her development. (This date is usually well past her due date.)

Bulking up

Preterm babies make NFL players look like picky eaters. Like full-term infants, premature infants eat every 1 ½ to 4 hours at birth, but they tend to prefer 1 ½- to 2-hour feeding intervals.

At first glance, your pint-sized sweetie's giant appetite may seem strange. But the reason is simple: A full-term baby spends that third trimester bulking up, and your tot's a little behind.

Babies need that extra padding to get by in the world. Without a cushion of fat, they have a hard time keeping warm enough, even in a 70-degree room. (That's why hospitals have those toasty incubators.) Even when your baby is big enough to leave the hospital and come home, he's often smaller than a full-term infant, and every ounce counts for staying warm.

Babies in the third trimester and full-term newborns gain as much as a pound a week. If he's healthy, your early bird will closely follow this rate. The younger and lighter he is, the faster he grows — and the more food he needs. Because he's catching up, he has the same intense eating habits as a newborn, but for a much longer time.

In short, when he's not sleeping, your cherub will be eating — day and night. So think of yourself as a 24-hour diner for now. Your reward comes as those little cheeks plump up, those little arms and legs get fat and dimply, and your sweetie stockpiles enough fat to snooze happily through the night.

Beating health setbacks

Medical problems for preterm babies tend to fall into two important categories — big and small. The major problems involve the function of critical organs (like the lungs, brain, and skin) and often lead to a long and complicated stay in NICU. The minor ones (such as maintaining temperature, establishing reliable breathing rhythms, and learning to eat) are less scary but can place big demands on you in the early days.

Big or small, medical problems affect your baby's sleep — and yours as well. Here's why:

✔ Preterm babies are vulnerable to infections that can cause sleep setbacks. The more premature an infant is, the less developed her skin and the more likely she'll need IVs and other lines. These vulnerabilities — in addition to an immature immune system — contribute to a much greater risk for serious bacterial infections of the bloodstream. And lung problems greatly increase the chance of developing pneumonia.

✔ Bringing a new baby home is exciting but stressful. That stress is multiplied if your infant comes home with monitors, feeding tubes, or medications because each of these interventions has a special way of disrupting sleep.

- Monitors are noisy. They go off frequently, causing loud noises and the commotion of worried parents rushing to wake Baby up.

- Feeding tubes are very uncomfortable, and that discomfort can easily interrupt sleep.

- Many of the meds for premature babies have side effects that disrupt sleep.

✔ The extra work of maintaining a temperature of 98.6 degrees in a smaller body can interfere with normal sleep cycling.

✔ Growth, although welcome, forces a premature baby to eat more, again interrupting sleep.

You can't do much about sleep disruptions due to medical problems and hospital stays. But as your little snookums gets bigger and healthier, those meds and monitors play less and less of a role — and you'll both be able to sleep easier. There *is* a light at the end of the 24-hour tunnel!

Top Priority: Keeping Your Premature Baby Safe

In many ways, premature and term infants aren't all that different. For example, all parents want their sweeties to grow up healthy, safe, and strong. Parents of on-time arrivals and early birds make safety a top concern. The difference is that keeping a premature baby safe is a tougher job, especially if Baby arrives very early. In this section we look at some of the big threats to your premature infant's safety and what you can do to reduce these risks.

Cutting the risk of SIDS

One huge worry for parents of preterm babies is sudden infant death syndrome (SIDS), but the very encouraging news is that SIDS is rare, even in babies who arrive early. Nevertheless, ⅓ of SIDS cases do occur in premature infants, so it's crucial to take every possible precaution.

 In Chapter 4, we outline the rules that can greatly minimize your baby's risk of SIDS. Read them, and follow each one to the letter — they're especially important when you're caring for a premature infant.

Swaddling your baby to keep him safe

Thousands of years ago, way before the invention of disposable diapers, parents came up with another smart idea, *swaddling* — that is, wrapping a baby snugly in a blanket, keeping his arms close by his sides. You can do this with a regular blanket or with a specially designed swaddling blanket.

Swaddling mainly adds comfort to your baby's life. But, because some features of swaddling *may* reduce the chance of SIDS, we discuss it in this safety section as well. Here are some of swaddling's big benefits:

- ✔ **It gives your sweetie a sense of security.** Swaddling may make babies feel a little like they're back in the womb, which is especially comforting for a preterm tot.

- ✔ **It promotes quiet sleep, which evolves into mature sleep.** Mature sleep is key to snoozing for longer stretches at night and staying awake longer during the day. (See the earlier section "Growing into a sleep pattern.")

- ✔ **It may help reduce the risk of SIDS.** Some researchers note that swaddled babies react more to sound (for unknown reasons), and this increased ability to rouse themselves may reduce their risk of SIDS. Also, when you swaddle your baby correctly, it keeps the blanket off his face — another important way to reduce the risk of SIDS.

 A premature baby is especially vulnerable, so keep a close watch over him. If you swaddle your baby, follow these precautions:

✔ **Check with your pediatrician to make sure swaddling is safe for your little one.** Of course, if your baby has an oxygen line or other tubes that can get in the way, you need to hold off on swaddling until your baby doesn't need these interventions anymore. Your pediatrician can be very helpful in letting you know the right time to begin swaddling.

✔ **Make sure your swaddled baby doesn't get overheated.** This condition can happen to swaddled babies who sleep in hot rooms (over 72 degrees). Suspect overheating if your infant seems uncomfortable, is flushed, feels hotter than expected, or is simply very fussy. If your baby has a fever, don't swaddle him until his illness passes.

✔ **Swaddle your baby carefully and properly.** Figure 12-1 shows the proper ways to swaddle a baby with a regular blanket or a special swaddling blanket. The main caution is to avoid swaddling so tightly that your baby is uncomfortable, has trouble breathing, or has trouble with blood flow to his hands and feet. (To double-check, squeeze his toe. The blood should flow back into it within a second after you release it. If not, the blanket's too tight.)

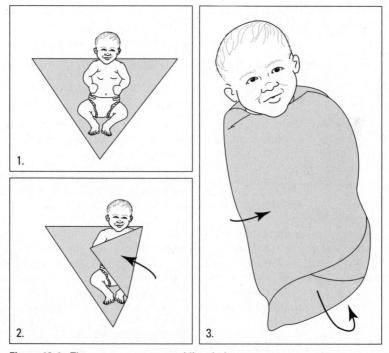

Figure 12-1: The proper way to swaddle a baby.

Dealing with an apnea monitor

Infants who leave the hospital earlier than five weeks before their due date often come home with an apnea monitor because their ability to remember to breathe in a reliable rhythm may not be fully developed. This deficiency can result in *apnea of prematurity,* a condition in which a baby breathes too shallowly or stops breathing altogether (different from *childhood* or *adult apnea,* which typically stems from structural obstructions to the airway.)

The beep of an apnea monitor can mean that Baby's breathing has stopped. However, it can also mean that the machine is malfunctioning (for instance, if a lead comes loose). When you respond to one false alarm after another, you may feel like throwing the machine out the window!

Apnea monitors can drive you crazy because they're prone to false alarms, but medical professionals have good reasons for recommending these monitors in certain situations. For example, your baby may need a monitor:

- ✓ If she comes home before she develops a highly reliable rhythm of breathing. The ability to breathe regularly all the time usually develops after five weeks before due date, and it's even more likely to be in place by three weeks before due date.

- ✓ If she has an abnormal windpipe or has a tube in her airway.

- ✓ If she's already experienced an event in which she stopped breathing for too long a time, threatening her safety.

- ✓ If she had severe breathing troubles in the hospital, requiring enough ventilatory support that her lungs developed scars and she now requires extra oxygen at home.

- ✓ If she has any additional medical condition that impairs her ability to breathe — for instance a neurological condition (from bleeding in the brain) or weakness (from difficulty in growing).

 Apnea monitors are designed to let caregivers know when a baby stops breathing. As it turns out, this is not the same as preventing SIDS. In 2003, the American Academy of Pediatrics reviewed studies on monitors and found that home monitors do not reliably prevent SIDS, suggesting that SIDS really is a different problem than the *forgetting* to breathe that occurs in very premature infants. So apnea monitors can be lifesavers for babies who don't have good breathing rhythms yet, but they're not helpful in preventing the different problem of SIDS.

If you and your doctor decide that a monitor makes sense, be sure the doctor prescribes a good model; this choice can reduce the number of false alarms you experience — without creating a risk of missing real ones. Your doctor can probably identify which monitors in your area are best. All good models also have the capability to record data each time the alarm goes off, so your doctor can analyze what's going on.

Adjusting Your Life to Accommodate a Preterm Baby

When your sweetie arrives early, the biggest challenge by far is the risk or reality of serious illness. If you avoid or overcome this danger, your baby's homecoming is a joyous occasion. Coming home is a dramatic sign that your baby, although premature, now is strong, healthy, and mature enough to thrive without all the supports of the hospital — and that's great news!

At the same time, coming home after a premature delivery puts a lot of pressure on you. You're waving goodbye to the hospital and its team of nurses and doctors — with its endless stream of tests and interventions — and replacing them all with little ol' you. Of course, the medical system stands by ready to help, but from this point on, you're in charge. That's why you need to have a good handle on what to expect as the next few weeks and months pass.

Watching your baby develop

Ever watch a science-class film of a flower blossoming? When the frames ran in real time, the flower didn't seem to budge. But time-lapse photography showed the bud steadily unfurling and the petals reaching out and opening up to the sun.

Watching your preterm baby grow and change is similar to watching that flower. His progress can sometimes seem slow, but in reality he's changing remarkably — inside and out.

If you feel frustrated when you see full-term babies gaining weight and hitting milestones earlier, stop and remember that your baby needs to devote much more effort to his internal functions. As a result, he often appears to be hovering at each developmental stage. For example, full-term infants often gain weight rapidly every day, starting at 3 to 4 days of age. Premature infants, on the other hand, frequently hover at one weight for a week or so before experiencing a burst of rapid growth. In the long run, however, healthy premature infants catch up to their peers — so patience pays off.

Both term and preterm infants grow; it just takes a premature baby a bit longer to do so. This hovering also means that he'll hit plateaus in his sleep development — so think in tiny steps if you're going to get your sweet-pea to sleep through the night.

Combating sleep difficulties in the early days

At the beginning of this chapter we look at how prematurity affects the life of an early bird and her family. Now we turn our attention to that big question: What can you do about sleep?

The first step in getting your little huggy-bear to sleep for longer stretches is simple: Sit back and wait till she's ready.

At a minimum, count on being up every few hours for the first four months *plus* the number of weeks your sweetie arrived early. During this time, she may need to eat as often as every 1 ½ to 2 hours. Her body has two jobs at this point — growing and eating. Sleep will follow later, when she can go for longer stretches without topping off her tank.

But while your little angel's busy growing up and filling out, you need to play the waiting game. At some point, your patience starts to pay off — you spot these signs that your darling is ready to switch from catnaps to real snoozes:

  ✔ Her medical issues are under control.

  ✔ She consistently puts on weight.

  ✔ She goes for longer stretches between feedings.

These visible signs mean that a big change is happening on the inside: Your little cupcake's sleep pattern is maturing. She's spending less time in immature active sleep and more time in quiet sleep (for a refresher on these terms, see "Growing into a sleep pattern" in this chapter). This maturation shifts her toward snoozing more deeply at night and becoming more alert during the day.

After these changes occur (about four months after her original due date, not her arrival date), you can follow the steps in Chapter 4 for reducing one feeding at a time to get your baby to sleep through the night. From that point on, simply follow the same drill we outline for full-termers. All systems go — full speed ahead!

Chapter 13

Sneezes, Sniffles, Aches, and Pains

• •

In This Chapter

▶ Adjusting the sleep routine when a minor illness strikes

▶ Wising up to the side effects of medicine

▶ Finding the best sleep solutions for long-term health issues

▶ Facing unique challenges: Snoring and sleep apnea

• •

*I*t's an all-too-common scenario: You work so hard to build an ideal sleep routine, and then along comes an illness — one of the top culprits for throwing a sleep schedule off-kilter. When you don't feel good, you don't sleep well, and that goes double for babies and toddlers. No one's more miserable at night than a stuffy-nosed infant, a tot with diaper rash, or a preschooler with an ear infection. (If you ever suffered an ear infection as an adult, you probably have deep sympathy for the young ones who get them all the time!) Worse yet, the whole family suffers when a tyke is sick or hurting because kids firmly believe in sharing their misery.

So what *do* you do when your little cherub wakes up in the middle of the night with a fever or your 2-year-old has an itchy throat? In this chapter, we describe the steps you can take to ease your sweetie into slumber when a bug, itch, or ouch is barring the door to Sleepyland. We also explain how some medications can keep your little one wide-awake (or conk her out) so you know which ones to give when, and we help you get your child back on track following an illness. Finally, we look at the special sleep issues of tots with long-term medical problems and sleep disturbances.

Coping with Garden-Variety Bugs and Ouches

Newborns are lucky when it comes to germs because the antibodies they pick up from Mom before birth protect them against many common bugs. But older babies and toddlers, just like grownups, get colds, the flu, and other icky stuff. In fact, kids just starting in preschool or day care are big targets for illness because a building chock-full of little tykes with dirty hands and runny noses is sheer heaven for germs.

However, viruses and bacteria aren't the only culprits that can keep your baby or toddler awake. There's also colic that comes from acid reflux or allergies (we cover this in Chapter 4) and vaccine reactions that can chase sweet dreams away. And then there's the irritation of diaper rash — one of the most-common occupational hazards of babyhood.

Any of these villains can easily derail a night's rest because a person normally cycles from deep sleep to near-waking and back. It doesn't take much to jar adults or babies from a light sleep; any little itch or pain can do the trick. (For a refresher on sleep cycles, check back to Chapter 2.)

Letting go of the schedule (temporarily)

The microscopic battle that's raging inside your sick cherub takes lots of energy, making her too wiped out to run around or digest food. That's why she drags through the day and picks at her dinner. And her stuffy nose, achy joints, and tummy woes intrude on her sleep at night, waking her up every few hours. Even when these symptoms quiet down, the inner war that her cells are waging can throw off her usual sleep patterns and make it hard for her to fall asleep and stay asleep.

When acute illness throws your child's sleep routine out the window, you need to suspend the sleepy-time rules and make healing your top priority. Allow your child to sleep when she wants, even during the day, and go to her any time she calls for you.

When the illness is over, resume your routine as soon as possible. Letting your child remain off-schedule much after the illness passes means you have more work getting her to resume the routine later. (For info on timing, see the "Resuming the routine" section later in this chapter.)

A mother's protection lasts and lasts

Newborns have a whopping advantage over older babies and toddlers during cold-and-flu season. For the first four to six months, they're shielded against many common illnesses by the antibodies passed on by Mom's body during pregnancy, and breastfeeding also offers some protection.

If Mom had a particular strain of cold virus last year, for example, Baby is safe from getting the same bug until around the 6-month mark. Ditto if Mom had chickenpox. So babies younger than 6 months tend to have no more colds or other viruses than their mothers, and often they have none at all. Some of this protection lingers for years, which is why illnesses such as chickenpox are milder in younger children and more severe for adults.

Caring for a sick, sleepy child: Comfort is key

Most common childhood illnesses are brief, harmless infections caused by one type of germ in particular: the virus. Of course, these illnesses don't seem harmless when your normally bright-eyed sweetie is sick as a dog, and they don't seem brief when he's runny-nosed and mopey for one to two weeks at a stretch. But these common bugs are no big deal, and before you know it, the symptoms are just a memory.

That quick turnaround is important because doctors don't have medicines to kill the viruses that cause common colds and stomach flu. Antibiotics, for instance, don't work because they don't kill viruses.

In the absence of a cure, the best remedy is to offer comfort. But what *is* comforting to a dribbly-nosed, coughing, feverish, or poopy little one? Here's our suggestion: Whatever works for your tot, whether it seems comforting to *you* or not. So if a humidifier makes you feel great when you have a cold, but it makes your child miserable, don't use it for him. If you love being propped up with lots of pillows when you're coughing but your child doesn't, don't do it. You get the idea.

Your sweetie will need the most comforting after sundown because his levels of cortisol (a natural comforter — see the sidebar "The cortisol connection" later in this chapter) drop after dark. As a result, all those aches and pains rev up, making him absolutely miserable, and you'll notice that he needs extra reassurance in the evening and the middle of the night.

Recognizing when to call for help

If your tot develops an illness, make sure it's not serious. Call your pediatrician or go to the emergency room if your baby or toddler:

✔ Is under 3 months old and has a temperature above 100.6 degrees

✔ Has trouble breathing

✔ Looks very ill

✔ Isn't eating enough to stay alert

✔ Seems limp

✔ Is in pain

✔ Has a very high fever — or, if she's under 3 months old, any fever

✔ Has a fever for more than two days

✔ Isn't producing a normal amount of urine

If you have any doubts at all, err on the side of caution and call the doctor. Also, if an ear infection has your tot howling in pain, ask your pediatrician for advice on treating it.

Using medicines and ointments to ease the discomfort

When your sweetie is droopy, you want to help — right now! To soothe his woes and help him sleep soundly, you may be tempted to reach for a cough syrup, fever medicine, or other over-the-counter remedy.

In reality, however, there's no magic pill for a cold or flu bug (remember that prescription antibiotics don't kill viruses either). The body's cells simply need time to win the battle against the bugs. Even after they do win, the resulting inflammation is much like a real burn — it takes a few days to heal. And no medication makes that healing any faster.

Fever reducers

A fever is one of the most common symptoms that make tots miserable during an acute infection. And the higher the fever, the more miserable your tot feels. *Note:* Fever itself is strangely harmless, but people often associate high fevers with danger (probably because everyone just feels far more miserable at 104 degrees than at 99). But the normal range for childhood fever is 100.6 to 105.8 degrees.

Fever isn't a concern as long as signs of more serious infection don't occur. What tells you if a more serious infection is present? See the nearby sidebar "Recognizing when to call for help" for important guidance on this question.

Fever is about the only problem that drugs *can* effectively treat when a garden-variety virus strikes. And because calming the fever can effectively reduce your tot's suffering, it's one of the best ways to help your acutely-ill infant or toddler get a little sleep at night.

Acetaminophen and *ibuprofen* are the best drugs to treat fever. These medicines only comfort your child — they can't cure him. So if your love-bug hates these medicines and refuses to take them, let him decide what's comforting; don't force him to comply. (Putting your foot down is necessary only for drugs that can *cure* — like antibiotics for bacterial infections — not for those that merely relieve symptoms.)

When giving your child acetaminophen or ibuprofen, give the right dosage. Too much of either med can be very toxic, so be sure to call your pediatrician for dosage guidance if you have any questions.

One common cause of fever is a reaction to vaccines, which can often result in a night or two of lost sleep. Today's vaccines are more pure than in earlier years, but some children still experience fever and aches that can interfere with a good night's rest. Live vaccines (measles, chickenpox, and flu) can cause symptoms for days, even a week or two. To comfort a child with a vaccine reaction, follow the drill for colds and other viruses that we outline in the following sections — the same measures help in either case.

Cold and cough meds

Of course, your grocery store shelves offer a host of over-the-counter cold and cough remedies that are longtime favorites. In fact, a recent study found that each month a third of all children in the United States under 3 years of age receive these medications.

Because parents are so accustomed to using these drugs, they're surprised to hear many experts don't think the meds pass muster on effectiveness or safety. The American College of Chest Physicians, for example, recommends that you don't use over-the-counter cough and cold drugs for kids because they don't do much good and can actually do harm, especially in young children.

Drugs can't cure viruses, so the best medicine is the low-tech kind: holding, cuddling, and distracting. Sitting or lying down with your little one is a powerful comforter. (Maybe your own parents relieved your suffering during those achy nights with that brand of medicine!) Distractions can include humming, singing, massaging, reading, or watching a favorite video. Together, these gentle moments can help soothe even the achiest child into a stretch of comforting sleep.

Petroleum jelly and soothing ointments

Infections aren't the only bad guys who disrupt your tot's sleep. Another common culprit for the not-yet-toilet-trained crowd is diaper rash. A widespread or very raw rash is (if you'll pardon the expression) a big pain in the rear — and every wiggle or turn during the night can make it burn like fire.

The best cure for diaper rash is a simple one: big globs of good, old-fashioned petroleum jelly. You can use more expensive diaper rash ointments as well, but they don't work any better.

If petroleum jelly or ointment doesn't work, leave your baby's diaper off and let him air dry. (Put plastic sheets under his bed sheets.) If the diaper rash looks at all serious, have your child's pediatrician check it out to make sure it's not turning into an infection.

Holistic methods

In addition to medications and other comfort steps, moms and dads use a wide range of holistic, alternative, herbal, or traditional substances to provide relief when colds or flu strike. Many of these (good old-fashioned chicken soup to clear a stuffy nose or yogurt to restore good digestive balance after a bout of the flu) can make a tot feel much better. Others — for example, some traditional folk remedies that contain high levels of lead — can be very harmful.

Rather than list all the possible holistic or folk treatments (there are hundreds, if not thousands!), we recommend that anything you try passes two simple tests:

1. **It works.**
2. **It causes no harm.**

In fact, we recommend that you apply these same simple tests to all treatments (holistic, alternative, herbal, and traditional), to all medications, and even to your methods of comforting.

In the case of colds or flu, set the bar pretty high for safety's sake. These illnesses are minor and pass quickly, so you don't really need to treat them at all. (Any benefit from a treatment is only minor and temporary, so why take even a tiny risk with one?)

Inflammation: The hero that looks like a villain

When germs invade your child's body, her tissues react by calling up an army of warrior cells to do battle. The result is inflammation: swelling, fever, pain, tenderness, a Rudolf-the-red-nosed-reindeer nose, and that extra mucus that makes her sound like she has a clothespin on her nose.

Inflammation can sound (and *feel!*) like a very bad symptom, but it has the very important task of killing bad germs. In fact, inflammation is a person's best line of defense against viruses. Although doctors can treat many *bacterial* infections with antibiotics, the body needs to rely on its own immune systems for *viruses*. The fevers, sweats, chills, sniffles, aches, and pains that your child suffers are no fun, but they're a clear sign that her cells are working hard to get her back in the pink of health.

Unfortunately, inflammation has its drawbacks. As we explain earlier, even when it does its job right, inflammation causes nasty symptoms. And if it goes wrong and starts attacking the body's own cells, it can cause a host of auto-immune diseases like asthma, arthritis, lupus, or Crohn's disease.

How can you tell whether a holistic treatment (or any treatment, for that matter) is safe? One good way is via very trustworthy sites on the Internet. We recommend the American Academy of Pediatrics (AAP) Web site at www.aap.org/sections/chim/. The AAP offers a Provisional Section on Complementary, Holistic, and Integrative Medicine and has extensive links to other very trustworthy sites.

Two words of caution:

- ✔ **Avoid any site that's trying to sell a product unless you know the company is unusually honest.** These companies usually offer biased (and sometimes very unreliable) information.

- ✔ **If you use an alternative treatment, be sure to tell your child's doctor about it, especially if your child also takes medications.** Herbal remedies can interact with drugs in potentially dangerous ways in addition to causing their own side effects.

Non-medicinal comforting methods

What else can you do to ease your cherub's path to Dreamland? Here are some good ideas:

- ✔ **Prop him up.** The more upright he is, the better he'll breathe. If he's old enough to have pillows in bed, use two or three to raise his head. Just make sure he's comfortable, or he won't be able to snooze.

✔ **Keep the drinks coming.** Give him lots of liquids, which can clear congestion and ease a cough. If he has diarrhea, be sure he gets plenty to drink so he doesn't get dehydrated. Also, if your child is old enough to sip a hot beverage, remember the old standby, chicken soup, does a great job of soothing a stuffy nose and sore throat. Milk is okay if your child wants it — it makes saliva thicker but doesn't create extra mucus.

✔ **Try steam.** Although some kids sleep easier with a humidifier in the room, others don't. Try it to see whether it helps. The same goes for humidifier additives like eucalyptus oil: If you want to know whether they comfort, try them out. (If you do use a humidifier, give it a good cleansing every day.)

✔ **Try a safe rub.** If you use a chest rub, make sure it's one specially formulated for babies or toddlers and doesn't contain camphor, which can be dangerous. Ask your tot's opinion — some kids breathe easier with a rub, and others object strongly.

✔ **Try suction.** See whether removing the mucus from your tot's nose with a suction bulb helps him breathe better. This step works for some kids and not for others. However, even if it is effective, don't force it on a tot who hates it with a passion — which many do.

✔ **Let your child sleep with you (or vice-versa).** Nothing is more comforting to a child than the presence of Mom or Dad, so if you're up for it, consider letting your child snooze alongside you.

Follow your child's lead because comfort measures are only as good as the comfort they provide (and he's the expert on that topic). Do whatever works, but steer clear of cough and cold meds if you can. Remember that hugs and cuddles trump any medical treatment.

Resuming your routine

If your tot is over 6 months old and was sleeping through the night before her illness, get her right back on track — the less delay, the better. Be on the lookout for the end of the illness so you know when to shift back to your sleep routines. Some of the signs include:

✔ Fever is gone.

✔ Other symptoms of illness are gone or so minor that they don't bother your tot.

✔ Energy level is back to normal or near normal.

✔ Appetite bounces back.

The cortisol connection

When people battle a bug, they almost always hit rock bottom at nighttime. Why? Blame *cortisol,* a natural body chemical.

Cortisol is a powerful steroid, a hormone that's also a powerful anti-inflammatory (think *natural aspirin*). Your body makes cortisol all the time, but it cranks out more in the morning, peaking around 8 a.m. Cortisol levels drop in the evening and at night.

At full strength, cortisol can help fevers, aches, pains, and drippy noses; even runny poops clear up. This improvement often leads Mom or Dad to say, "Oh, good — you're all better now!" But all those symptoms return with a vengeance when the sun goes down and cortisol levels plummet. The drop explains why, at midnight, your poor little tyke feels like something the cat dragged in.

However, don't assume that your tot's on the same page as you. In fact, expect a few sleepless nights when she recovers. She's enjoyed your company so much that now she misses you — and hopes you'll forget that silly old rule about sleeping through the night! So she's likely to come padding into your bedroom at 3 a.m. or call for you in the night.

Don't be surprised if this happens, and don't get mad. After all, this plan makes perfect sense from a young child's point of view (if something wonderful happened the last time you called out, you'd be nuts not to try it again!). The key to success is realizing that your child may *want* you, but she doesn't really *need* you at night any more. (Yep, it's that want-versus-need issue again — see Chapter 3 for more on this.)

If your sweetie slept peacefully before illness struck, it was because she comforted herself back to sleep — probably thanks to hard work on your part! She also knew that you wouldn't come hopping every time she peeped. Her illness, however, created a new expectation: Mommy or Daddy is on call all night, so I don't need to get myself back to sleep. To get her back in the groove, you need to change that expectation. In Chapter 5, we explain just how to do that so everyone can sleep snugly again.

We strongly recommend standing firm — well, actually, lying firm if you're in bed! — when your tot summons you at this stage. Even if *you* rationalize that you're just checking or taking a peek, *she* knows that you've come to see her and will sense victory. (If you need help following through on the no-peek plan, see Chapter 5 for advice. The techniques in that chapter work for older toddlers as well.)

When Meds Keep Your Tot Wide Awake — or Zonked Out

These days, there's a pill for everything. Even toddlers get their share of prescriptions — everything from antibiotics for strep throat to antacids for acid reflux.

These drugs can make kids feel a whole lot better, and most prescribed medications are very important. However, each one has a downside: side effects. In particular, many children's meds can ruin a night's sleep — or, conversely, drop your tot in his tracks like a tranquilized ape. This section gives you the lowdown on how prescription and over-the-counter meds can upset your child's sleep schedule and how you can counteract the problem.

All drugs have two names — a generic and a brand name. Most drugs are sold under a variety of brand names, but each one provides the generic name in the *Active Ingredients* section on its package. *Note:* In the following list, we provide *only* the generic names. Be sure you read the Active Ingredient list on the brand you choose to verify its generic drug name.

Drugs that make kids wired

Some (but not all) of the biggest culprits in making kids wacky are drugs that contain chemicals similar to your body's *adrenaline* (the chemical your body cranks out when you're under stress — say, if you're being chased by a bear). Adrenaline makes your heart beat faster, raises your blood pressure, increases your blood sugar, and gets your muscles ready to run.

What happens when your child takes a medication containing an adrenaline-like chemical? Pretty much the same thing. So don't be surprised when your child turns into a human tornado, sometimes for hours.

Here are the most common drugs that make kids wired — all but the last two are adrenaline-derived. Also note the tips on how to circumvent the problems they can cause:

 ✔ **Drugs for wheezing and asthma:** *Albuterol* is the biggest offender, but the longer-acting asthma meds (for example *salmeterol* and *pirbuterol*) can jazz up your child and block sleep for hours. *Note:* These drugs are crucial for kids with asthma, so don't stop giving them!

Inhaled steroids for asthma like inhaled *fluticasone* and *budenoside* don't appear to interfere with sleep and can sharply reduce the need for albuterol-like drugs.

Solution: If your child is using a lot of the adrenaline-like asthma drugs and not inhaled steroids, ask your pediatrician whether inhaled steroids are an appropriate alternative. For many children, inhaled steroids cut down on the need for albuterol-like drugs and can aid sleep. If this switch isn't possible, ask about other choices for the albuterol-like medicines. One form, *levalbuterol,* seems to have less chance of causing agitation or interfering with sleep. Some pediatricians use *ipratropium,* which also has less chance of bothering sleep.

✔ ***Phenylephrine* (the ingredient in over-the-counter decongestants):** This drug shrinks blood vessels, and less blood supply to the nose means less mucus. But that adrenaline rush also means you pay big time for a clear nose.

Solution: Stop using it. Over-the-counter cold remedies have little proven benefit.

✔ **Stimulant drugs for hyperactivity or attention problems:** This is usually a problem for older kids, but some preschoolers are taking *methylphenidate* or other stimulants that can quash sleep.

Solution: Never discontinue such medications without first talking with your pediatrician. Also, remember that sleeplessness is sometimes a temporary side effect that lasts only a week or two. If your tot's sleep loss is mild or tolerable, wait a few days to see whether the problem passes. If it doesn't, or if sleep problems are severe, talk to your pediatrician about adjusting the dosage or selecting an alternative medication.

✔ ***Amoxicillin* and oral steroids:** These meds can put the kibosh on sleep.

Solution: Check with your doctor if the med is turning your tot into a whirling dervish, but don't stop giving one of these drugs without consulting the doctor first. With luck, your pediatrician can offer other choices that are less stimulating.

✔ **Immunizations:** Shots can make kids hyper for a day or two.

Solution: Fortunately, the effect has a time limit, so just sit back and wait for the excitement to wear off.

Drugs that make kids snoozy

As you can guess, some drugs can knock your child out. Allergy and cold medicines head the list here.

✔ *Diphenhydramine:* This antihistamine is one of the most sedating medicines and is actually sold in another form as a sleeping pill. It can make a tyke drop like a KO'd boxer.

Solution: Newer antihistamines such as *loratadine, cetirizine,* and *fexofenadine* are designed not to make users groggy. If your tot needs allergy meds, talk to your doctor about these alternatives.

✔ *Dextromethorphan:* This is by far the most common cough suppressant in over-the-counter cold remedies. In fact, it's available under dozens of different names. Whatever its brand name, this drug also acts like nap-in-a-bottle for many toddlers.

Solution: Like other ingredients in over-the-counter cold and cough remedies, dextromethorphan has very limited proven benefits— so solve the drowsiness problem by discontinuing this med.

✔ *Ibuprofen:* This drug, along with *acetaminophen,* is the most common medication used to control fevers. You may be surprised to know it also makes some tots sleepy.

Solution: Think about using acetaminophen instead.

✔ *Trimethoprim/Sulfamethoxazole*: This antibiotic causes grogginess in rare cases.

Solution: If your child has this sleepy response, tell your pediatrician. The doctor can help you decide whether a different antibiotic is appropriate.

✔ Immunizations: Although shots make some kids hyper, they can knock the stuffing out of others for a day or two.

Solution: Unless your tot is so zonked that you can hardly rouse him, sleepiness is a normal side effect — and one that's worth the side effect. The protection that immunizations provide is critically important. If you think your child's reaction is extreme, however, call your pediatrician.

Sleep and Kids with Long-Term Health Issues

Colds and flu last just a few days, but other health problems can last for months or even a lifetime. If your child has one of these issues, you're not alone; tens of millions of children in the United States have long-term problems affecting their health or development. The most common are:

✔ Problems related to prematurity — for instance, breathing difficulties, developmental delays, or problems related to bleeding in the brain (we cover these in Chapter 12)

✔ Problems caused by a haywire immune system (the body's defenses revving up when they shouldn't) — for instance, the chronic inflammation of asthma, allergies, or eczema (a common skin problem in tots)

✔ Gene abnormalities — for example, sickle cell anemia, hemophilia, or metabolic disorders (disruptions to the body's chemical reactions)

✔ Problems affecting the brain — such as hyperactivity, autism, seizures, or cerebral palsy

In addition to the stress that long-term health problems add to your daily life and routine, they can make it tough for a tot to get a solid night's sleep. And because they're chronic, they can make getting a good night's rest a big challenge well into adulthood.

The good news is that you can take active steps to help your child sleep through the night, as we explain in this section. But first, because these obstacles may affect your youngster for the long haul, we explain *why* chronic illness can disturb slumber.

Understanding how long-term health issues affect sleep

Chronic medical problems are very different from a passing illness. By their nature, they're long-term or permanent, or they can recur regularly over many years. As a result, maintaining good sleep routines can be very tricky for everyone in the family. Here's why:

✔ Parents of tykes with health issues have lots of worries that sap their energy and make them toss and turn at night. Toddlers pick up on their parents' worry and tension, so your sleeplessness can be contagious.

✔ Tots worry too. Hospital visits, lab tests, and doctor's appointments can leave them with questions and fears — and those fears can lap over into the nighttime.

✔ Many medical problems cause pain or discomfort. Whether it's the itch of eczema, the wheezing of asthma, or an inability of a child with cerebral palsy to roll over and get comfy, health issues can keep your sweetie wide-awake.

✔ Typical sleep strategies don't always work for toddlers with impairments to their thinking, behavior, or language skills.

Knowledge is power!

The more you know about your child's health problem, the better you can cope and the more secure you'll be. Your increased confidence, in turn, helps reduce guilt and helps your child relax during the day and sleep better at night.

The first step in gaining control over your child's health issues is to turn to his doctor. Cultivate a strong relationship with a doctor who knows your child well and is committed to helping him. In addition, you need to trust her to

✔ Quarterback the team of specialists your child needs

✔ Arrange for special therapies

✔ Stay up-to-date on new developments involving your child's illness

✔ Give you the information you need in a way that makes sense to you

But don't stop there. You can find loads of information at your library or on reliable Internet sites. In particular, we recommend PubMed (www.ncbi.nlm.nih.gov/entrez/query.fcgi?DB=pubmed) sponsored by the National Library of Medicine; it gives you access to the latest medical literature on just about any topic.

Another great site is from the American Academy of Pediatrics (www.aap.org); it provides links to truly trustworthy sites for a variety of chronic conditions.

Tufts University also hosts a wonderful site (www.cfw.tufts.edu/topic/5/124.htm); it's full of great links on managing chronic illnesses in childhood.

You can also seek out support groups because moms and dads with hands-on experience are truly the best experts around. If there isn't a specific group for your child's problem, try contacting *Parent-to-Parent*, a wonderful group that has a chapter in nearly every state. You can get info on chapter locations at www.p2pusa.org.

Be sure that you and your child's doctor explore every treatment option. Any therapy that helps your child feel or communicate better also helps him sleep more snugly at night (or helps you figure out why he can't). Ask your doctor whether any of these approaches may be right for your child:

✔ Medications to treat the health problem

✔ Special services such as orthopedics or neurology consults

✔ Medical equipment like breathing treatments or braces

✔ Speech, physical, or occupational therapy

✔ Aquatic therapy or other exercise programs

Clearly, you can't just wave a magic wand and make these problems go away. But you can take steps to reduce both the emotional issues and the physical problems that rob you and your tot of sleep.

Reducing the effects of chronic illness on sleep

The word *chronic* means *long-lasting, always present,* or *habitual.* In other words, a chronic problem doesn't go away (at least not for a while). Nonetheless, you can often reduce the effects of your child's chronic problem on her sleep.

For example, if your child has asthma, you can toss out carpets and stuffed animals and wrap her mattress or pillow in plastic and a hypoallergenic cover. For tots with painful nerve and muscle problems, the right mattress and a new arrangement of pillows and bedding can make all the difference in the world. Kids who are hyperactive can benefit greatly from calming activities in the evening and soft music or white noise at bedtime; adjusting the type or timing of their meds can also reduce sleep problems.

To identify sleep problems you can address successfully, ask yourself these questions:

- ✔ **Is my child's disability related to this sleep problem?** Knowing how a medical issue affects sleep can suggest solutions. For instance, blind children often have trouble establishing a day/night schedule, so their parents use cues like music to mark the transition from light to dark. Their doctors sometimes prescribe *melatonin,* a sleep-inducing chemical.

- ✔ **Can medication, surgery, or other approaches solve the problem?** Talk to your child's doctor about these options. Most medical centers offer programs to help kids and adults deal with chronic pain, and sleep clinics can address other issues like apnea (See "Snoring and Sleep Apnea: Not Just Grownup Problems!" later in the chapter).

- ✔ **Can other parents help?** Check the Internet or ask parents at support groups. One good trick is to join Internet discussion groups where you can query other parents about your tot's problems (see the nearby sidebar "Knowledge is power!" for helpful links to get you started). Odds are you're not the first parent with these problems, and somebody else may have a bright idea for solving them.

- ✔ **Do any stores offer special equipment to help solve this problem?** It's amazing how many gadgets you can find for kids with sleep issues: special beds that can help prevent bedsores, blanket cradles for sensitive skin, ropes for toddlers to pull themselves out of bed, and so on. Ask your insurer what your plan covers.

✔ **Can my child's strengths compensate for her problems?**
A child with limited leg strength, for instance, can have leg pain as well — a problem that can make sleep elusive, especially if turning over in bed is tough. But the same child may have excellent upper-body strength. A good therapy team may be able to design a program that uses those strong arms to compensate for aching legs. The result: a better and longer night's sleep.

Physical therapists and occupational (daily living skills) therapists often have great advice. Be sure to ask your child's therapists for ideas and suggestions.

If your child has a developmental disability like autism or Down syndrome or she's hyperactive and can't settle down at bedtime, see whether her doctor or school can steer you to a specialist in *behavior modification*. These professionals have special tricks up their sleeves that can sometimes solve stubborn sleep issues, and they may come to your home to design a tailor-made plan.

Snoring and Sleep Apnea: Not Just Grownup Problems!

Most people think of snoring and *sleep apnea* (when breathing stops long enough to cause problems) as grownup problems, but they sometimes affect little people as well. That's why you need to know the difference between harmless, run-of-the-mill snoring and the more serious problem of sleep apnea — you can ignore the former, but you need to handle the latter.

Snoring

Snoring occurs when the soft tissues at the back of your throat touch the throat when you breathe. Anything that brings these tissues together can cause snoring noises. Common culprits include: anything that leaves those tissues swollen (like colds and allergies); being overweight; or a mouth structure that brings these tissues very close to each other.

Snoring isn't the same as sleep apnea (see the following section), but it can sometimes be a *symptom* of it. About 10 percent of all kids snore, but only 10 to 20 percent of these snorers have sleep apnea. If a snoring child's oxygen levels don't drop, he doesn't have sleep apnea and you have no need to worry.

The only way to be sure whether it's snoring or apnea is to measure oxygen levels during sleep with a simple device that snugs onto a person's finger or toe. ***Note:*** Only a sleep lab can do this reliably.

If your tot's snoring is fairly quiet and he seems very comfortable (he's not thrashing around like he's hungry for air), then the snoring is probably just that — a mild noise that's not of much concern.

Sleep apnea

If your tot suffers from sleep apnea, she has abnormally long pauses in breathing. The biggest concern is that her oxygen supply drops to unhealthy levels. Here are potential warning signs of sleep apnea:

- ✔ **Distressed snoring:** These are red flags:

  - **Very loud snoring:** Your tot wakes everyone in the house, and people think a bear has gotten into her bedroom!

  - **Snoring every night:** Mild snoring doesn't usually occur this often.

  - **Snoring in every position:** Mild snoring usually goes away if your tot rolls over one way or the other.

  - **Thrashing during snoring:** A child with sleep apnea may toss and turn violently and look as if she's hungry for air.

  - **Snoring that wakes up your child:** Regular snoring doesn't usually do this.

- ✔ **New or reactivated bedwetting:** This condition can happen with or without snoring, but it raises concern when it has no other explanation. Sleep apnea can actually increase urine production.

- ✔ **Sleep shortage:** If your sweetie drags around like an over-partied teenager, acting moody and irritable, it can be a sign of sleep apnea.

- ✔ **Attention deficit:** A surprising percentage of kids diagnosed with attention deficit/hyperactivity disorder actually have sleep apnea (at least 5 percent). If your toddler seems hyperactive and has snoring or sleep deficiencies, consider sleep apnea as the source.

- ✔ **Slowed growth:** Sleep apnea can actually slow a tot's growth and leave her shorter than she would have been. This effect takes years to notice, so don't wait to see this effect.

Most sleep apnea stems from the lymph nodes in the back of the throat getting too big. (Think swollen glands, but inside the neck; the glands on the sides of the throat are *tonsils,* and the glands just above the roof of the mouth are *adenoids.*) When these nodes get too big, they obstruct breathing when your tot sleeps — a problem called *obstructive sleep apnea syndrome* (OSAS).

If your child has enough symptoms to concern you, ask your pediatrician to check for sleep apnea. Doctors can treat this problem with several methods that may include nasal steroids (nose spray) and, if needed, surgery to remove the tonsils and adenoids.

Chapter 14

When Life Changes Keep Your Child Awake

Kids thrive on consistency — the sandwich you cut exactly the same way each time, the book you read so many times that its pages are tattered. Parents often discover the hard way that disrupting these *little* routines can result in chaos, so imagine how upsetting a truly *big* change is to your tyke! Count on an earth-shaking event to affect every part of his life, including sleepy-time.

Big changes can chase away a child's sweet dreams and replace them with bedtime squabbles and middle-of-the-night awakenings. But even anticipated events such as a vacation or a birthday can torpedo some little ones. In this chapter, we look at why life changes affect tots even more than grownups and offer some words of wisdom on handling the big and little changes that can stop sleep in its tracks.

Understanding Your Youngster's Stress Over Change

As your child grows up, you're likely to discover that she handled change better when she was a baby. When separation anxiety enters the picture (see Chapter 6), changes get trickier because they often involve partings. But they really get interesting when she's 2 ½ to 3 years old.

From your 2- to 3-year old's point of view, everything revolves around her. As a natural outgrowth, she believes that she *causes* everything that happens to her or her loved ones. For example, if the babysitter leaves for a new job or a sibling breaks a leg, your little one is likely to think it happened because of something she did, said, thought, or wished.

Experts call this concept *magical thinking,* and it contains so little adult logic that parents often underestimate its power. But in reality, this irrational (although perfectly age-appropriate) thinking is often the underpinning of a tot's peculiar behavior.

Self-centered thoughts can play a big role in how your child deals with a difficult issue like divorce or illness. If your tot believes she's the cause of an upsetting or confusing event, her feelings can be so intense that she can't calm down at bedtime or sleep through the night.

Good changes (like vacations) and neutral changes (like time zones) can also cause routines to jump off track. Anticipation and excitement can keep anyone awake, but they're an especially potent mix for tots who can't really talk out their feelings.

The bottom line is that expected and unexpected changes — whether they're life-changing (like a divorce) or simply fun (like a vacation) — can turn your angel's world topsy-turvy. And for sensitive tots, even a birthday party can be cause for a meltdown.

Common Life-Changes Most Children Face

Any life change that breaks routines, adjusts settings, or brings new people into your toddler's world can knock the sleep train off its tracks. To keep your child on track, prepare him by

✔ **Talking the situation over.** You can explain something really big (like Mom and Dad separating) more formally and a less-earthshaking change less formally. For instance, if you're planning a move and you pass a moving van on the street, say casually, "Soon the van will come to our house, and that's how your toys and bed will get to the new house." Then follow up later with a detailed discussion.

Children need to hear info again and again. Bring the topic up when it's appropriate by looking and listening for clues your child gives you. One obvious clue can be sleep problems, and one good solution is to bring up the topic up during your

bedtime ritual. For instance, if you're divorcing, reassure your tot that you understand that he's confused and sad *but* that Mom and Dad love him and will always be there to keep him safe.

✔ **Creating visual aids.** Use homemade books, calendars, and parallel stories to help give your child a concrete idea about the changes. These techniques are simple and sure hits with the toddler set:

- **Homemade books:** Libraries offer books designed to help children through difficult situations, but nothing works better than a book that you create just for your child. The book can help explain big issues like a divorce or serious illness or little issues like vacations and moving to a big bed. Follow these suggestions:

  In a photo album, illustrate the change with photographs or even pictures from magazines or the Internet.

  Write important words on index cards and slip them into place. *Note:* These words are important because you want everyone who reads the book with your tot to give the same message.

  The book can be short — a few pages — but make sure it includes info about your sweetie's feelings. For instance: "Joey will miss Mommy and Daddy when they are away and they will miss Joey, but they will come back." (Turn back to Chapter 10 for more details on homemade books and an illustration of one.)

  Bind the pages with electrical tape so little hands can't take the book apart.

- **Parallel stories:** These *social stories* are a wonderful way to talk about events and feelings as if you're talking about someone else (like changing the names to protect the innocent!). Make up a name (keep the sex and the age the same as your star), or use a real person that your child knows, or even use yourself. For instance, if you want to prepare your babe for a move, start with, "When I was 3, my family moved to a new house. I was afraid my toys wouldn't get packed and that I couldn't find my room!"

  Calendars: Children in this stage are getting a sense of time, so a calendar helps them get a better grip. Use your calendar as a countdown ("This many days until your birthday party") or to clarify his schedule ("This is a day Mommy picks you up; this is a Daddy day").

In the following sections, we look at two of the most common of exciting life events — a move to a new house and a vacation — and help you minimize their damage to your tot's bedtime routine.

It's moving day!

If you're planning a move (especially if it's to a bigger and better house), you probably expect your little dumpling to be thrilled when you tell her, "You're getting your own room!" or "Our new place has a great big yard." But adult logic is often lost on a child. So the move that has *you* all excited can have *her* up at night, worrying or clinging to you tearfully.

To make the move to your new digs easier, follow that all-important rule: Tell your sweetie all about it every step of the way. Let her know when you start house-hunting and give her a tour of the new place as soon as you know it's yours.

Before and during the move

Here are some other tips that can make moving day and those first few nights in a new home more fun and less stressful:

- ✔ **Break out the camera.** Put pictures of your old house in an album or use them for your homemade book about the move. After you move, put pictures of the new house opposite pictures of your former place. If you're moving too far away to regularly see your old friends and neighbors, put their pictures in the album, too. That way, your tot doesn't think they just disappeared.

- ✔ **Ask your tot to pitch in.** Even an 18-month-old can put some toys into a box. As she's packing her treasures, reassure her that all of them — and her pets and siblings! — are going to the new house. If she needs new bedroom items, let her help pick out sheets, comforters, and so on.

- ✔ **Let your sweetie watch on Moving Day.** It's tempting to outsource your child on this hectic day, but at the very least, let her see a few boxes or pieces of furniture go into the van. This transition helps her understand that her possessions don't just vanish, only to reappear somewhere else.

- ✔ **Have the movers pack your child's stuff last.** "Last in, first out" is a good motto in this situation. If your child's furniture and toys are the last items to go in the truck, then they can be the first in your new home. This plan allows you to get her room in order before bedtime. She'll sleep much better if her crib or bed is all set up and she's not surrounded by a confusion of boxes and cries of "Where are the pajamas?"

- ✔ **Stay close.** If a move takes several days and involves complicated travel arrangements, keep your child with you. A separation at this time only adds to daytime behavior problems and nighttime upsets later on. Too busy to watch your sweetie while you're handling last-minute details? See whether Grandma or the babysitter can come along.

✔ **Postpone the crib-to-bed switch if you haven't already made it.** Let your sweetie adjust to one big change at a time. If it's time for the crib to go, wait until a few weeks after the move.

After the move

No matter how smoothly your move goes, expect a few sleepless nights when you first arrive. Here are a few of the reasons and their possible solutions:

✔ **Look and listen from your little one's point of view.** A new house means new shadows, new noises, and an unfamiliar floor plan. Kids can wake up and not get back to sleep because of their still-strange surroundings. Two suggestions:

- Place nightlights and furniture where they cast few shadows and can't put on a scary light show.

- Spend a little time walking your child between her room and other parts of the house so she gets the feel of her new digs.

✔ **Expect some plaintive calls at first.** Even the best sleepers can have trouble settling down due to the excitement of the move and the newness of their rooms. For a week or two (at the most!), go in to reassure your child. After that, re-establish your standard nighttime routine.

✔ **Anticipate a midnight visitor.** Even if your little one goes willingly at first, she may find her way into your bedroom later on. If she does, keep your ultimate goal in mind:

- Allowing her to sleep in your bedroom gives her the A-OK to a new arrangement.

- Walking her back into her room — every time she comes out — tells her you want her in her own room.

  Be reassuring but firm, and let your gut guide you. If she really seems scared, you may want to sit nearby until she nods off. ***Note:*** After a few days, wean her from this expectation or you may be sitting in her room until she leaves for college! Wean her slowly by moving your chair closer to the door and then into the hallway. Or go cold turkey when you feel she's *wanting*, not *needing* you.

✔ **Seize the moment.** If your child wasn't getting to sleep on her own in the old house, a move may provide the perfect opportunity for you to establish a new routine. If so, make sure that you're in the new house for at least two weeks and have a semblance of organization before you start a routine to help your tyke get herself to sleep (see Chapter 5 on getting a bed-time routine going).

✔ **Expect the unexpected.** The exciting news "You're getting your own room!" isn't so great when it becomes a reality. Frequently kids find it harder than they expected to give up each other's company.

If your children balk at sleeping in separate rooms, start grad-ually by having them nap in their own rooms while sharing the same room at night. Usually they just need a little time to get used to the idea. (If they really don't like it, put them back together and presto! You have a new den!)

Traveling with (and without) your tot

You may remember wonderful vacations that left you relaxed, refreshed, and ready to take on your world. But add *parent* to your job title and you add a different kind of vacation experience. With or without your little bundle of joy, vacations have both their ups and downs.

If you bring your child along

Vacations with your child create a lifetime of memories. One day you may look fondly back at the picture of your tot looking adorable in his sunglasses and floppy hat, shaking hands with Mickey Mouse or watching Old Faithful blow. Of course, by then, you'll have forgotten all the horrible nights you spent crammed into a hotel room, listen-ing to your spouse snore and your tyke say, "I can't sleep." "When are we going to the lake tomorrow?" "I'm hungry!"

Those restless nights are part-and-parcel of the vacation experi-ence, so you can't totally avoid all the sleep chaos. However, here are a couple of ways to minimize the madness:

✔ **If your budget can handle it, spring for a hotel suite with a small kitchen and two or more rooms.** It'll give you extra pri-vacy, and the kitchen can help to keep meals on track (which in turn can keep sleep schedules smooth).

✔ **Avoid overdoing it.** You can always come back to the same vacation spot another year, so don't cram in too many activi-ties each day. Give your tyke plenty of time to unwind and just hang out; he'll be less likely to have a bedtime meltdown.

✔ **Factor your child's age into the equation.** Very young infants are actually the easiest to travel with, and they often sleep as soundly on the road as they do at home. Toddlers are typi-cally the worst travelers because they acutely feel changes and don't have the language to tell you what's worrying them. That means you have to do some extra preparation:

- Bring your babe's favorite transitional object with him. Your little tyke doesn't have a special lovie? Then be sure to bring his own sheets or blanket so he feels more secure. (This is a good idea for all kids.)

- Make a book about the trip (see our advice on making personalized books earlier in this chapter).

- Let him pack a few special items in a small backpack to take on the plane if you're flying.

- If he's still in a crib, try to get one at your hotel so he feels more at home.

- Try to keep his naps and bedtime on schedule. This goal may be impossible some days, but the more consistency the better. Babies can generally snooze anywhere, and older children can understand the special occasion, but those 2-year olds . . . they thrive on consistency.

✔ **Expect two or three off-schedule nights when you return.** It's normal, and it'll pass if you keep the bedtime rules consistent.

If you leave your child at home (or elsewhere)

A different situation arises when you go on a trip and your angel stays behind. It's a rare child who doesn't give Mom or Dad some payback for taking a kid-free vacation, but you can keep problems to a minimum if you follow these rules:

✔ **Set the stage for your goodbye.** Prepare your child ahead of time by telling him where you're going, who's taking care of him when you're gone, and when you'll be back. We strongly suggest creating a personalized picture book (see tips earlier in this chapter) that he can look at before and after you leave.

- The book should contain specific information about who will care for your child and where.

- A calendar showing when you'll return is especially helpful; have your sitter put it on the fridge and mark off the days until you come back.

✔ **Don't be afraid to call.** Sometimes the sitter says, "Don't call" because your tot gets upset after you hang up. True, but your little angel feels lots better knowing that you're OK, you're thinking about him, and you're coming back in a few days!

✔ **Make sure you say "Goodbye."** Slipping out while your sweetie's snoozing may seem easier, but this plan can leave him feeling scared and abandoned. Wake him up, even if it's just for a quick goodbye kiss.

✔ **Keep the home fires burning.** Whenever possible, have the sitter come to your home so your cherub is in his own environment. However, if your little one needs to move:

Explain to him where he's going (a personal book is handy for this — see our advice earlier in this chapter).

Give him a trial night or two before you leave to help him acclimate if your tyke is staying with someone in town.

Make the sleeping arrangements as close as possible to the way they are at home.

If your parents (or in-laws) have an old crib, it may not be up to current safety standards. For instance, it may have leaded paint or rails that are too close together. If you're not sure, it's safer to rent a new crib.

Parents often ask how long they can leave a young child. A good guide is one to two nights for every year of a child's age. So when your babe turns 1 year old, a weekend away is just about what he can handle.

Saving daylight time

One minor issue that causes headaches for just about everyone with kids is daylight savings time. Whether you're springing forward or falling back, changing the clocks — even by just an hour — can throw a young child's schedule completely out of whack. The problem of waking too early or getting to bed too late usually resolves itself in a couple of days, but here are some tricks you can use to hasten the process:

✔ Start manipulating your child's bedtime about two weeks before the clocks change. For instance, if your child's 7 a.m. wake-up call will change to 6 a.m. in the fall, try moving her bedtime up 15 minutes every three or four days until she goes down an hour before her usual bedtime.

In the spring, do the opposite.

✔ If you're trying to get a toddler to bed at 8 p.m. but it's not dark outside, try blackout shades for her room and the other rooms she uses right before bedtime. Start your bedtime routine in these darkened rooms so she'll associate the darkness with sleepytime.

✔ Aim for middle-of-the-day naps instead of later ones so they don't push back bedtime till the midnight hour.

If a stay-at-home parent returns to work

When a parent who's been home full-time returns to work, it changes a tot's life as well. Going back to work almost always involves a separation, so his bedtime (which is yet another separation) is especially likely to take a hit. In Chapter 11 we discuss the relationship between your sitter or child-care facilities and your tot's sleep. In this chapter, we focus on preparing your little one for the change.

For the under-6-months crowd

If you need to return to work shortly after your child's birth, the partings will be harder on you than on your baby. These suggestions can make them easier:

- **Choose wisely.** If you're confident in your choice of caregivers (see Chapter 11 for choosing just the right fit for your family), your baby can sense this and will probably develop sleep patterns just as if you were around him full-time.

- **Keep the connection close.** Send in a receiving blanket that's been close to your body so your baby has your scent nearby.

- **Come and visit.** If you work near your baby's child-care center or home, don't hesitate to stop in to feed or play with your baby. Building an attachment is all-important in these early months, so spend as much time together as you can. Don't worry about your little one making a scene when you leave — those are a few months away.

For the older baby or toddler

If your baby's 7 to 12 months old, you may deal with *stranger anxiety* (see Chapter 6); your angel's probably reacting with heartrending tears when you leave. But with preparation and time, even the most sensitive tot can adjust happily to a care situation. Here's how to help:

- Help your little one to get comfy with his caregiver. Bring your toddler to visit your caregiver before you return to work so you can make this stranger seem not-so-strange.

- Keep schedules consistent. By this time, you child has firm likes and dislikes and probably has a sleeping routine. Make sure your caregiver is aware of the details of putting Junior down for a nap.

A 2-year-old benefits from your telling him exactly what's going to happen and where he's going to be.

Dealing with Illness and Death

Think back to a time when you had a cold or the flu and you weren't quite yourself. Even if you told your child, "Everything's fine," she probably picked up on your sick vibes and fussed more than usual — just when you needed peace and quiet the most!

If someone close to your child is facing a major illness, expect this same reaction from your child — only more so. The upheaval that a serious illness causes in your household can rock your baby's world, and it's not uncommon for a tot to handle the situation just fine during the day and then fall apart at that sleepy-time separation.

Keeping your child in the loop

Many parents think (kindly, but incorrectly) that they should protect their kids by hiding big problems like illness. But even if you're an Oscar-winning actor, your baby or toddler has such a strong connection to you that you can't conceal your feelings from her. And those feelings are immediately felt by your children. *Note:* Children may not understand their parents' feelings for years, but they still feel them immediately.

In fact, hiding bad news from your child makes matters worse, not better. When you don't keep your child in the loop, her confusion and anxiety increase, making it that much harder for her to cope during the day and sleep well at night. And she's not going to miss all of these clues:

- ✔ Lots of doctor visits for the ill family member

- ✔ Long absences when a loved one is in the hospital

- ✔ Changes in your tot's schedule (for instance, if a different person picks her up from preschool)

- ✔ Special medical equipment around the house

- ✔ A change in the ill person's personality — depression, lack of energy, and so on

You can't expect your smart cookie to miss these signs and signals that something's up. She won't. So take steps to help her cope — for her own good and for yours. And keep in mind that much of your game plan depends on your child's age and ability to understand. Read on.

Maintaining normalcy for a baby or very young toddler

You can't really explain a complicated issue like illness to a baby or 1-year-old. However, you can help your tyke through this difficult time in two ways: First, realize that he knows something's wrong and be patient when he's extra-fussy or sleeps poorly; second, reassure him by keeping his routine as calm and normal as possible. Here's how:

- ✔ **Keep familiar faces around.** Friends and neighbors may offer to help out by babysitting during a crisis, but stick to your usual caregivers if you can. Also, if your child is happy in his day-care program, keep him there to help stabilize his life.

- ✔ **Spend as much time with your child as you can — even when you're the one who's sick.** If you're hospitalized, ask your doctor whether this is possible. If you're home, try to keep your little one close by, even if you can't help with his physical care. Simply singing or reading to him can keep the bond between you strong.

- ✔ **Keep your little one at home.** Although you may be tempted to send your tyke off to Grandma's until a rough patch passes, your child will feel more secure and keep his habits on target when he can sleep in his own crib on a regular schedule.

  If you can't care for him yourself, see whether Grandma (or another caregiver) can come to your house. Children separated from their parents for long periods during difficult times often develop sleep problems, and bedtime can be even more of a struggle after everyone's reunited.

Helping an older toddler or preschooler cope

An infant or very young toddler may just sense the feelings of the grownups in her life, but when your little one begins to use and understand language, a serious illness or death can have a greater impact on her; this child of 18 months or older *knows* something big is changing in her world. When this happens, she depends on the important adults in her life to guide her through the maze of confusing and unsettling emotions.

Explaining the situation

Now that your tot is old enough to have some language under her belt, you can take additional steps to help her adjust to the new reality of a loved one's illness. The most important step — and the hardest one — is telling her what's happening.

Stories from the crib: Feelings that make you go bump in the night

Two-year-old Ari wasn't at all sure he *loved* his new sister, Beth. She fussed and cried, and Mommy and Daddy said they couldn't take him to the park because it was too cold to take the baby out.

Ari wasn't happy — he wished that Beth had stayed at the hospital and not come home with Mommy. Then, one morning, Ari came downstairs for breakfast and found Grandma there. Grandma told him that Beth got sick in the middle of the night and Mommy and Daddy had to take her to the hospital.

That night, Ari couldn't fall asleep and Grandma had to sit in his room. Even when Mommy and Daddy brought a healthy Beth home a few days later, Ari couldn't go to asleep. In fact, he seemed terrified to be alone and literally clung to his parents when they tried to put him down.

Mom and Dad realized that Ari was reacting to his sister's illness and that he was worried that his jealous thoughts had harmed her. Dad sat down with Ari and told him a story: "Ari, when I was just about your age, Aunt Janey had to go to the hospital and, you know, I was really worried. Sometimes Aunt Janey made me mad and sometimes I wished I was still the only kid. So I worried that I was the reason she got sick and had to go the hospital.

"But do you know what my Mommy — your Grandma — told me? She said that *all* big brothers sometimes get mad at their baby sisters and that no matter how mad or angry I was, those feelings never, ever made someone sick."

Ari listened with wide eyes and open ears. That night, he fussed a little but seemed much less upset. Within a few days, his sleep schedule was back to normal.

When she knows the score, she can ask questions, get reassurance, and, as a result, spend less time worrying and more time sleeping. Because your child immediately feels what you do, your explanation can't create an emotional surprise. Instead, the explanation actually solves a troubling mystery. Now she knows what's wrong and can work with you to understand and adapt.

This conversation is very difficult because parents instinctively want to shield their children from hurtful and scary news (especially when they can't promise a happily-ever-after). But your toddler will be even more worried and afraid if she senses the shadow hanging over your household and doesn't understand the cause.

Here are some tips on approaching this sensitive topic:

✔ **Explain the word *sick*.** Most children past the 18-month mark have some experience with being sick. When you tell your tot that someone she loves is sick, help her see the difference between

- The kind of sick that gets better with pink medicine

- The kind of sick that lasts a long time and can make a loved one look or act very different

✔ **Let her know she's okay.** Your toddler may worry that she or other family members may be sick, too. Assure her that this isn't the case.

✔ **Tell her that experts are on the job.** Explain that the doctors are helping her loved one get better. If Grandma's in the hospital, simply say that sometimes it's easier to make a person feel better in the hospital, where there are lots of doctors and nurses to help.

✔ **Explain obvious changes.** For instance, if Daddy undergoes chemotherapy and loses his hair, you can say, "The medicine Daddy needs to get better is so strong that it made his hair fall out. But after he's done taking the medicine, his hair will grow back in." (And then assure your tot that her own medicine isn't that strong and that her hair will be okay.) Your sweetie will notice a lot (a sick person's new symptoms, the arrival of new medical equipment, and so on), but she may be too afraid to ask. Your simple, matter-of-fact comments can ease her mind about these changes.

✔ **Ward off guilt.** Kids this age can believe that their wishes or angry thoughts cause bad things to happen, and these sneaky feelings can wreak havoc with sleep. (Check back to "Understanding Your Youngster's Stress Over Change" for more on this magical thinking.) You probably know how hard it is to fall asleep if you think you're to blame for a family crisis — and it's even harder to handle those big feelings if you're tiny. For instance, little Abby may think that her brother got sick because she got mad at him for taking her toy. Or maybe she thinks Daddy had to go to the hospital because she got angry when Dad wouldn't give her ice cream for breakfast.

Make sure your child understands that her thoughts, wishes, or ideas did not and cannot cause illness. Parallel stories (more on these earlier in this chapter) are particularly helpful in letting your child know that she's off the hook, no matter how big and angry her feelings are.

Easing the anxiety

No matter how gently you deliver your message, expect your child to have some trouble dealing with the situation, especially if the person who's ill is Mom, Dad, Brother, or Sister. If your tot's in the throes of separation anxiety (see Chapter 6 for an explanation of this phenomenon), any kind of parting is hard. A parent's illness sends her anxiety levels sky-high, and the effects of parting each night at bedtime can be overwhelming.

Although it's a tough time for a tot, you can help your child over this obstacle:

- **Stick to familiar routines.** If your tot's in school or childcare, keep her there if you can. School staff members tend to be understanding about serious illnesses, so talk to them if you need to extend your child's day to meet your schedule demands. (Keeping your tot an extra hour longer at a place where she's happy and comfortable is better than making her learn the ropes at an unfamiliar place when she's already upset.)

  Do your best to follow normal bath-time and bedtime routines; this gives your child a sense of stability in the midst of chaos.

- **Carve out time for day-to-day needs.** Sometimes tots get lost in the shuffle when parents are overwhelmed by making treatment decisions, caring for a sick child or spouse, and handling financial and job worries all at the same time. Even though your own life is turned upside-down, try to find time to attend to your healthy child's needs — whether it's a new pair of shoes, a story time, or a trip to the playground.

- **Break the rules sometimes**. We usually praise *consistency,* but some days *comfort* needs to take top billing. For instance, if Mommy just got home from the hospital, your tyke may not want to say, "Goodnight" and go to her own room. If that happens, a shared bed (or cot or sleeping bag in your room) can feel like the Ritz to her.

- **Keep your family intact.** You may need to travel to another city for your spouse's or sick child's treatments. If possible, take all your children along. Many big-city hospitals have special apartments where an entire family can stay when one child needs an extended hospital stay. This arrangement can add to your workload, but it's less traumatic (and usually results in fewer long-term sleep issues) than leaving a child behind.

- **Use local and extended resources.** Many cities now have centers or organizations (for instance, the Wellness Community for families of cancer patients) that offer programs to help kids cope with illness affecting a family member. Also, most large hospitals have a child life worker who can offer advice on helping your child to make sense of a confusing time. Here are two good Web sites as well:

- www.bbc.co.uk/relationships/coping_with_ grief/bereavement_helpchildren.shtml

- www.cbn.com/family/parenting/OConnor_ ChildrenFear.aspx

If a loved one dies, most parents want to talk with their toddlers about it — but they worry about scaring their tots or causing some psychological harm. In reality, pretending that nothing happened is more harmful because this leaves the child feeling confused and helpless. So, where to begin?

- ✔ If a parent or sibling is ill with a serious disease, let your child know what's happening and what your little one can expect. If you know that the loved one has a terminal illness, you can begin to explain that Daddy is so sick that the doctor's can't make him better. Make it clear that this isn't the same as when your little one gets an ear infection.

- ✔ Don't be afraid to use the word *die*. Your child will hear it from people around her and should have some idea of its meaning.

- ✔ Avoid describing death as "just like going to sleep." Such analogies make the compared event terrifying. In this case, sleep becomes like dying, and such confusion can often cause severe sleep problems.

- ✔ Let your toddler know that when someone dies, the person doesn't talk or eat or sing or play. Explain that you can't see the person anymore but that you can look at the person's picture and remember the fun you had together.

- ✔ You can make a memory book with pictures of your tyke sharing good times with the person who died. Children love and need concrete reminders, and this book may become a favorite possession.

Children under 5 or 6 years of age see death as reversible. One day they seem to understand that Grandma died, but the next day they ask whether she's coming to their birthday party. Don't be surprised if a tot who doesn't grasp this concept jumps out of bed at the slightest sound in the hopes that her loved one is returning.

Also, expect (and allow) some regressive behavior. For instance, a child who's totally potty-trained may start wetting the bed at night. Be patient because this regression is normal and will pass as she adjusts to her loss.

The death of a close family member or friend is a terrible trauma, and your child will experience disturbed sleep for some time. At this point, your child's need for security and support takes precedence over independent sleep routines. So if she needs to co-sleep with you for a few months or camp out on your floor, let her do it. It'll probably be a comfort to you as well.

The Big Split: Divorce and Your Little One

Divorce isn't rare these days, and it doesn't carry the stigma it once did. Nevertheless, children still react strongly when it happens to their family.

Your child's self-centered thoughts (see "Understanding Your Youngster's Stress Over Change" earlier in this chapter) play a part in this reaction. He may wonder, "Was I so bad that it made Daddy want to leave?" or "If I wish hard enough, will Mommy and Daddy get back together again?" With these thoughts swirling through your little cub's head, it's no wonder the sandman often can't get a foot in the door.

Some general tips to start

If you're going through a divorce, the advice we offer earlier for talking about illness or other serious issues with your tot can steer you in the right direction. Below are some helpful ideas for breaking the news about a divorce. These simple steps can't solve all sleep problems, but they can definitely help.

1. **Explain the situation in simple terms and without blaming your ex.**

   • Mommy and Daddy are going to live in separate houses now because we are not going to be married anymore.

   • Mommies and Daddies can stop being husbands and wives but they *never* stop being Mommy and Daddy.

2. **Reassure your child that although the divorce is a big change, their love is not changing.**

3. **Reassure your child that he is not the cause of the divorce in any way.**

Shared custody: Bouncing from bed to bed

Telling your child about a separation or divorce is just the first step — and not the hardest, by far. The real challenge is working out custody issues. As you're struggling with these thorny issues, your little one is trying to figure out where he fits into this jigsaw puzzle with questions like "Where will I live? Where will I sleep?" Whether you decide on a 50/50 time split or one parent to have full custody while the other gets weekends and vacations, you can count on lots of moving back and forth. The result: lots more chances for sleep upset! Here are a few tips that can minimize the bedtime battles when your child's sleepy-time place changes frequently.

Create a schedule your child can live with

If your child is under 18 months old, let him sleep at one parent's home all of the time, with the other parent spending ample time with him during waking hours. Children this age have a hard time switching gears when their caregivers and surroundings change, and frequent moves can put a big crimp in your efforts to create a bedtime routine.

Moving an under-5 child every other day will almost certainly throw a monkey wrench into his sleep patterns. If you can, create a schedule that allows your child to stay at least three consecutive nights at each house.

One week at Mom's home and one week at Dad's works for some families, but a week without seeing a parent is a very long time for children under 3 years of age. If you do choose the week-at-a-time plan, make sure your child gets to see and spend time with his other parent during off weeks. For instance, during Mom's week, Dad can pick up Junior from preschool and take him out to dinner one night.

Make a calendar

One of the best ways to help a young child understand and remember which parent he'll be with and where he's going to sleep is a simple calendar. Put a picture of Mom or Dad or their homes in each square so she has a visual reminder of that day's routine (see Figure 14-1).

Keep a copy of the calendar at each house and look at it with your child in the morning. Let your child use a sticker to highlight the day as you review the plans. For instance, you can say, "You see Daddy's picture. He'll pick you up from school and take you to his house, and you'll sleep there tonight."

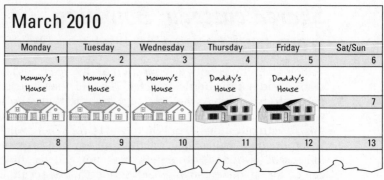

Figure 14-1: A calendar helps your child know where he'll sleep at night.

Make two cozy nests for your sweetie

Kids need a special place of their own in both Mommy's and Daddy's homes. Each house should have a child-friendly room with lots of toys, kid-sized furniture, and good lighting. (Also, buy or borrow an extra crib if your tot's not yet in a big bed.)

Try to use this room solely as your child's bedroom so your sweetie doesn't feel like an afterthought. However, if your child is with you only every other weekend or a second bedroom just isn't in the financial cards, it's okay for a room to do double duty. Just make sure that when your sweetie's comes for a visit, you convert it into his special place for his special time with you. Also, siblings can share a room, but be sensitive about their ages and sexes.

Use discretion when considering co-sleeping

Divorce is often a lonely and confusing time for both adults and children. So snuggling up together in bed can be comforting for you and your little one, especially in those first days when your life's been turned upside down. It's perfectly natural for both of you to need this close connection. If your tot's less than 18 months of age, co-sleeping for several weeks or months can ease sleep for both of you in this transitional time.

However, as your child grows older, continuing to share a bed can make him feel like he's taking the place of the missing parent. If your child gets this idea, he may feel it's his responsibility to take care of you and make you feel better.

This isn't your child's responsibility, and his misguided ideas can lead to confusion and inner conflict on his part. On the one hand, he wants to be the missing parent; on the other, he worries about what it means to take Mommy's or Daddy's place.

To avoid laying this big burden of imagined responsibility on your child's tiny shoulders and still keep him close to you, consider the sleeping-bag-on-the-floor routine. This way you don't send any wrong signals.

Figure out what stays and what travels

Kids settle in better when they have some clothes and toys that stay at each house and a few small items that they can carry back and forth (like a favorite Teddy bear). Make sure you have a set of the basics — pajamas, toothbrush, comb, a couple of changes of clothes — at each place.

Agree on a consistent bedtime routine

Okay, we know this isn't easy. After all, the fact that you and your spouse are divorced is a big clue that you don't always see eye-to-eye! But the bottom line is simple: The more you can agree on nightly routines, the more peace you can expect at both households. So try to come to a consensus on your child's bedtimes, nightly baths, and so on.

If this agreement isn't a possibility, then tell your child, "These are the rules at this house. When you sleep at Mommy's (or Daddy's), there are different rules." Your child soon learns what to expect at each house. You can use the sleep schedule in Chapter 5 to help your tyke keep the rules straight at each house.

Relegate adult sleepovers to your off nights

If you're planning a romantic rendezvous at your house, save it for a time when your little sweetie is away. It's confusing and disturbing for your tot to see a stranger sleeping in your bed, and he's likely to get up several times during the night just to let you know he's concerned.

Remarriage: Adding Another Member (Or More) to the Mix

Divorce or widowhood rocks your world, and it takes time for you and your child to put the pieces of your lives back together. Then, if romance and remarriage enter the picture, all of your routines take another giant hit. This is a much happier time, but it can still cause friction during the day and tensions at night.

The following examples highlight some of the challenges:

- ✔ A child accustomed to co-sleeping can find herself out in the cold if your new partner thinks the master bedroom is off-limits to tykes.

- ✔ Your new better-half may take a dim view of nighttime wake-ups by a tot who's used to seeing Mommy and Daddy in bed.

- ✔ You and your new partner likely have some different ideas about your child's bedtime routine.

- ✔ Even a child who takes this big life change well is going to find your new relationship unsettling enough to disturb her night-time sleep.

To get your little one back on the sleep track, follow these guidelines:

- ✔ **Engage your new partner in some straight talk.** Surprise parties are fun, but middle-of-the-night surprises aren't the right way to start off a new marriage. (Well, at least not surprises that involve the kids!) To avoid them, discuss your current setup with your new honey and come to some decisions about the kids' bedtime routines. For instance, do you allow your child to come to your room in the night? Do you have a firm bedtime or a flexible one? Thinking about these questions beforehand can make it a smoother ride.

- ✔ **Plan ahead when you're blending children.** If you both have kids, you may need some heavy-duty negotiations to create a routine that works for everyone. The closer in age the children are, the more important it is to have similar expectations. (If one child is 4 or 5 years older than another, you can always say, "Well, he's older — that's why his bedtime is later." If they're three months apart, however, this line definitely doesn't work!)

- ✔ **Separate bedrooms are ideal, but often blended families mean blending bedrooms as well.** All children, regardless of age, need time to get used to a new family arrangement. Luckily, kids under 3 usually don't object to sharing a room; in fact, they may welcome a roommate. School-aged kids accustomed to their privacy are much more likely to have problems sharing with a step-sibling. Soothe prickly feelings by using screens to divide rooms and setting firm rules about not messing with a roommate's stuff.

- ✔ **Involve your new spouse in the nighttime routine.** There's nothing like a snuggle and a shared book to begin cementing an important relationship.

Part V

The Part of Tens

"Okay, the lawn chair seemed to quiet him down, but don't go anywhere with that ladder."

In this part . . .

*E*ach *For Dummies* book features a special section called "Part of Tens" in which you find helpful tips and good-to-know facts. In Chapter 15, we offer a quick list of our best bedtime tips along with advice on how to make them work even better. Chapter 16, on the other hand, lists ways that parents *prevent* their tots from getting a good night's sleep — just so *you* know what big mistakes to avoid! And Chapter 17 has our favorite bedtime stories, games, and songs that help put a smile on your tot's face when evening rolls around.

Chapter 15

Ten Tips for Getting Your Tot to Sleep

In This Chapter

▶ Playing the right roles

▶ Taking your calming techniques to the next level

▶ Creating a sleep-friendly environment

*I*n other chapters, we give you the big picture for getting your sweetie to snooze. Here, we zoom in on some of the little details — because often the subtle tricks make the difference between an on-schedule bedtime and an extra hour of fussing.

In this chapter we cover the established bedtime strategies like bathing and noise-proofing and offer brand-new tips as well.

Know Who's the Boss

Confusion about a single question — *Who's in charge?* — is at the heart of all struggles between parents and children at bedtime. Because expectations are the key to successful parenting, everyone can do their jobs so much more easily when their roles are clear. So when bedtime arrives, here's the scoop:

✔ You're in charge of major clock and space decisions. (When does the bedtime routine begin? When is head-on-the-pillow time? Where's the bed? Where do the parents sleep? When is wake-up time?) All children look to their parents for guidance and answers on these questions.

✔ Your tot's in charge of getting herself to sleep. Many sleep problems stem from parents trying to relieve children of this task. But only the person who's falling asleep can get herself to sleep. If you try to do it for her, you only create confusion and struggle.

When both you and your cherub know your roles, harmony can reign, and everyone can get that precious gift — sleep.

Snack Smart

Warm milk and some light snacks (a few raisins, a few apple slices, or a whole-wheat graham cracker) can promote sleep. Stay away from colas and chocolate; you don't want your babe waking to a caffeine rush. For ideas on healthful snacks, see *Baby & Toddler Meals For Dummies* by Dawn Simmons, Curt Simmons, and Sallie Warren (Wiley). Of course, you'll skip this tip if your child is a young infant!

Cuddle — Try a Sling

If your newborn has lots of trouble calming down in the evening, remember that many babies and toddlers love to cuddle and be rocked. (You'll know early on whether your infant likes lots of touch. If not, skip this tip.) If he's a cuddle-bug, be sure to snuggle with him at bedtime because it'll help him make the leap into sleep. Using a sling is an easy way to get closeness and movement, and it still gives you a free hand!

Make Bath-Time a Joy

Tubby time is a muscle-relaxing, stress-relieving way to wind down after a long day. To be sure you're solving sleepy-time problems rather than creating them, try these tips:

- ✔ Assemble everything you need before you start so you're not rushing around at the wrong time.
- ✔ If you like to add oils, consider plain baby oil. Use fragrances only if they don't cause irritation. Be sure to avoid bubble baths, the number one cause of bath-related skin inflammation.

Bathing with your tot can be calming and a great way to bond. But a wet child is a slippery child! If possible, have your partner bring Baby to you in the tub, and then pop her into her infant seat (covered with a towel next to the tub) when she's done. And think twice about breastfeeding. Your angel may love it, but it often stimulates a poop — wrong time, really bad place!

After the bath, wrap your sweetie in a big, fluffy towel and rub her down gently. Finish off with a soothing massage and bedtime stories . . . ZZZZZ (see Chapter 17 for good story ideas).

Go for a Stroll

Sometimes a little journey can be a wonderful addition to the bed-time routine. A stroll, a bike ride (for older infants and toddlers), or even a short ride in the car can be very relaxing and lots of fun. Strolls in particular are a great way for families to spend time together (toddlers can wear their p.j.s). Remember to keep the stroll calm; this is a chance to wind the day down, not wind the kids up.

Use Warm, Comfy Sheets

On a cold night, make your child's bed more welcoming by putting a warm towel over the sheet just before tuck-in time. If your tot's old enough to have a blanket, toss it in the dryer for a few minutes to take off the chill. And here's another idea: Wrap Teddy in a pil-lowcase and give him a quick dryer tumble as well.

Read a Story (or Make Up Your Own!)

Telling or hearing a story is one of the most simple and powerful joys of life. Finding a great bedtime book (see Chapter 17 for ideas) allows you and your tot to share that joy with each other, and that can have powerful benefits. For example, reading to even very young children (or narrating your own stories) clearly promotes language and reading development, and it seems to improve sleep, even after your baby or toddler nods off. Tender moments together, great stories to share from your lifetime, improved inter-est in books, better language skills, and a better night's sleep — that's well worth the read! See Chapter 17 for ideas.

Dial Down the Noise; Dial Up the Calm

As we mention in Chapter 5, soft, predictable noise can mask annoying sounds and lull your child to sleep. You can buy special white-noise tapes at baby stores, but any noise — from a ticking clock or metronome to a DVD of soft music — can do the trick.

Then again, your little one may have trouble falling asleep when you *stop* using a heater or air conditioner. Try playing a tape of quiet rain or other soft nature sounds, or turn on a fan in her room. *Note:* Many a newborn is soothed by the gentle slosh of the washing machine or the chug-chug of the dishwasher. Plunking your little angel in a safe spot next to (*not* on top of) one of these noisy appliances may soothe her more than the sweetest lullaby.

Squelch the Squabbles

If you're itching to scold your partner about a credit card bill or a missed anniversary, put your disagreements on ice till your cherub is sound asleep. Even then, put some distance between you and the nursery before you start arguing, and keep your voices low and civil. Tots have amazing radar; if they overhear tense words, they lie awake worrying.

Check the Thermostat

Unless your baby is premature, he's snug and happy at the same temperature as you. But houses can warm up or cool down during the night, so a room that's cozy at 7 p.m. can be too cold or too hot six hours later. If you find yourself reaching for a robe or kicking off the covers just as your tot wakes you up, consider a trip to the thermostat instead of your little angel's room. And if you do pop in to see him, make sure his room feels comfortable to you.

Chapter 16

Ten Pitfalls to Avoid at Sleepytime

. . . .

In This Chapter

▶ Sabotaging your routines with timing mistakes

▶ Straying off course

. . . .

*I*n the previous chapter, we talk about the right moves to make if you want your tot to sleep. Now, we're switching gears to tell you what *not* to do. Here's a look at ten big bedtime no-no's.

Forgetting to Let Your Tot Wind Down

Picture yourself coming home at night after a fantastic party or an exciting movie. Do you immediately throw on your jammies and turn out the lights? Probably not. Most likely, you kick off your shoes, prop up your feet, and savor a little quiet time with a book or a late-night show.

Your tot feels the same way. He doesn't have an on/off switch, so he needs time to slide gently from the excitement of his day into the total quiet of the night. Send him to bed all wound up, and your whole household may be in an uproar for hours.

As a general rule, 20 to 25 minutes is the outside limit for the pre-bed routine, but the wind-down can start as much as an hour before. Here are some ideas:

  ✔ Turn off exciting or noisy television shows or videos.

  ✔ Turn on soft music.

  ✔ Turn down the lights — get your house *ready for bed*.

✔ Prepare your child for the trip to dreamland with soft, encouraging words such as, "When this CD is finished, it will be time for your bath and jammies."

Encouraging Your Tot to Rev Up

Some parents make a bigger mistake than skipping the wind-down stage; they actually re-energize their little rug rats by watching loud or violent shows, inviting noisy company over, or cranking up the video games as bedtime approaches.

Obviously, you can't run your house like a monastery, especially if you have lots of friends who drop by in the evening. But try to keep noisier activities out of earshot or mask them with lullabies or white noise (see Chapter 15).

Stretching Out Bedtime

Foot-dragging at bedtime is a favorite kid ploy, and a tot who moves at the speed of light in the day hours can suddenly turn slow as molasses as the clock ticks toward tuck-in time. If your sweetie tries to slow your beddy-bye ritual to a snail's pace each night, don't let him get away with it. One good trick is to schedule the least favorite parts of his bedtime ritual right before the best parts. This way he hurries through the icky stuff like teeth-brushing to get to story time or a massage.

Being Inconsistent

Fred toughs it out on Tuesday night, resisting the urge to go to his daughter when she wakes up and fusses. On Wednesday, he turns into a marshmallow and pays her a quick visit. He gets his courage back on Thursday and stays in his own bed, but his angel tortures him by hollering twice as hard and twice as long as usual.

What's setting her off? Fred is because he keeps changing his mind! She doesn't know what to expect from him, so she tests him. When he fails the test by going to her, he's really telling her to try even harder.

Consistency is key here. If you know your little kitten is hale and hearty, dry as a desert, and has a full tummy, you can feel comfortable sticking to your guns and letting her find her way back to sleep. Every time you poke your head in her room or go in for one more cuddle, you're telling her that you're still at her beck and call.

That said, trust your own instincts when you think you *should* break your own rules and go in to check. If you suspect that your little one may be coming down with a bug or if she had a particularly upsetting or exciting day, then don't hesitate to follow your gut and make sure that your precious gem is okay.

Answering Too Many Callbacks

Tell your sweetie, "You can get a drink, read, or go to the bathroom any time you want — *before* you go to bed." After that point, keep your responses to his plaintive whines — "I need a drink," "I'm scared of the dark," and so on — to an absolute minimum.

Obviously, you need to respond to real emergencies, large or small, after lights-out time. But ignore the obvious ploys for attention. And if your sweetie's old enough, let him know that he can get a drink of water or go potty all on his own.

Losing Your Cool

In the last chapter, we talked about avoiding quarrels with other family members when your angel's trying to doze. That same rule applies to all tense words as well.

If your computer crashes, the cable goes out, or the dog throws up on the carpet, resist the urge to raise your voice. If you let your temper get the best of you, you'll have two problems. One is that your tot won't sleep well. The other problem is that she's going to remember the bad words she hears and repeat them to Grandma.

If your tot's the cause of your trying day, make sure you reassure her that you love her and you're not mad at her (even if she did try to flush her toothbrush down the toilet). A child who thinks Mommy or Daddy is angry at her isn't able to calm down and go to sleep easily.

Missing the Obvious

Too often parents forget that holidays, a vacation, a visit from Grandpa, or an illness can disrupt a tyke's sleep schedule. If your cherub's routine suddenly falls apart, ask yourself: "Did something big change in his life?" If so, take steps to put the schedule back on track. (See Chapter 14 for good ideas.) Change is one of the biggest and most overlooked culprits in broken bedtime routines.

Turning the Couch into a Bed

To your child, the couch is an ideal place for some shut-eye because Mommy or Daddy is right at hand. But it's not ideal because she can't become independent when she doesn't sleep in her own room. If you're watching television together and you see your little sprout start to get droopy, move up your bedtime schedule and hustle her off to the sack before she keels over.

Missing Milestones

Bedtime routines aren't cast in stone, and they need to change along with your tot. For instance, you need to bump back bedtime as your sweetie gets older and needs less sleep. Also, you want to give your tot more and more control over his routine. If not, you may wind up still tucking your 11-year-old in bed!

Avoiding That First All-Nighter

Loving parents do almost anything to avoid upsetting their little ones. If your child is used to *you* in the middle of the night, you know exactly what to expect when that doesn't happen: a reaction strong enough to unnerve even the most laid-back parent. Fearing this meltdown, many moms and dads never let their tots learn to sleep on their own. Instead, they just wait it out — sometimes for years.

But, as the cliché goes, you never know until you try — and if you don't let your tot try to sleep through the night, you'll never know whether she can. (And after four months of age, she can. Trust us.)

Chapter 17

More than Ten Great Bedtime Stories and Songs

*T*ots can't go from 60 to 0 in a minute, so you need to provide time for your sweetie to wind down before he hits the pillow. You want to avoid activities that excite your child — especially tickling, running, and the old throw-your-baby-in-the-air game.

In this chapter, we offer a great alternative: a list of tried-and-true songs and books that signal lights out to your tot. If you bring out these favorites night after night, your biggest problem will be keeping your *own* eyes open long enough to offer a goodnight kiss.

The #1 Bedtime Story: *Goodnight Moon*

A million babies and toddlers can't be wrong, and at least that many kids count *Goodnight Moon* by Margaret Wise Brown (HarperCollins) among their favorite bedtime stories of all time. It first appeared in the 1940s, and it's been going strong ever since — and for good reason. This sweet tale follows a little rabbit as he says "Goodnight" to everything in his bedroom. It beautifully sets a sleepy pace that will have everyone yawning in *your* house.

Sheer Poetry

Warm and fuzzy and absolutely delightful are the poems found in *When We Were Very Young* by A. A. Milne and Jon J. Muth (Hyperion). Older children love the engaging verses of Shel

Silverstein, whose books include *A Light in the Attic, Where the Sidewalk Ends,* and *The Giving Tree* (HarperCollins). Jack Prelutsky is a big hit with the young set too. Who can resist titles like *It's Raining Pigs and Noodles,* and *The Frogs Wore Red Suspenders* (HarperTrophy)? But don't overlook the real classics, *Mother Goose* stories — just pick the ones with the not-so-scary words!

Rhymin' the Night Away

Everybody loves a rhyme, and your tot will delight to the rhythmic sounds of *Brown Bear, Brown Bear, What Do You See?* by Bill Martin, Jr. and Eric Carle (Henry Holt). Kids love to help you read the predictable lines, and the repeating patterns can magically soothe a fussy baby to sleep. Three other rhyming favorites are *The Very Hungry Caterpillar* by Carle, *Peter's Chair* by Keats (Puffin Books) and *Dr. Seuss's Sleep Book* (Random House).

Talkin' About Tuck-In Time

Books that center on bedtime are always winners because they get your tot's mind focused right where you want it — on sleep. In addition to *Goodnight Moon,* other good books include

- *A Child's Good Night Book* by Margaret Wise Brown, Jean Charlat, and David Diaz (HarperFestival)
- *Time for Bed* by Mem Fox and Jane Dyer (Harcourt Brace)
- *If You Were My Bunny* by Kate McMullan and David McPhail (Scholastic Inc.)
- *Can't You Sleep, Little Bear* by Maring Waddell (Candlewick)
- *Love You Forever* by Robert Munsch (Red Fox Books)

Rockin' Songs for the Rocking Chair

Wonderful albums of lullabies abound, from classical collections featuring Bach and Brahms to *Rockabye Baby! Lullaby Renditions of Led Zeppelin* (we kid you not). One of our personal favorites is *I Will Hold Your Tiny Hand* by Steve Rashid, which will have your tot bee-bopping happily off to bed with catchy but calming numbers like "My Baby Loves to Rock" and "The Porkpie Lullaby." Evie Tornquist's album *Gentle Moments* includes some lovely songs just made to help your tot tumble into dreamland.

Best Hit Single

We give our award for Best Bedtime Song Ever to "Hush Little Baby," a song that's been around since the dawn of time. This little ditty has many variants, depending on what part of the country you hail from, but here's a favorite version.

> *Hush, little baby, don't say a word,*
> *Papa's gonna buy you a mockingbird*
> *If that mockingbird don't sing*
> *Papa's gonna buy you a diamond ring*
> *If that diamond ring turns brass,*
> *Papa's gonna buy you a looking glass*
> *If that looking glass gets broke*
> *Papa's gonna buy you a billy goat*
> *If that billy goat won't pull,*
> *Papa's gonna buy you a cart and bull*
> *If that cart and bull turn over,*
> *Papa's gonna buy you a dog named Rover*
> *If that dog named Rover won't bark,*
> *Papa's gonna buy you a horse and cart*
> *If that horse and cart fall down,*
> *You'll still be the sweetest little baby in town.*

It's Showtime!

Somehow, the same show tunes that set audience's toes to tapping can help a baby drift off to dreamland, so try some of your favorites on your tyke. (But we recommend skipping *Stomp!* or *Phantom of the Opera*.) Classical music is great, too — but forgo the "1812 Overture" and go with something like Pachelbel's restful "Canon in D" instead.

Reachin' for the Stars

We bet you still remember the first verse of "Twinkle, Twinkle Little Star," but here are the rest of the lyrics in case you're an overachiever. This one's a big favorite with babies, and if you forget the words in midstream you can always switch to the "ABC song" because these golden oldies share the same melody.

> *Twinkle, twinkle, little star, how I wonder what you are.*
> *Up above the world so high, like a diamond in the sky.*
> *Twinkle, twinkle, little star, how I wonder what you are!*

When the blazing sun is gone, when he nothing shines upon,
Then you show your little light, twinkle, twinkle, all the night.
Twinkle, twinkle, little star, how I wonder what you are!

Then the traveler in the dark thanks you for your tiny spark;
He could not see which way to go, if you did not twinkle so.
Twinkle, twinkle, little star, how I wonder what you are!

Bilingual Beddy-Bye

Impress your tot with your worldly ways by offering up both the French and English versions of the classic song, "Frere Jacques:"

Frere Jacques, Frere Jacques,
Dormez-vous? Dormez-vous?
Sonnez les matines, sonnez les matines
Ding ding dong, ding ding dong.

Are you sleeping, are you sleeping?
Brother John, Brother John?
Morning bells are ringing, morning bells are ringing
Ding ding dong, ding ding dong.

If you can't pronounce the French lyrics, just fake them. It's not like your baby will know!

Appendix
Sleep Logs

· ·

Sometimes tracking your baby's trends can help you get a good handle on a sleep problem. Other times, more information simply gets in the way. So break out the sleep logs in this appendix if you think they'll help you spot trends and create strategies, but don't feel like you need to use them if you're not into lists and forms.

The first log helps you get an in-depth look at your tot's sleep patterns right now so you can spot good changes and problem areas. The second log covers an extended period of time so you can detect long-term patterns.

The Week-Long 24-Hour Sleep Watch

The first log (see Figure A-1) simply charts when your child is awake and when she's asleep, all day every day, for a week at a time (see Chapter 5 for an example). It's most helpful when you're fine-tuning the sleep routine and want to be able to spot patterns. To use this chart, simply color in sleepy hours with a pen or pencil (or crayon, if one's handy!). Then at the end of the week, look at the overall pattern for clues. For instance: Are naps getting more or less consistent? Are nighttime calls getting farther apart or closer together?

If necessary, track your child's routine for several weeks so you can get a long-term view of her sleep habits. Given this information, you can work on problem areas (like naps that are all over the map instead of relatively on-target or bedtimes that get later each night). This chart can also help you anticipate developmental leaps that coincide with sleep disruptions.

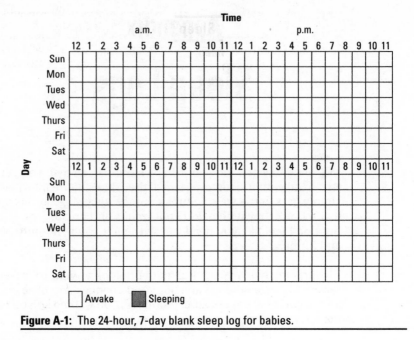

Figure A-1: The 24-hour, 7-day blank sleep log for babies.

The Developmental Sleep Assessment

The second sleep log lets you detect patterns over weeks or months so you can connect sleep situations to big or little milestones or changes in routines. For an example, refer to Chapter 6.

Don't fill out this log daily (who has time for that?); instead, make quick notes on it whenever you notice a change in sleep routines. The log can then provide a bird's-eye view of long-term trends so you can see what's disrupting your baby's once-firm sleep routines.

Table A-1 is a blank table for you to copy and use.

Table A-1	Sleep Log and Milestones		
Date	*Duration of Sleep and/or Sleep problems spotted*	*What's new? (company visiting, new sitter, etc.)*	*Milestone Reached*

Index

• C •

Notes

BUSINESS, CAREERS & PERSONAL FINANCE

0-7645-9847-3

0-7645-2431-3

Also available:
- Business Plans Kit For Dummies 0-7645-9794-9
- Economics For Dummies 0-7645-5726-2
- Grant Writing For Dummies 0-7645-8416-2
- Home Buying For Dummies 0-7645-5331-3
- Managing For Dummies 0-7645-1771-6
- Marketing For Dummies 0-7645-5600-2

- Personal Finance For Dummies 0-7645-2590-5*
- Resumes For Dummies 0-7645-5471-9
- Selling For Dummies 0-7645-5363-1
- Six Sigma For Dummies 0-7645-6798-5
- Small Business Kit For Dummies 0-7645-5984-2
- Starting an eBay Business For Dummies 0-7645-6924-4
- Your Dream Career For Dummies 0-7645-9795-7

HOME & BUSINESS COMPUTER BASICS

0-470-05432-8

0-471-75421-8

Also available:
- Cleaning Windows Vista For Dummies 0-471-78293-9
- Excel 2007 For Dummies 0-470-03737-7
- Mac OS X Tiger For Dummies 0-7645-7675-5
- MacBook For Dummies 0-470-04859-X
- Macs For Dummies 0-470-04849-2
- Office 2007 For Dummies 0-470-00923-3

- Outlook 2007 For Dummies 0-470-03830-6
- PCs For Dummies 0-7645-8958-X
- Salesforce.com For Dummies 0-470-04893-X
- Upgrading & Fixing Laptops For Dummies 0-7645-8959-8
- Word 2007 For Dummies 0-470-03658-3
- Quicken 2007 For Dummies 0-470-04600-7

FOOD, HOME, GARDEN, HOBBIES, MUSIC & PETS

0-7645-8404-9

0-7645-9904-6

Also available:
- Candy Making For Dummies 0-7645-9734-5
- Card Games For Dummies 0-7645-9910-0
- Crocheting For Dummies 0-7645-4151-X
- Dog Training For Dummies 0-7645-8418-9
- Healthy Carb Cookbook For Dummies 0-7645-8476-6

- Home Maintenance For Dummies 0-7645-5215-5
- Horses For Dummies 0-7645-9797-3
- Jewelry Making & Beading For Dummies 0-7645-2571-9
- Orchids For Dummies 0-7645-6759-4
- Puppies For Dummies 0-7645-5255-4
- Rock Guitar For Dummies 0-7645-5356-9
- Sewing For Dummies 0-7645-6847-7
- Singing For Dummies 0-7645-2475-5

INTERNET & DIGITAL MEDIA

0-470-04529-9

0-470-04894-8

Also available:
- Blogging For Dummies 0-471-77084-1
- Digital Photography For Dummies 0-7645-9802-3
- Digital Photography All-in-One Desk Reference For Dummies 0-470-03743-1
- Digital SLR Cameras and Photography For Dummies 0-7645-9803-1
- eBay Business All-in-One Desk Reference For Dummies 0-7645-8438-3

- HDTV For Dummies 0-470-09673-X
- Home Entertainment PCs For Dummies 0-470-05523-5
- MySpace For Dummies 0-470-09529-6
- Search Engine Optimization For Dummies 0-471-97998-8
- Skype For Dummies 0-470-04891-3
- The Internet For Dummies 0-7645-8996-2
- Wiring Your Digital Home For Dummies 0-471-91830-X

Separate Canadian edition also available
Separate U.K. edition also available

SPORTS, FITNESS, PARENTING, RELIGION & SPIRITUALITY

0-471-76871-5   0-7645-7841-3

Also available:
- Catholicism For Dummies
  0-7645-5391-7
- Exercise Balls For Dummies
  0-7645-5623-1
- Fitness For Dummies 0-7645-7851-0
- Football For Dummies 0-7645-3936-1
- Judaism For Dummies 0-7645-5299-6
- Potty Training For Dummies
  0-7645-5417-4

- Buddhism For Dummies
  0-7645-5359-3
- Pregnancy For Dummies
  0-7645-4483-7 †
- Ten Minute Tone-Ups For Dummies
  0-7645-7207-5
- NASCAR For Dummies 0-7645-7681
- Religion For Dummies 0-7645-5264
- Soccer For Dummies 0-7645-5229-9
- Women in the Bible For Dummies
  0-7645-8475-8

TRAVEL

0-7645-7749-2   0-7645-6945-7

Also available:
- Alaska For Dummies 0-7645-7746-8
- Cruise Vacations For Dummies
  0-7645-6941-4
- England For Dummies 0-7645-4276-1
- Europe For Dummies 0-7645-7529-5
- Germany For Dummies
  0-7645-7823-5
- Hawaii For Dummies 0-7645-7402-7

- Italy For Dummies 0-7645-7386-1
- Las Vegas For Dummies
  0-7645-7382-9
- London For Dummies 0-7645-4277
- Paris For Dummies 0-7645-7630-5
- RV Vacations For Dummies
  0-7645-4442-X
- Walt Disney World & Orlando
  For Dummies 0-7645-9660-8

GRAPHICS, DESIGN & WEB DEVELOPMENT

0-7645-8815-X   0-7645-9571-7

Also available:
- 3D Game Animation For Dummies
  0-7645-8789-7
- AutoCAD 2006 For Dummies
  0-7645-8925-3
- Building a Web Site For Dummies
  0-7645-7144-3
- Creating Web Pages For Dummies
  0-470-08030-2
- Creating Web Pages All-in-One Desk
  Reference For Dummies
  0-7645-4345-8
- Dreamweaver 8 For Dummies
  0-7645-9649-7

- InDesign CS2 For Dummies
  0-7645-9572-5
- Macromedia Flash 8 For Dummies
  0-7645-9691-8
- Photoshop CS2 and Digital
  Photography For Dummies
  0-7645-9580-6
- Photoshop Elements 4 For Dummies
  0-471-77483-9
- Syndicating Web Sites with RSS Feeds
  For Dummies
  0-7645-8848-6
- Yahoo! SiteBuilder For Dummies
  0-7645-9800-7

NETWORKING, SECURITY, PROGRAMMING & DATABASES

0-7645-7728-X   0-471-74940-0

Also available:
- Access 2007 For Dummies
  0-470-04612-0
- ASP.NET 2 For Dummies
  0-7645-7907-X
- C# 2005 For Dummies
  0-7645-9704-3
- Hacking For Dummies
  0-470-05235-X
- Hacking Wireless Networks
  For Dummies
  0-7645-9730-2
- Java For Dummies
  0-470-08716-1

- Microsoft SQL Server 2005
  For Dummies 0-7645-7755-7
- Networking All-in-One Desk
  Reference For Dummies
  0-7645-9939-9
- Preventing Identity Theft For Dummies
  0-7645-7336-5
- Telecom For Dummies
  0-471-77085-X
- Visual Studio 2005 All-in-One Desk
  Reference For Dummies
  0-7645-9775-2
- XML For Dummies
  0-7645-8845-1